AUTHOR'S NOTE

No attempt has been made in this book to give a scholarly transliteration of Arabic names for people or places. The style adopted is the one generally used in British or French newspapers, which it is thought would be most familiar to readers of this work in the English language.

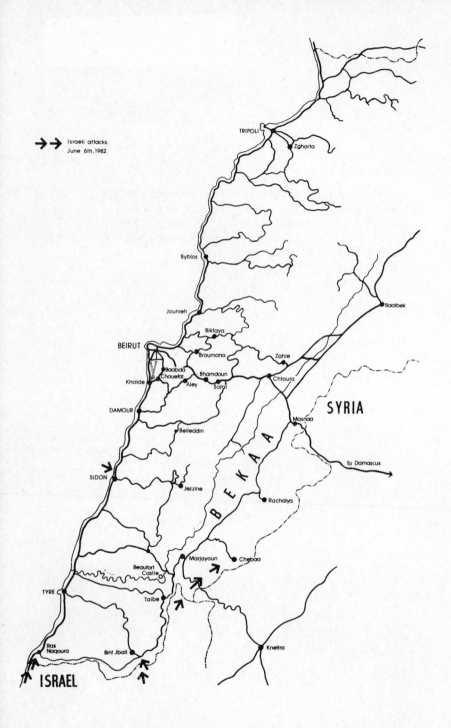

→→ Israeli attacks,
June 6th, 1982.

TRIPOLI
Zghorta

Byblos

Baalbek

Jounieh
Biktaya
BEIRUT
Broumana
Zahle
Baabda
Bhamdoun
Choueifat
Khalde
Aley
Sofar
Chtoura

SYRIA

DAMOUR
Beiteddin
Masnaa

SIDON
To Damascus

Jezzine

Rachaiya

B
E
K
A
A

Marjayoun
Chebaa

Beaufort
Castle

TYRE
Taibe

Ras
Naqoura
Bint Jbail
Kneitra

ISRAEL

BEIRUT

ACKNOWLEDGEMENTS

The chapters dealing with Israeli actions in Southern Lebanon, and with the situation inside Israel, were contributed by Hugh Davies, who reported the war from Jerusalem for *The Daily Telegraph*. The author also wishes to express his gratitude to the editors and staff of *L'Orient*, the daily French language newspaper in Beirut, and the *Middle East Reporter*, the digest of Arabic language broadcasts and newspapers. Both publications performed an invaluable service throughout the siege of Beirut, continuing to publish in spite of the most appalling difficulties, and regularly giving a balanced and comprehensive account of events.

Final Conflict

THE WAR IN THE LEBANON

John Bulloch

CENTURY PUBLISHING

LONDON

FOR JILL
who shared it all

Copyright © John Bulloch 1983

First published in Great Britain in 1983
by Century Publishing Co. Ltd,
76 Old Compton Street, London W1V 5PA

British Library Cataloguing in Publication Data

Bulloch, John
  Final conflict.
  1. Israel-Arab Border Conflicts, 1949- – Lebanon
  2. Lebanon – History – Civil War, 1975-
  I. Title
  956.92'044   DS87.5

ISBN 0 7126 0171 6

Photoset by Rowland Phototypesetting Limited
Bury St Edmunds, Suffolk

Printed in Great Britain by
Redwood Burn Limited
Trowbridge, Wiltshire

FINAL CONFLICT

Since this book went to press in January 1983, the Kahan Enquiry has reported on the Beirut Massacres. As a result of its findings, there have been personnel changes in the Israeli Army and Government.

PREFACE

The Israeli invasion of Lebanon and the siege of Beirut was the final battle in Israel's longest war – its vain struggle to subdue the people displaced from Palestine to make way for the Jews. That was formally begun in 1965, when Al Fateh launched its first military operation into Israeli territory, a weak and ill-organised effort which resulted merely in the blowing-up of a water culvert. Eighteen years later, Al Fateh and the other seven groups in the Palestine Liberation Organisation had grown into a formidable fighting force equipped with sophisticated weapons and able to hold off the full strength of the Israeli Defence Forces for months.

In the period from 1965, the Palestinians had been subdued and thrown out of Jordan by King Hussein's Bedouin Army, controlled and regimented in Syria, barely tolerated anywhere else in the Arab world, and only in Lebanon allowed to flourish. It was not through any government decision that the Palestinians were given such a free hand in the Lebanon, which was one of the most advanced, cosmopolitan and democratic states in the Middle East; quite the reverse. Successive Lebanese cabinets refused to regulate the Palestinian presence at times when they were capable of doing so, and only tried to do so when the Palestinians had grown strong enough to impose their own conditions. Thus it was that the PLO was given a formal status in Lebanon in 1970 through the Cairo Agreement, which, with the following Melkart Convention, permitted the PLO a free hand in much of Southern Lebanon, gave them complete autonomy in the fifteen sprawling refugee camps scattered all over the country, and guaranteed them a steady supply route. It was a virtual abrogation of authority by the Lebanese Government, and it led in the end to the *de facto* partition of the country, giving the PLO total control of some areas of the south, and the dominant role in West Beirut.

The growth in power of the PLO was largely the result of the Lebanese Civil War of 1975–76, for which the Palestinians were blamed by the Christian half of the population; but that conflict was not of the Palestinians' making, nor was it to their advantage. The Civil War was entirely the outcome of the breakdown of the Lebanese political and social system. In Lebanon, a National Covenant gave a permanent position of superiority and advantage to the Christians of the country, and in particular, the Maronites of Mount Lebanon, the ancient Turkish Christian wilayet to the north of Beirut. That Covenant had been based on demographic as well as historical considerations, though the census on which the whole edifice rested had been taken as long ago as 1932 and by 1975, when the civil war began, there was little doubt that the Christians of the country were in a minority. Also, it was obvious that the distribution of wealth throughout Lebanon had gone seriously wrong. A tiny proportion of people from the old Maronite and Sunni establishments enjoyed disproportionate riches and had too much say in the way the country was run and the economy manipulated. The Shia Moslems of the south – 'the disinherited', as they were called by a new leader, the Imam Moussa Sad'r – were the poorest of all, yet they lived in the most sensitive area, along the border with Israel; once driven out of there, they were forced to set up home in shanty towns next to the Palestine refugee camps which ringed Beirut. The civil war was brought about because the Maronites wanted to retain their dominant position and the Shia wanted a fairer share of the national cake, while the Sunnis saw an opportunity to win greater political power for themselves while the other two groups were preoccupied with their own particular affairs.

The Palestinians were peripheral to this internal struggle, though they provided the catalyst when war finally did break out. The 1968 influx of refugees from the territories seized by Israel was joined in 1970 by the great bulk of Palestinian fighters expelled from Jordan by King Hussein's army. This pushed the Palestinian population of Lebanon up to some 300,000, of whom about 10,000 were trained, full-time irregular soldiers, with that number rising to some 30,000 when the Palestinians were mobilised. The majority of these people were

Sunni Moslems, which further upset the balance of groups in the Lebanon, worried the Christians and heartened the Moslems.

When the Lebanese Civil War first began, the Palestinians tried hard to stay out of it; they could not do so for long. The Christians, led by the Phalangist forces, were winning in Beirut and in the country, so the PLO had to join in to prevent their allies being defeated: for they knew that if the Christians won, their first move would be to destroy the armed strength of the PLO and disperse the Palestinians. So the PLO joined in on the side of the leftist, mainly Moslem groups in Lebanon, and tipped the balance. Now Syria had to take steps to save the Christians, for no government in Damascus, no matter how radical it claimed to be, could afford to have a state on its border dominated by the radicals of the PLO and capable of provoking a war with Israel – a war which would be bound to involve Syria.

The Syrians' intervention in Lebanon expanded their influence physically, but also diminished their capabilities, by tying down a large part of their forces in areas they could not defend and did not want to hold. The Lebanese experience also had an effect on the Syrian troops who served in the country, and may well have done something to stiffen the resolve of the insurgents in Syria who were conducting an armed uprising against the government. This rebellion culminated in the battle of Hama, in which approximately ten thousand people were killed by Syrian special forces – not only to subdue the rebellious town, but also as a warning to others. In Lebanon, Syria had the worst of all worlds: it had stepped in to prevent the installation of a government whose policies might have been a danger to Damascus, but it found itself fighting those elements which it had gone in to protect. It also failed in its primary purpose, for Israel refused to allow Syrian troops to be deployed in Southern Lebanon, thus still leaving the possibility for the Palestinians to provoke a war, or for Israel to use their presence as a reason to launch an invasion of its own.

Twice that happened. On the first occasion, the Litani Operation of 1978, the Israelis were half-hearted, seeking only to encircle and kill as many Palestinian fighters as possible and not to subdue the PLO totally, or to drive north to destroy the organisation and its leaders. That incursion resulted firstly in the formalisation of Major Sa'ad Haddad's 'Free Lebanon', a buffer strip along the border commanded by a former Lebanese Army officer who was a puppet of the Israelis, supplied, controlled and paid from Tel Aviv; and secondly, in the establishment of the United Nations Interim Force in Lebanon – UNFIL – a three thousand-strong army which was supposed to prevent Palestinian infiltration into Upper Galilee, and thus remove any excuse for Israeli action in Southern Lebanon. However, UNFIL never managed to establish full authority over the area given into its care. It could not stop the PLO firing rockets into Israel over the heads of its troops, and was both powerless to prevent Israeli action and lacked the will to do so.

The growing might of the PLO in Lebanon was mirrored by the increasing strength of the Phalangists, the main Christian party and militia. Under the ruthless direction of Bachir Gemayel, the Phalangists became the dominant force in East Beirut and 'the mountain', bloodily subduing their only rivals, ex-President Camille Chamoun's National Liberal Party, and incorporating the smaller, previously autonomous groups.

The Phalangist militia, some 25,000 strong, was a professional army, supplied and trained by Israel, and stronger than the Lebanese Army, which was forced to operate under severe handicaps. Following the Civil War, the Lebanese Army had been built up in numbers; but it could never be used, because in any conflict in Lebanon there were always sectarian overtones, and army units would break up if ordered to act against homogenous groups. Nor could the Lebanese Army be used to fend off the Israeli attackers – which, even if it had failed militarily, might have been effective in rousing world opinion and forcing Arab assistance. Such an action would have been perceived as offering protection to the Palestinians, not defending national territory. It would also have been likely to cause conflict in the armed forces, as within the army, as in the country, some half of the people sympathised with the Israeli aim of destroying the PLO.

In Israel, the much tougher policies adopted in the occupied territories and towards the PLO were seen as the work of the

Prime Minister, Mr Menachem Begin, and the Defence Minister, Mr Ariel Sharon. But these men were elected members of a government chosen by one of the most democratic, if complicated, electoral systems in the world. Their accession to power reflected a trend in Israel, a change in national attitudes: gone were the early days of socialism, idealism, when to be an Israeli was an adventure, a challenge and a privilege. Now the number of immigrants had diminished to an unwilling trickle, and the native-born and oriental Jews were becoming the majority. In the army, in particular, this pattern was all too clear, with some sixty per cent of Sephardim (oriental Jews) in the ranks, and a similar proportion of Ashkenazim in the officer corps. Israel was becoming a genuine country of the Middle East, but one still ruled by Poles, Russians and Rumanians, who felt they had to take extreme positions to reflect the wishes of the people they led or commanded.

The change in the national attitude in Israel gave rise to extremist factions which were exemplified by Gush Emunim, ostensibly a religious organisation, but increasingly a pressure group and political lobby, often used by cabinet ministers for their own purposes. It was Gush Emunim which established the illegal settlements later legalised by the Begin government, and it was Ariel Sharon who encouraged them in their efforts, with his dream of a million Jewish settlers on the West Bank at a time when there was difficulty in persuading ten thousand to live there. The extremists, the zealots and that small number of Israelis who believed in Mr Begin's concept of Eretz Israel, the expansion of the state to the biblical borders, were in a minority in the country: but they were a highly vocal minority who could shout down the quieter, saner majority.

One of the most important effects of the war in Lebanon was to make those who objected to what was going on much more vocal. The Peace Now movement and its offshoots became a power in the land, and Israelis of all sorts were forced to think deeply about what was going on, the direction their country was taking and the way they wished it to go in the future. For the first time in decades, a real national debate began, a questioning of accepted ideas and a profound examination of the philosophy of the Likud government led by Mr Begin. It was an examination of fundamental concepts which took place not only in Israel, but in Jewish communities throughout the world. The Israeli actions in Lebanon, the ruthlessness with which the army acted, the brutality with which the siege of Beirut was conducted, the immorality of denying food, water and power to a city which housed 400,000 civilians as well as some 15,000 combatants, prompted much soul-searching by every Jew and every Jewish community. For non-Jews everywhere, the issue seemed much clearer: it was once again a David and Goliath contest in the Middle East, but this time Israel was Goliath and the Arabs, the Palestinians, were the Davids; it was a role-reversal which shocked the world and which led to a vast loss of sympathy and support for Israel.

As the three-month invasion of Lebanon went on, every country of the region became involved to some extent, with the superpowers, America and Russia, trying to salvage what they could from the débâcle. Syria was the one Arab country directly affected, just as it had feared it would be. The Syrians did not want a war with Israel, and were not prepared for one. Their aim was to build up a credible Arab alliance around themselves, something which might just make up for what they saw as the defection of Egypt from the Arab camp. They were far from achieving their objective, and so had no desire for the military adventure forced on them. The result was that they lost, both militarily and politically. Their army, air force and air defence systems were found to be no match for the Israeli technology, Israeli weapons, or Israeli soldiers; and because of the defeat, they lost credibility with those they were wooing, countries they were trying to persuade to join them in a Soviet-protected bloc – for Russia itself was shown to be ineffectual in a crisis, politically ham-handed, and the provider of armaments which could not stand up to those supplied to Israel by America. The Syrians sought to make capital out of the fact that they alone among the Arab nations fought on the side of the Palestinians in Lebanon, but their inept performance and continuing troubles at home gave them little leverage. President Hafez Assad emerged a weaker and a sorrier man from the conflict.

The other Arab nation closely involved was Saudi Arabia.

The Saudis as usual worked quietly – but work they did on this occasion. They rightly saw that their strength lay in the pressure they could bring to bear on the United States, and after a hesitant start caused by a misjudgement of events, as well as a secret, perhaps subconscious, willingness to see the PLO diminished, the Saudis acted consistently. Their aim was two-fold: to save Lebanon, and Beirut in particular, from total destruction by the Israeli sledgehammer; and to extricate the PLO in an organised, coherent and acceptable form, not as a defeated rabble without leaders or organisation. On both these counts they succeeded to a degree, though the time taken was much longer than they had expected or wanted, and in spite of their hopes, the PLO eventually emerged as divided as ever.

Yasser Arafat, leader of Al Fateh and chairman of the PLO, held onto his position within the movement and in the Arab world by being the perfect consensus politician. Sometimes it seemed he had no opinions or views of his own, apart from the ever-present platitudes which lard the speeches of every politician. He was the man who infallibly detected the majority view, and acted on it; he was not a leader in the sense of initiating policies or even discussions, for all his undoubted skill at holding his men together during the siege, in taking every propaganda advantage possible and in dealing with friendly governments. Once it was over, Arafat had the opportunity to capitalise on all that had happened. There was a vast surge of sympathy for the Palestinians and their cause throughout the world, and most important of all, in America. Arafat missed his chance. He could have ditched the wild men in the movement, George Habash of the Popular Front, Nayef Hawatmeh of the Democratic Front, and the rest. For a time, it seemed as if he was going to do so: the extremists all gravitated naturally to Damascus before setting out on the wanderings around the Arab world which seemed destined to be the lot of Palestinian leaders for years to come; Arafat, however, steadfastly refused to go to Syria, and instead very properly sailed immediately to Tunis by way of Greece. As the headquarters of the Arab League, Tunis was the place to put the stamp of legitimacy and respectability on the PLO, turning it into a Goverment in Exile which would quickly have been recognised by most countries of the world. At the last moment, unable to face the internal dissension which such a move would bring, Arafat passed up the chance. Perhaps after so many years, he had simply become tired. Whatever the reason, Arafat fumbled the opportunity of a lifetime. That chance is unlikely to come back, for never again will the Palestinians enjoy quite the standing they did in the Autumn of 1982.

In the end, there were clear winners and losers from the conflict: the winner was America, and the loser Russia. The United States, by its close involvement through the immense mediating efforts of Philip Habib, risked appearing to be the champion of Israel, yet managed to avoid that; the swift and timely sacking of Al Haig as Secretary of State, and his replacement by George Schultz in the middle of the war was a graphic demonstration that the administration was changing tack. Equally, President Reagan's well-publicised comments to Mr Begin and his obvious personal concern, did much to still criticism in the Arab world. Of course, at a popular level, America was blamed for what was going on, for having armed Israel, and for allowing it to do what it was doing. But the governments of the Arab countries took a more sophisticated view: they noted the superiority of American arms; they watched with admiration as America skilfully gained all the diplomatic advantages it could; and many quietly welcomed the increased involvement of America in the region.

America's objectives in the Middle East have always been clear: to safeguard the oil wells, preserve the 'friendly and moderate' regimes in charge in the countries where the oil is produced, to keep the Soviet Union out and diminish its influence in those countries where governments considered unfriendly to the West are in control. By its dominant role during the invasion of Lebanon, America furthered those aims and expanded its influence in the area. At the same time, the Soviet Union was seen as being a loser on the battlefield, inept diplomatically, and as being unable, or even worse, unwilling, to help its ally Syria in time of trouble.

To some extent, paradoxical as it may sound, Lebanon was a winner. Yet again, the country suffered immense damage, with Tyre and Sidon dreadfully knocked about and 25 per cent of all

buildings in Beirut affected. Exact casualty figures may never
be known, but those compiled by various international agencies
are probably the most reliable. These show that some 19,000
people died during the Israeli operation, almost 7,000 of
them in Beirut. Throughout the country about 30,000 were
wounded, again with the majority in Beirut. Of the total dead
and injured, only about 16 per cent were fighters, a statistic
illustrating the blanket nature of the Israeli offensive, in which
no attempt was made to spare areas containing high propor-
tions of civilians, so long as those places also harboured small
numbers of combatants. Those displaced, too, were almost all
civilians, mainly from the refugee camps of the south. The
United Nations estimated that some 60,000 people had their
homes destroyed and were forced to move. Yet for all the
physical destruction, there was hope for the Lebanese. At the
end of it all, they were able to elect a new president who had the
support of both the Moslem and Christian establishments; the
army, for all its lack of activity during the invasion, was intact,
though it did little to enhance its reputation during the first
days of its move into West Beirut; and among the Arab states
and throughout the world, Lebanon was assured of help,
support and goodwill to an extent unknown before.

The great question mark was over the Palestinians. Their
troops, the regular forces of the Palestinian Liberation Army
and the irregulars, the guerrillas of all the different factions, had
fought well and bravely, and had succeeded in holding off the
Israeli Army – admittedly, largely because of Israel's reluctance to risk heavy casualties on the streets of Beirut. In the
end, they were driven out, not by Israeli force of arms, but
because the leaders of the civilian population of West Beirut
told them they had to go, that the people of Beirut had
sacrificed enough for them, and that it would be unreasonable
and counter-productive to hold on any longer. The Palestinians
accepted that, and agreed to leave. It was then that Israel
committed as serious a war crime as anything that followed, or
anything that had gone before. For despite firm, categorical
and written assurances from the Palestinians and the Americans that the PLO would quit Beirut, the Israelis kept up their
attacks, bombing and shelling the city, maintaining the block-

ade and so depriving the inhabitants of the most basic necessi-
ties of life, and continuing the threat of an all-out assault. It was
brutal, it was unjustified, it was unnecessary and it was uncivil-
ised.

So, in the end, the Palestinians created the legend many of
their leaders wanted, and were sent into exile, dispersed around
the Arab world, separated from their families, with a future at
best uncertain and at worst hopeless. Their leaders were back
where they had started, with little real muscle to back up their
public attitudes and once again were totally dependent on the
uncertain political charity of the more powerful of the Arab
states. Still unwilling to settle for the possible, they missed the
chance presented by President Reagan's new initiative, and by
encouraging the Fez summit conference to settle for a hard-line
declaration which would take Syria along with the majority,
probably postponed for years any real negotiations. During the
Israeli invasion of Lebanon and the siege of Beirut, the
Palestinian leaders had been effective, efficient, personally
brave and politically astute. Once it was over and they were out
in the world again, they were divided, bickering, extremist,
ineffectual and inept. Arafat, in particular, must bear the
responsibility for missing a golden opportunity, for squander-
ing in weeks the gains for which Palestinians and Lebanese
alike had given their lives over the months.

As for Israel, it was, of course, the military victor – though
not as convincingly, quickly or cleanly as both Israelis and their
supporters would have liked. The Israeli forces had used
massive firepower near-indiscriminately; for all their talk of
trying to minimise 'enemy' civilian casualties, they had made
no attempt to avoid heavily populated areas. Alongside the
bombing went what appeared to be deliberate attempts on the
part of Israeli leaders to 'dehumanise' the Palestinians and to
equate their leaders with Nazis. When Mr Begin was questioned about the bombing of an apartment block in Beirut used
as a meeting place for the Palestinian leadership, in which more
than a hundred women and children died, he asked rhetorically
if it would have been wrong to refrain from bombing a building
containing Hitler if it also housed twenty other people. Neither
the analogy nor the facts seemed correct. The Israeli Army was

intent on finishing the Palestinians once and for all, and cared little for the damage done in the process. The Israelis claimed that those who stayed in Beirut had only themselves to blame – an argument which ignored the fact that people were being forced out of their own homes, and blamed and punished for events over which they had no control.

In the end, Israel lost: it lost because it forfeited the sympathy and support of the world on which it depended for so much: it lost because the action taken in Lebanon tore apart the fabric of Israeli society, creating divisions where none had existed before, and exacerbating those which had always been there. Above all, Israel lost because it went to war for an objective which could not be achieved: for the basic Israeli war aim was to destroy not just the PLO, their leaders and their infrastructure, but the concept of Palestine itself. Israel wanted to expunge from people's minds the idea that one day a State of Palestine might exist; that the three million Palestinians of the world might have a homeland of their own like so many others. The Israelis tried to use guns to shoot a dream; not surprisingly, they failed.

Finally, the awful aftermath of it all: the massacres at the Sabra and Chatila refugee camps in Beirut. There can be no doubt that although the Christian militiamen of the Phalangist Party and Sa'ad Haddad's men from the south wielded the knives and pulled the triggers, the Israelis were responsible. They were in physical control of West Beirut, they sent the Christians in to do their work for them, they lit the area to make the task easier and they failed to stop what was going on, or to attempt to stop it, until it was too late. The military argument that there were two thousand PLO fighters left in the camps was shown to be false, and the lame defence that no-one could have known what would happen, if accepted, would have been an admission that the Israeli Army commanders had no knowledge of recent Lebanese history and no up-to-the-minute intelligence assessments. Twice before, the Christians had acted as they did at Sabra and Chatila: at Karantina in 1975 and at Tal Zaatar in 1976. Every child in the Middle East, including in Israel, knew of those events; yet the Israeli army commanders chose to ignore them, or to plead ignorance. Similarly, Israeli officers had attended the burial of Bachir Gemayel at Bikfaya, and had heard his brother Amin speak of vengeance for his murder. Israeli agents had also reported Christian plans to take such actions as would 'induce' up to 250,000 Palestinian civilians to leave Lebanon, settling old scores in the process.

The massacres were a horrific end to a horrific period. Unlike many other events of this desperate time, they were completely, damningly, the responsibility of Israel.

CHAPTER ONE

The siege of Beirut began with flowers and cheers; it ended sixty-eight days later with tears, gunfire, and a macabre aftermath of carnage, evasions and hypocrisy. In the long weeks between, this major city of the Middle East, a city of high-rise buildings, fashionable shops and sophisticated people, more Western than oriental, experienced a blockade more reminiscent of medieval times than of modern warfare. According to a strategy which had been worked out long before, the Israeli Defence Force deliberately bombed, shelled and rocketed the civilian population of West Beirut, so that their leaders would put pressure on the Palestinians to leave. The prime Israeli objective was to get the Palestinians out of the city: to do so, they used their massive firepower against the ordinary people, both Lebanese and Palestinian.

The siege began on the evening of Sunday, June 13th, when the first Israeli tanks rolled into Baabda, the small town above Beirut whose only claim to fame is that it houses the Lebanese Presidential Palace. The Israeli armoured brigade had trundled up the road through Shemlan after establishing a tactical headquarters at Dar el Qamar, and reached Baabda by early evening. The tanks met no resistance, for there were no Palestinians there, and though the Lebanese Army headquarters was only a few miles away, there were no Lebanese troops in the area either – not that they would have been likely to fight even if they had been there. As it was, the Lebanese gendarmerie men stationed in Baabda merely gathered on the verandah of their police station to watch the tanks swing into position.

Soon, other Israeli military vehicles brought in infantry; then, an hour later, a new convoy pulled into the small square of the town, crowding it with trucks and jeeps, and out of the command car stepped the unmistakable portly figure of General Ariel Sharon, Defence Minister of Israel, architect of its thrust into Lebanon and hero of the 1973 war with Egypt. Wearing the distinctive brimless helmet of a tankman, the general strode into the police station and into the Gendarmerie commander's office. 'Out', he snapped at the startled and probably frightened commander. And then 'Arik', as he is known in Israel, sat down in the Lebanese officer's chair to have his picture taken by attendant Israeli photographers. The general then ordered the Lebanese officer to provide twelve rooms for the night for himself and his entourage; and finally he set off on a lumbering tour of inspection of the positions his men had taken up.

Next day, the word had spread to both East and West Beirut, and journalists from West Beirut set off in their dozens across the Green Line dividing the city, crossing from the last Moslem-Palestinian checkpoint to the Lebanese Army post, and then on to the Phalangist roadblock. Once there, they found they were not the only ones eager to see the Israelis. The roads were jammed with cars as thousands of Lebanese Christians from the east of the city set out to visit this newest tourist attraction. Girls in off-the-shoulder dresses, smiling and waving, gave the whole affair a carnival atmosphere; men cheered and shouted 'shalom' to the Israeli troops as they reached Baabda; and bemused taxi-drivers from the western half of the town asked incredulously of their journalist fares: 'Are those *really* Israelis?'

They were indeed – and a tremendous reception they were given. Lebanese children asked them for autographs and climbed up on the tanks to be photographed with the invaders. Policemen milled about, trying to find Israelis who could speak Arabic or French. And eventually, the crush became so great that the same policemen had to institute a one-way system for traffic, and to start doing point duty, while two hundred yards away, President Elias Sarkis sat in his palace, fingering his worry beads and asking everyone around him what was going to happen next.

In the short term, the answer was: nothing. The Israelis moved their tanks about, and in the following few days set up an armoured vehicle park just below the palace, with volley-ball courts for the soldiers, tents for the officers and petrol dumps to keep the armour moving. The most important move had already been made. Baabda is no more than a few miles from the main Beirut-Damascus highway, as well as being a bastion of the Christian-controlled areas of the country. By their unopposed entry into the town, Israel had effectively cut the main supply route into Beirut from Syria, had prevented the Palestinians or Syrians getting out of the city, and had linked up with their effective but discreet allies, the Phalangist militia led by Mr Bachir Gemayel. By taking Baabda, the Israelis had encircled Beirut and made possible the blockade of the city which they were to impose three weeks later. They also put themselves in a position from which they could apply direct, physical pressure on the Lebanese leaders; Israeli guns were literally pointing at the presidential palace, as well as at the western half of the city spread out in a panorama below Baabda.

The move into the small mountain town was the culmination of the first part of the Israeli invasion of Lebanon which began on June 6th, anniversary of the blitzkrieg Six-Day War of 1967. It also represented Israel's first mistake in Lebanon – if the invasion itself did not count as a mistake. For the Israelis stopped at Baabda – probably at the behest of the more moderate members of Mr Menachem Begin's cabinet. If they had gone on that day, as General Sharon and the Chief of Staff, General Rafael Eytan, had wanted, they could have motored down into West Beirut with no more than token opposition from the disorganised Palestinians, and none at all from the Moslem militias. Instead, they halted, and in so doing let themselves in for almost ten more weeks of war. Another result was that as the weeks went by, and it became progressively more difficult for the Israelis to move into the city, General Sharon was increasingly apt to say to his colleagues, 'I told you so.'

It was the first days of the Israeli thrust into Lebanon which had led General Sharon to put into effect the second stage of his plan. Originally, he and others in Israel had said they wanted to clear a twenty-five-mile strip north of the Israeli border; all Palestinians were to have been driven out of the area, because it was from here that PLO gunners had fired their rockets into the Israeli settlements of Upper Galilee, Metullah, Kiryat Shmona, Maalot and the rest. As early as the Spring of 1981, Mr Begin had made a solemn promise to the people of that region: soon, no more rockets. He gave that assurance to the settlers while on a tour of Upper Galilee, and he meant it. It was the first warning of what Israel intended to do, and it was taken very seriously by both Lebanon and the Palestinians. Unfortunately, there was little they could do to guard against what was to come later.

While it was the Israeli cabinet which took the decision to move into Lebanon, it was General Sharon and his field commanders who had day-to-day control of operations; and they had ideas rather different from those held by many of General Sharon's ministerial colleagues. The Israeli military had a much clearer idea of what should be done than the civilians: they wanted to destroy the PLO once and for all. To the military mind, it seemed that physical destruction of the men of the PLO, and if possible of their leaders, would put an end to the threat which had plagued Israel for so long. The plan concocted by General Sharon and General Eytan was to surround as many Palestinians in the south as possible, and to 'liquidate' them – a word used by General Eytan with apparent disregard for its sinister echoes of the Nazi Holocaust. At the same time, the Israeli military planners were well aware of what had happened during their previous incursion into Lebanon, in the Litani operation of 1978; that time, the Palestinians had resisted where possible, and faded quietly away when resistance became foolhardy. They had then regrouped, and as soon as Israel withdrew, set about once again causing as much trouble as possible. This time, General Sharon and his men were determined to prevent that happening, so a second phase of the plan for the invasion of Lebanon was drawn up. This involved a drive right up to Beirut itself, the city where the Palestinian leaders lived and had their offices, where the PLO was as much an authority as the state itself – often more – and where so many of the Palestinian fighters had their homes in the teeming refugee camps surrounding the Lebanese capital.

General Sharon had not told his cabinet colleagues his plans in any detail, nor were the objectives of the invasion set out in any Orders of the Day to his men. Rather, the general improvised, making plans as he went along. An invasion, once successful, carries its own momentum, he said, and the situation had to be exploited. In this way, Israel's war aims quietly expanded to include the destruction of the PLO, and then the expulsion of Syrian forces from the country, and finally, the establishment of a stable government in Lebanon which would sign a peace treaty with Israel. A considerable advance from the original position, the establishment of a twenty-five-mile-wide security zone in Southern Lebanon.

That day in Baabda, everything must have seemed possible to General Sharon and his men. Their advance into Lebanon had been no walkover, but they had done what they set out to do quickly, ruthlessly, and fairly efficiently. Above all, they had avoided a confrontation on the border with the United Nations forces there, an incident which might have aroused world opinion against the Israelis and forced them to stop before they had properly begun. The risks had been there, despite the small numbers and lack of strength of the UN force. One of the component groups of UNIFIL, the UN Interim Force in the Lebanon, had been provided by the Dutch. Now, Holland had always been the most pro-Israeli country in Europe, just as Israel had always had more regard for the Netherlands than for any other European State, an attitude deriving from the Second World War, when the Dutch and the Norwegians probably did more and risked more than the people of other nations in their efforts to save and protect the Jews among them. In Southern Lebanon, the Dutch unit was armed with a number of anti-tank missiles, as well as side arms, machine guns and a few mortars and bazookas, and it was through the Dutch positions that one of the three Israeli invasion columns moved on June 6th. What would have happened if the Dutch commander had ordered the lead tanks to stop, and had threatened to open fire if they did not do so? Of course, the tanks would have closed down and kept going. But suppose the Dutch had used one of their anti-tank weapons, successfully; the logical course for the Israeli column commander would have been to call in an air-strike to clear the way ahead. Would the world have accepted that? Large numbers of Dutch dead as a result of strafing runs by American-supplied Israeli planes? It would have been unthinkable.

As it was, nothing of the sort happened. The Dutch, the French and the Norweigians all stood aside – though one Norweigian soldier was killed 'by accident'. With no opposition and little protest from the international peacekeepers, the Israelis swung into Lebanon in the wake of their planes, which for the previous forty-eight hours had been pounding Palestinian positions all over the area between Beirut and the Israeli frontier. One column of invaders began heading up the Bekaa Valley, the traditional route to outflank the Syrians for an army on the march to Damascus; the second force advanced on Beaufort Castle, the old Crusader fort which had been used as a firing platform by the Palestinians for years and which was a constant menace to the positions of Major Sa'ad Haddad, Israel's puppet commander in Southern Lebanon; the third Israeli column headed towards Tyre, a Palestinian pocket enjoying near-complete autonomy within the area supposedly under UN control.

It was Beaufort Castle which was of most symbolic importance to the Israelis. For years the Palestinians there had defied all attempts to bomb them out. Perched at the top of a 1,200-foot sheer cliff, built of volcanic rock taken from the mountain itself and honeycombed with laboriously dug passages and cellars, the castle seemed near-impregnable – as solid as when it had first been built by the Crusaders in the twelfth century. Israel had constantly bombed and shelled it, but each time the Palestinians merely disappeared into their deep shelters under the castle, to re-emerge and return to their guns as soon as the bombardment was over.

So, after hours of hard pounding, the Israelis knew they had to go in if they were to take it this time. The assault was straight up the cliff face, with helicopter gunships forcing the Palestinians to stay under cover once the Israeli commandos were on the bare mountaintop stronghold. Some hundred and fifty Israelis went in, while sharpshooters fired down from the gunships at any Palestinians they saw. However, few of the defenders were visible outside, so the Israeli assault team had to go down into the underground labyrinth to winkle them out. This they did in the classic manner: first, CS gas grenades were thrown in, then hand grenades, and finally the Israeli commandos ventured into the rooms and tunnels themselves, spraying the way ahead with Uzzi machine gun fire and making sure every last area was clear. In the end, Beaufort belonged to the Israelis; not a single Palestinian remained alive, not a prisoner taken. The Israelis had killed every one of the thirty-five Fateh men defending the castle.

News of the fall of Beaufort was a tremendous boost to the Israeli troops as they advanced on Tyre and Nabatiyeh, the two southern strongholds of the PLO. It was also the one item allowed to be reported in full by the strict Israeli military censors, and within hours of its capture, there were pictures of Mr Begin himself at the castle, congratulating the men who had taken it. General Sharon was there too, and in a significant, though perhaps unintended remark, Mr Begin told Major Haddad, the leader of the 'Free Lebanon' border strip: 'Now Beaufort is yours.'

But Israel did suffer some significant casualties as it advanced northwards into Lebanon. First was a helicopter, shot down with the loss of both its two-man crew. Second to go was a Skyhawk, piloted by Reserve Captain Aharaon Ahigaz. This was shot down by a Sam Seven missile near Nabatiyeh, and proved to be the only Israeli plane to fall victim to the Palestinians' main anti-aircraft weapon. The pilot ejected safely and was picked up by some farmers near a small village. He said later that this caused 'a bit of a problem'. In fact, the peasants began beating and kicking him, but by good luck, local PLO units had seen exactly where he landed and a jeep-load of fighters was quickly on the scene. They took him prisoner, sent the local people away and took Ahigaz to their headquarters. 'From then on there was no trouble,' he said.

The shooting down of the Skyhawk and the capture of the pilot was almost as great a boost to the Palestinians as the taking of Beaufort was to the Israelis. Ahigaz was immediately taken to Beirut to be shown off to the Press, the main object being to get him on to local television, so that the fighters could see that this was one claim which *could* be substantiated.

At the end of Day One of the invasion, the Israelis had taken a major objective and were at the gates of Tyre and Nabatiyeh. That night, they landed from the sea near Sidon to threaten that town as well, and in the morning the Israeli troops who had been pounding Tyre and Nabatiyeh all night, moved forward under cover of massive air-strikes. In both places they found surprisingly light resistance, with most of it around Nabatiyeh being put up by men of Amal, the Shia militia group, rather than by the Palestinians. Soon, the tanks were moving into the main streets of both towns, with Israeli soldiers setting up checkpoints and examining everyone's documents in order to try and identify PLO members. Just before the troops went in, Israeli planes had dropped leaflets urging the people of Tyre and Nabatiyeh to flee, and the lead tanks were fitted with loudhailers which Arabic-speaking officers used to issue the same message. Soon, the same tactics were being adopted at Sidon, as the Israelis signalled their intention of moving in there as well.

The Palestinians were clearly disorganised, and their resistance was poor in most areas of the south. So bad was the picture coming into PLO headquarters in Beirut that Khalil al Wazir, known as Abou Jihad, the overall commander of the Palestinian fighting forces and number three in the PLO command structure, decided to go to Sidon himself and try to sort things out. He got into Sidon with no trouble, found the local Fateh commander, had a blazing row with him as the bombs and shells crashed in, gave a series of orders, none of which were carried out, then set off again for Beirut. But by this time the Israelis had surrounded the town and there seemed to be no way out. Abou Jihad decided to stay in Sidon and take command himself, but the local Fateh men would not have it. They insisted that Abou Jihad was needed back in Beirut, and that if he were killed or captured, as seemed likely if he stayed in Sidon, it would be of great help to Israel and a bad blow for the PLO. So a friendly undertaker was summoned, a coffin was brought, air holes were drilled, and Abou Jihad was shipped off to Beirut as a casualty of war. The ambulance, one of the flat-topped Moslem kind always used to transport the dead, was stopped twice by Israeli patrols, but on both occasions the soldiers did not bother to open the coffin. Abou Jihad reached Beirut safely.

The relatively low level of resistance to the Israeli attacks in the south were not the result of any lack of will on the part of the Palestinians; their fighting spirit was shown in operations which continued for months after the Israelis had occupied the towns of the area. Rather, it was because they had organised for a different kind of attack and a different sort of defence. The Palestinian officers, like generals everywhere, based their strategy on what had happened before. They thought that the Israelis would try to do as they had done in the Litani Operation – sweep in with two columns, in an attempt to encircle and kill as many Palestinians as possible. So the Palestinian leaders had trained their men in mobile warfare: they were to hit where they could, but to withdraw as soon as they were in any danger of capture or encirclement. Thus they had few static defensive positions, and the Israelis met little of the trouble they had expected from fixed anti-tank positions, which could have been established along the small number of invasion roads the Israelis were forced to take. In the towns, particularly Tyre and Nabatiyeh, individual groups of fighters did cause the Israelis trouble, but the response was always the same – massive pounding by tank fire, or recoilless rifles at minimum range. With their guerilla training, this was something the Palestinians had not expected – nor could they stand up to it.

When the invasion of Lebanon had first begun, Mr Begin had sent a number of messages to the Syrians, both by his public pronouncements and via the Americans, calling on them to stay out of the conflict. Israel, he claimed, would only take on the Syrians if President Assad ordered his men to fight. Naturally enough, this was answered with a number of bellicose statements from Damascus, but it was talk alone, matched by little real activity on the ground. As the Israelis began pushing into the Chouf on the third day of the attack, the Syrians did put up some sort of a fight near Jezzine, with helicopter gunships attacking the advancing Israeli columns. But the Syrians quickly pulled back as the Israelis came on, and there was nothing which could be called a battle there.

It was on this third day of the invasion that Israeli tanks rolled into the main square of Beiteddin, once the site of the old capital of the area when it was ruled by Prince Fakrheddin, and now the summer presidential palace. In this pleasant, quiet little town, one foolish or brave individual – no-one ever found out who it was – did fire a single shot as the Israelis moved in. At this stage, the tanks were opened up and soldiers were sitting relaxed on top of them. Immediately the Israelis answered with concentrated bursts of machine gun and small arms fire. The message was clear: the only weapons used in Beiteddin from then on were cameras.

By this time the scope of the Israeli objectives was beginning to emerge – not through any statements made in Jerusalem, but through Israeli activity on the ground. For now they were extending their operations far beyond the twenty-five-mile security zone they had at first been talking about. Israeli gunboats were strafing the coastal highway all the way up to Beirut itself, while the jets were making repeated strikes on Damour, a major Palestinian stronghold thirteen miles south of Beirut. Damour was once a prosperous market town in the centre of a rich farming region supplying Beirut with much of its fresh food, and had been populated entirely by Christians. After the Phalangist massacre at Qarantina in the Lebanese civil war in 1976, it was attacked by Palestinian and leftist forces in retaliation, and the Christians living there were forcibly expelled or killed. Finally, the refugees from Tal Zaatar camp who escaped the massacre committed there by men of Camille Chamoun's National Liberal Party militia were re-settled in Damour, and came to serve as a screen for the Democratic Popular Front for the Liberation of Palestine, the extremist group led by the former Syrian Army officer, Captain Ahmed Jabril. Three months later the wheel was to come full circle, when a detachment of the Phalangist militia made up entirely of men from Damour went into the Palestinian refugee camps of Sabra and Chatila.

In Damour, Ahmed Jabril had at first been supported by Syria, but he had fallen out with President Hafez Assad and had turned to Libya for help. Colonel Gaddafy had supplied him with a number of batteries of Sam Nine missiles, plus some

Libyan 'volunteers' to man them. It was perhaps this which so concentrated Israeli attention on Damour.

The situation in the east of Lebanon was now causing concern, too, for the Israelis were within range of the Damascus Road, which meant that Syria could not risk sending reinforcements into Beirut, even if it wished to do so. There was also the risk that Syrian forces in the west of the country would be cut off; later, this was to become a reality.

Through it all, the steady pounding of Sidon went on. The town was now surrounded, and the terrified population had no way of responding to Israeli exhortations to flee except by rushing down to the sand dunes at the edge of the sea. When they did so, many were killed as shells from Israeli gunboats fell short – a pattern which was to be repeated over and over again in the coming months, until the gunboats, with their notorious inaccuracy, came to be seen almost as a terror weapon.

There were other times of terror in the south too. In the village of Ketermaya near Sidon, the Druze inhabitants had always resisted having Palestinians amongst them; so much so that when a Palestinian unit had set up an anti-aircraft gun just outside the village, the people had persuaded them to move it. So when the Israelis dropped leaflets calling on people to show white sheets or towels on their houses if they did not intend to resist, every house in the village soon had its fluttering signal of surrender. Yet the Israeli planes came over and deliberately shot up the place; and hours later, when the people were burying their dead, the jets came back on another strafing run and killed more people. An Englishman working nearby, Paul Templeman, who went up to see what he could do to help, was almost lynched on being mistaken for an American. Already the identification of Israel with America was taking hold.

While the Israelis were sweeping into Southern Lebanon, the world was clicking its tongue, but doing little else. From Arab countries came the usual ringing denunciations but again, nothing more. Only America did anything positive, and that was to speed up the mission of Mr Philip Habib, the special American envoy who had arranged the ceasefire between the PLO and the Israelis in Southern Lebanon a year earlier. Mr Habib had been due back in the area in any case, but once the

Israelis moved, he was summoned urgently to France where
President Reagan and Mr Haig, the Secretary of State, were
attending the Versailles conference. He left immediately for
Israel, made no headway there at all, and moved on to Damascus. He arrived in Syria just in time for one of the real turning
points of the whole affair – the Israeli attack on the missile sites
in the Bekaa Valley. What with Israel claiming the fall of Sidon
on the same day, the fourth of the war, this was a time of
spectacular reverses for both the Palestinians and the Syrians.

The Sam Six missile sites in the Bekaa Valley near the
crossroads town of Chtaura had been installed in the Spring of
the previous year. They were intended to protect the Syrian
forces holding a defensive line halfway down the southern
portion of the Bekaa Valley, the natural Israeli invasion route
into Eastern Lebanon and thus into Western Syria. The missiles had originally been put in place after Israeli planes shot
down two troop-carrying Syrian helicopters during the Syrian
siege of the Christian town of Zahle – a siege almost as savage as
that of Beirut in the coming months; on that occasion it had
been the Syrian forces who were the aggressors as they had tried
once again to limit any expansion of the power of the Lebanese
Christians.

To the Syrians, the slim white missiles with their sinister
black nose-caps were symbols of their defiance of Israel, as well
as a practical means of defence. They sited them ostentatiously
beside roads and on small hills so that everyone could see them.
And they fired them off whenever Israel sent over one of its
small pilotless drones. That was what caused all the trouble. In
the second or so between the firing of the missiles and the
destruction of the target, the drones had radioed back to base
in Israel the frequency of the radar beam being used and all
the other electronic data which the most sophisticated of
American-supplied equipment could collect. When the time
came, the Israeli planes were fitted out with electronic counter-
measures that rendered the missiles totally ineffectual.

It was a spectacular sight. Wave after wave of Israeli planes
came over, the advanced F16s hitting the targets, the F15s
flying top cover, and circling lazily in the sky above them all,
one of Israel's Hawkeye command planes, crammed with

electronic gear, directing operations and jamming the Syrian radar. As the Israelis attacked, so the Syrians came in with their Mig 21s and 23s. The Israeli 'guard planes' saw them off, closing in on the Syrians and firing their missiles at short range, while the Syrian pilots tried to use theirs from a considerable distance. One Israeli plane literally flew his Syrian opposite number into the ground: hot on the tail of the Syrian Mig, in classic dog-fight fashion, the Israeli pilot closed in so much on the Syrian that the Mig pilot flew his plane directly into a hillside.

The Syrian missiles were launched, but not a single hit was registered. As each Sam went streaking towards its chosen target, so at the last moment it curved away, to explode harmlessly somewhere miles from any Israeli plane. The ECMs were totally effective: it was a day of triumph for American technology.

And it was a black day for the Syrian Air Force: they lost 22 of their planes, and 17 of the 19 missile batteries then in place were knocked out. To make things worse, the following day, Israel did it again, knocking out two more missile batteries and shooting down 25 Syrian jets and two helicopter gunships. Again, no Israeli losses.

It was after these two days of total disaster that Syria decided to pull out of the fighting altogether, though it was not announced at the time. At a council of war in Damascus, General Mustafa Tlas, the army commander, told President Assad and the political leaders that the Syrian Air Force was outclassed, the ground-to-air missiles useless, and that without air cover, the army could not fight on. What he did not add, but what was becoming obvious was that the Syrian tanks, some of them the latest Soviet T72s, were no match for the Israeli Chieftains. Syria was finding itself unprotected, outgunned and outclassed, so the decision was taken to pull out as soon as a reasonable opportunity presented itself. In the meantime, President Assad ordered that maximum publicity should be given to Syria's role in the war. A far-seeing and able politician, he correctly anticipated events to come, and hoped that by emphasising the fact that Syria had been the one Arab state to play an active role in the war, he would be able to wrest some political advantage in the future. His forecast proved right.

In Lebanon itself, Israeli troops stormed into Sidon after another massive bombardment, once more preceded by the now-familiar calls to the inhabitants to flee while there was still time. There was some heavy fighting and some Israeli losses in the battle for Sidon, but the disorganisation of the Palestinians there made things easier for the invaders. There were stories of treachery among Palestinian commanders, and at least one who was captured said publicly that he had long disagreed with PLO policies and had wanted to abandon 'the military struggle'. He appeared to have done so very quickly when the Israelis arrived. Another Palestinian officer from the area was 'executed' by a hit squad on suspicion of having collaborated with the invaders, and there were constant reports of uncannily accurate Israeli intelligence, which served to heighten suspicion of Palestinian leaders and officers.

By Day Six of the war, again with unhappy memories of 1967, Syria had had enough. The Syrians accepted a ceasefire offer made through the good offices of Mr Habib, and in Eastern Lebanon the guns fell silent at noon on Friday, June 11th. Next day, the PLO agreed to abide by a ceasefire call made by the United Nations. The UN had also demanded Israeli withdrawal – but it takes two to make an effective ceasefire. The Israelis soon made it plain that they considered Syria alone to be an 'official' body, a state capable of entering into direct negotiations which could result in a truce. The PLO, Israel held, were merely a band of terrorists, so they felt justified in doing what they wanted and taking no notice at all of Yasser Arafat's announcement that his men would adhere to the UN resolutions. The result was that Israeli troops went ahead with their mopping-up operations in Tyre, Nabatiyeh, Sidon and the other occupied areas; bulldozers were brought in to raze the Ain Hilweh and Rashidiyeh refugee camps, which had long been centres of recruitment and training for the PLO; and busloads of handcuffed and blindfolded suspects were taken off for interrogation. These men were denied the small comfort of International Red Cross visits since they were not considered prisoners of war, but 'administrative detainees'.

It was at this point, six days into the war, that General

Sharon announced that Israel had accomplished all its objectives: a twenty-eight-mile strip of Lebanese territory had been
occupied, he said, and Israel was determined to keep this buffer
zone clear of Palestinian fighters to make good Mr Begin's
earlier promise that no more rockets would ever fall in Upper
Galilee.

General Sharon also revealed that Israeli Army spokesmen
had been less than frank in the details they had given of their
casualties. Up to that time, the spokesmen had been talking of
68 Israeli soldiers killed in the invasion and 424 wounded;
according to General Sharon, the true cost up to the time of the
ceasefire was more than 100 killed, and more than 600 injured.
Such discrepancies were to turn up again in the future, and
were never accounted for, either by Sharon or anyone else.
Palestinians also took heart from the Israeli admission that
among those killed were General Yekutil Adam, a former
deputy chief of staff, and a colonel, Haim Fella. The Palestinians felt they had acquitted themselves well, and warned that
they still had operational units behind the enemy lines who
would not observe any ceasefire. This proved to be true, and
these small groups of guerrillas did attack the Israelis when
they could in the next few weeks, though the damage they
inflicted was minimal.

After a week of war, the Israelis were effectively in total
control of Southern Lebanon. They were at Khalde at the
southern entrance to Beirut, and they were within striking
distance of the main Beirut-Damascus highway in the east of
the country. They had taken over more than a third of Lebanon, established their security zone, and killed or captured
large numbers of Palestinian fighters.

CHAPTER TWO

As Lebanese and Palestinians alike began talking about the results of the Israeli invasion, counting the cost, and generally assuming it was all over bar the politicking, General Sharon quietly added a new Israeli war aim, which was to prolong the conflict for months: the complete destruction of the PLO, elimination of their infrastructure in the country and an end to their power. Thus it was that hours after the first ceasefire was supposed to have gone into effect, Israeli forces were hard at it south of Beirut, trading fire with the Amal units who were the main defenders there, and quietly moving up into the hills above Beirut airport to ensure that the Palestinians could not use the roads there as an escape-route towards Syria. At the same time, Israeli tanks and self-propelled guns were being moved closer to the Damascus road, so that if the need arose, the Israelis could interdict traffic there whenever they chose.

On Sunday, June 13th, Day Eight of the war, General Sharon sent his tanks into Baabda and followed them in person. This was a move reminiscent of yet another war, that of 1973, when Israel took advantage of the ceasefire with Egypt to complete the encirclement of the Third Army on the East Bank of the Suez Canal. Now Beirut was surrounded, with Israeli troops to the south and east, and the Christian Phalangist forces to the north – soon to be reinforced by Israelis there too. Though it was to be a few more weeks before Israel resorted to the blockade in an effort to starve the Palestinians out, the siege of Beirut had begun. In the meantime, the fighting and the talking went on.

Months before the invasion, Palestinians and Lebanese alike had been warning of what was in store. Israeli troops were massed all along the border, they said, merely waiting for the right moment to attack. But there had been too many false alarms before, so few people took any notice, even when American intelligence reports confirmed the presence of large Israeli units. Israel, it was said, was merely applying political pressure through her military presence; after the débâcle of the Litani Operation of 1978, which had achieved little and resulted merely in the establishment of the UN force in Lebanon, Israel could not afford another large-scale incursion, the argument went.

Thus the experts. The reality was that Israel was completely determined to make good Mr Begin's promises to the settlers in Upper Galilee, and General Sharon was equally intent on ending the power of the PLO. As early as January, 1982, General Sharon had given notice to the Americans that he intended to send his troops into Lebanon, and weeks before the invasion took place, American diplomats were quietly telling their European allies that Israeli action was imminent, and that the only matter in dispute was the timing.

As it turned out, the date of the invasion was dictated by an event beyond Israel's control: the attempted murder of the Israeli ambassador in London, Mr Shlomo Argov. One of the most active, outspoken and effective of Israel's envoys. Mr Argov was hit in the head by a bullet fired from a 9mm Polish-made machine pistol. The bullet lodged close to his brain, and was removed by specialists at the Central Middlesex Hospital. For weeks Mr Argov was on the critical list, then gradually he began to recover, until he was eventually well enough to be taken home to Israel. One of Mr Argov's assailants was shot and also wounded in the head when the Ambassador's bodyguard and his British Special Branch guard opened fire as the attackers ran away. Eventually, three men, two of them carrying Jordanian passports and one an Iraqi, were charged with the attempted murder of the ambassador.

It did not take long to establish who the men were: they were from the Abou Nidal group, a terrorist organisation established by a dissident Fateh officer, Hassan Sabry al Banna, who had been condemned to death *in absentia* by Fateh after an abortive mutiny against the authority of Yasser Arafat and the other leaders. Units of the Palestinian Armed Struggle Command, the military police of the PLO, had moved against his troops stationed in Southern Lebanon, and Abou Nidal, as he was known, had fled to Baghdad, taking with him a number of followers who were as disenchanted as he was with the Arafat style of leadership. In Baghdad they were made welcome, largely on the Arab principle that anything which serves to divide a powerful neighbour must be useful. Soon Abou Nidal and his men were being trained by the Iraqis in clandestine operations, sabotage and general mayhem. Though they were often allowed to select their own targets, they were also used as an arm of Iraqi Intelligence; thus, while it was often Abou Nidal's men who pulled the trigger when some Palestinian official in Europe was assassinated, it was usually the Iraqis who had given the orders.

In 1981, Abou Nidal apparently fell out with the Iraqi authorities and moved from Baghdad, this time to Damascus. Again, he was made welcome, largely because the Syrians thought they could use him against his old Iraqi friends in the constant war being waged between these two Ba'athist states. Once more Abou Nidal was supplied with weapons and money, and this time was set to attack Israeli as well as Palestinian targets. The aim was to provoke the Israelis into action against the PLO, which President Assad felt was getting too powerful and too independent – in other words, Arafat was refusing to do as Assad wanted. A sure sign of this was that Abou Nidal renamed his force Assifa, the storm, the same name as that given to the fighting forces of Al Fateh, Arafat's own group.

Now, however, there was a complication, for some of Abou Nidal's men had remained in Baghdad, staying loyal to the Iraqis, and they too were in the field, carrying out actions against both Palestinians and Israelis. The question was: which group was responsible for the attack on Shlomo Argov? The machine pistols used in the attempted murder had previously been used on the Continent in attacks on Jewish targets, but all that proved was that the same small number of weapons were being shunted around Europe in someone's diplomatic bag. What was obvious was that the results of the attack in London could be of benefit only to the Iraqis: President Siddam Hussein's army was being mauled by the Iranian forces and thrown back inside Iraqi territory; yet at that time, the President still had hopes of holding a non-aligned summit conference in Baghdad in the autumn, so that anything which would cause trouble to Iran was bound to be of benefit to Iraq; if trouble could be caused to Syria at the same time, then so much the better.

Certainly the Iraqis never repudiated Abou Nidal. After it was all over, President Hussein was asked directly if he condemned the terrorist acts committed by Abou Nidal's men. He replied that he did not consider what they had done was 'terrorism'; Abou Nidal had come to Baghdad as a refugee, and could not be turned away; what he did, the Iraqi leader claimed in a remarkably disingenuous reply to a question, was entirely up to him.

The fact remained that Western Intelligence agencies were certain it was the Iraqis who had allowed their diplomatic bags to be used to move guns about. If it was indeed the Iraqis who ordered the attack, and the circumstantial evidence is strong, then the results were everything they hoped for: Syrian military strength was set back years, the threat to Iraq in the north was removed, and all Syrian aid to Iran dried up.

The Iraqi calculation – if it was Iraq which was responsible – must have been that given sufficient provocation, Israel would carry out its long-threatened sweep into Lebanon. Then, the argument must have run, Syrian troops were bound to become involved, since the Israelis would go deeper into the country than ever before. Syria might then become bogged down in the kind of war of attrition which had taken place on the Golan Heights after the 1973 war. Other Arab countries took the same view: everyone was certain that Israel would act, and no-one was very alarmed at that prospect. Most of them, for all their public protestations, were quite happy to see the PLO cut down to size.

In the West, a different attitude prevailed. In both Washington and London, there was advance knowledge of what the Israelis intended to do. Even while many in the Middle East were watching the forty-eight hours of bombing in Lebanon which preceded the invasion and thinking that it was the Israeli 'punishment' for the London attack, diplomats and intelligence men in America and Europe were quietly warning of what was to come. This time, they said, Israel had prepared a spectacular offensive. When pressed, the small number of people in the know accurately forecast an Israeli move into Beirut, and an attempt to eliminate the leadership of the PLO.

These warnings were being given while Mr Begin and General Sharon were still talking of the establishment of a twenty-five-mile-wide security zone as their main war aim. Clearly, the real objectives of the war had been set much earlier, went much further than most people realised, and had been communicated to the Americans well in advance. All the evidence suggests that it was the American Secretary of State, Alexander Haig, who had given the go-ahead.

Mr Haig was one of that most dangerous of animals, a political general, and he was also a man obsessed with the East-West conflict, who saw everything in terms of advantage or loss 'for the West'. On his first tour of the Middle East, only weeks after taking office in 1980, he had lectured such people as King Fah'd of Saudi Arabia and King Hussein of Jordan about the dangers to the Middle East from the Soviet Union, ignoring their arguments that it was the Palestinian issue which was the key to the situation in the area. In Jerusalem, Mr Haig had stood happily by while Mr Begin made some of his more outrageous remarks about the Arabs, and had himself been trapped into condemning the Syrians at a time other American diplomats were quietly trying to mend fences with that country.

After a year in office, however, Mr Haig had a clearer grasp of things: he accepted that the Palestinian question had to be settled if there was to be peace in the Middle East, though he shared Israel's view that the establishment of a Palestine state would lead to the creation of a Soviet surrogate in the area. Mr Haig's idea was that a measure of autonomy in the West Bank, plus links between that area and Jordan, would be quite enough to satisfy Palestinian aspirations, if the power of the PLO could only be broken. The PLO, whom he saw as a mixture of a terrorist organisation and a Soviet front, *had* to be destroyed. So when General Sharon arrived in Washington in January of 1982 with his quiet plans for doing just what Mr Haig wanted, the Israeli Defence Minister was given a warm welcome. The two generals thought alike.

Even the Arab countries were not averse to the PLO being put in its place. The Saudis honestly believed that a political settlement of the issue was possible, arguing that the weight of Arab influence – that is, oil – was enough to persuade the Americans to exert pressure on Israel. The Saudis had always been bitterly opposed to terrorism, rightly believing that they themselves were as vulnerable as anyone else; Syria was angry because the PLO would not fall into line and form an alliance with Damascus; Iraq feared that precisely that might happen, and so was happy to see the PLO militarily reduced; Egypt believed it could once again resume leadership of the Arab world if peace could be established, and saw the Palestinians as the main obstacle. Only such isolated states as the Libya of Colonel Gaddafy genuinely supported the Palestinian cause, and the Libyans were too far away and too few to have any real influence on affairs.

The Palestinians themselves appeared not to realise just how isolated they were, or to understand the damage they had done by their actions in Lebanon. In Beirut the situation was not too bad, for the Palestinian 'state within the state' was matched in East Beirut by the Phalangist administration, which had taken over the functions of government in just the same way as the Palestinians. It was in the rest of the country, and particularly in the south, that the Palestinians had made themselves so unpopular. By regularly firing rockets into Upper Galilee from Beaufort Castle and other strong points, they immediately drew Israeli counter-fire, which invariably killed Lebanese villagers or damaged Lebanese homes and crops without hurting the Palestinians. That was bad enough, but the Palestinians went further: they extorted money, they meted out rough and provocative 'justice', they seized what they needed, they sited their guns near villages, they sought shelter near the border, and they made little contribution to the welfare of the area. It was the Palestinians, too, who had been the cause of the 1978 Israeli invasion, the Litani Operation, which had led directly to the setting-up of the UN force. This in itself had caused resentment among Lebanese villagers, who found themselves constantly subject to checks, their fields traversed by military vehicles, and their homes used first by one faction and then by another.

The Litani Operation had been in effect a dress rehearsal for the invasion of 1982, and it taught the Israelis a number of lessons. Chief of these was that a frontal onslaught into Southern Lebanon was ineffective and counter-productive. For that was what the Israeli forces had done in 1978. In March that year, prior to the Israeli incursion, a band of Palestinian terrorists crossed the border into Israel, and in a wild drive down the road from Haifa to Tel Aviv, killed thirty-two people as they sprayed indiscriminate fire at buses, cars and lorries. Naturally, this mass murder drew the regular Israeli response, for by that time the pattern of terrorist attack followed by reprisal raid was well established. However, on that occasion, bad weather forced the Israelis to delay their counter-strike, so that it was some days before the Israeli forces moved. When they did, they attacked straight across the border, with no troops landing further up the Lebanese coast, and no helicopters putting men into position behind the Palestinian lines. Because of this, and as a result of the delay in mounting the operation, it failed in its objectives.

These objectives had been set out at some length when the invasion began. A military communiqué ran as follows:

> The Israeli defence forces have opened a purifying operation along the length of the Lebanese border.
>
> The goal of the operation is to root out the bases of the terrorists near the border and to hit the special bases from which the terrorists leave for operations deep inside the territory of Israel.
>
> The Israeli Defence Forces do not intend to harm the population, the Lebanese Army or the Pan-Arab Force, but rather the terrorists and their helpers, in order to guarantee life and security to the residents of Israel.
>
> The goal of the operation is not reprisal for the crimes of the terrorists, because there is no reprisal for the murder of innocent civilians, men, women and children, but to defend the State and prevent attacks by people of Al Fateh and the PLO, who use the territory of Lebanon in order to attack the citizens of Israel.

Thus the Israeli command when the attack was launched. The reality was very different; for on this occasion, Israel displayed a ham-handedness and lack of finesse quite out of keeping with its image and with its past performance. Units did not reach their start positions on time; tank commanders lost their way, and squadrons were broken up; infantry showed unwillingness to move forward in the face of only moderate resistance; and the whole planning of the operation seemed inefficient.

The real objective, as it emerged later, was to cut off and kill as many Palestinians as possible, and in order to do that, the Israelis swept in a wide arc from the slopes of Mount Hermon across to the sea at Tyre. But with no stop-line along the Litani River to prevent the guerrillas moving back, no helicopter-borne troops in position, and no landings along the coast, the Palestinians were able to fade away before the Israeli advance. In the event, very few Palestinian fighters were killed in the operation; as usual, those who bore the brunt of the Israeli attack were the Shia villagers of Southern Lebanon, for rather than going in on foot, with the consequent risk of casualties, the Israelis used their tanks and artillery to pound villages and towns as they advanced. Very few Palestinians were caught in this way, but hundreds of peasants were – men, women and children, to echo the Israeli Army communiqué. Again, the Israeli infantry, fearful of casualties, resorted to the bad old Army practice of 'rifle reconnaissance' – firing indiscriminately at any area which might conceal enemies; again, it was the Lebanese civilians, not the Palestinians, who were the victims.

The original Israeli intention appeared to have been to carry out a neat surgical operation, encircling and destroying the Palestinian fighters. The Israeli talk of rooting out guerrilla bases was pure propaganda, since the guerrillas maintained no bases close to the Israel border – an obvious precaution. Then, as the operation went on and was seen to be failing in its objective, a second contingency plan seemed to have been put into action. This was to occupy the whole of Southern Lebanon up to the Litani River, with the object of forming a buffer-zone along the border. This the Israelis did, eventually inducing the United Nations to send in the peace-keeping force. In theory this meant that Israel had extended its security zone up to the Litani River. In practical terms things did not work out like that: the UN men proved incapable of stopping the Palestinians from infiltrating into Upper Galilee, and were powerless to prevent PLO gunners from firing rockets over their heads into Israeli territory. All that Israel achieved by the Litani Operation was to put in place an international force which could, in theory and possibly even in practice, prove a deterrent to any further Israeli incursion.

Naturally, Israel learnt from its mistakes. The man in charge of the Litani Operation had been General Rafael Eytan, a man long concerned with Lebanon, who had led the commando squad which had landed from helicopters at Beirut Airport at Christmas, 1968, and destroyed thirteen planes of Middle East Airlines in one of Israel's first reprisal raids. By 1982, General Eytan had risen to become Chief of Staff of the Israeli Army, and it was he who was largely responsible for planning the 1982 invasion – 'Operation Peace for Galilee,' as it was called. Eytan showed he had learned from the past. This time, helicopters were widely used to drop troops in position ahead of the main advance, and there were landings on the coast to the north of Tyre, Sidon and Damour, as those towns were attacked in quick succession. Tanks were used, as in the past, but now they were backed up by infantry.

In only one respect did General Eytan not alter his tactics: once again, the Israeli forces took no heed of possible Lebanese civilian casualties. The Air Force was used to bomb and rocket positions without regard to the safety of the local population, and Israeli gunners laid down interdiction fire on roads used more by civilians than by guerrillas. Tyre, Sidon, Damour and eventually Beirut were all shelled mercilessly, often by the notoriously inaccurate gunboats lying just over the horizon or by smaller patrol boats using 40mm machine guns. Israeli troops responded massively to the slightest provocation, opening up with heavy weapons even when only a few rifle shots had been fired at them; again, one policy which remained consistent was to try to minimise Israeli casualties.

Israel also made little attempt to abide by the conditions laid down by America when certain weapons were supplied. The

United States had stipulated, for example, that cluster bombs and cluster shells should be used only 'for the defence of Israel'; in fact, both were used right from the beginning of the war, though Israel at first denied this. Naturally, from a military point of view, it made good sense to use these weapons, which were highly effective against large concentrations of troops. The trouble was that they were not used against large concentrations of troops, but large concentrations of Palestinian men, women and children. Cluster bombs were dropped on the Ain Hilweh refugee camp and on the Rashidiyeh camp; cluster shells were fired into densely populated areas of Beirut; cluster bombs were dropped wherever the Israelis planned a sea-borne assault, in order to clear the way for the troops.

The Israeli defence to these accusations was that the Palestinians had deliberately situated their headquarters, stores and artillery positions in populated areas. This was certainly true. Originally the Palestinians had sited their defensive weapons not in anticipation of Israeli attacks, but to guard against assaults by the Lebanese Army or the Phalangist militia. Their aim had been to protect their camps. Later, certainly, the Palestinians did move heavy weapons into a number of Lebanese villages in the south, often in the face of active opposition by the inhabitants. However, this was often unavoidable; the Palestinians had to have somewhere to live, to train, to plan and to house their headquarters and back-up staff. Tents on the bare, rocky mountainsides of the south would have been an invitation to the Israelis to destroy them, so they moved into the towns and villages, using quarters indistinguishable from the civilian buildings around them. In Nabatiyeh, there was undoubtedly a high concentration of Palestinian offices and depots, though thousands of civilians lived there as well. The criticism of Israel was not that it bombed or shelled such places, but that it took the precaution of bombing or shelling whole areas, just in case there were Palestinian targets hidden there. As to the Israeli accusations that the Palestinians deliberately sited their weapons near churches, mosques or hospitals, no evidence of this could ever be found. On occasions, of course, artillery was positioned close to such places. But as the war went on and the Palestinians were penned into smaller and smaller areas, it was often difficult to find somewhere to site a gun where it would be effective and where it would not invite return fire onto some sensitive area. In Beirut, most of the Palestinian guns were mobile, and were constantly moved about; those that were static were often deliberately sited in open pieces of land where they were highly vulnerable, in order to refute the Israeli charges that advantage was being taken of civilian shelter.

It was noticeable, too, that when the Israelis moved into an area, they rarely set up tented camps. Instead, like the Palestinians, they requisitioned houses, schools or offices in the towns they had seized. When they did once set up a big tank park just below the presidential palace at Baabda, they soon had to dismantle it. At this stage, journalists and reporters were still able to move from one side of Beirut to the other, and soon pictures of the park, complete with lorries, armoured vehicles, staff cars and all the rest, appeared in newspapers in West Beirut. That night, salvoes of Katyushas crashed in and a considerable number of vehicles were destroyed. The next day everything was dispersed: the Israeli command had learnt the folly of underrating Palestinian intelligence or the ability of the Palestinian gunners to target accurately.

CHAPTER THREE

For thousands of Israelis, it all began with the ominous ringing of a telephone on the Shabbat, June 5th. Devout Jews only allow the telephone to interrupt Sabbath worship in times of national crisis, so this had to be something serious. It was. The message brought by the phones was from military headquarters in Tel Aviv, and always it was the same: 'This is the Army. Get your things together and come down right away.' One hundred thousand of the country's 325,000 reserve officers and soldiers were being mobilised, and all knew without being told exactly where they were going, for only eleven days before, during a visit to New York, Arik Sharon had spelt it out. In a speech to newspaper editors which had been widely reported inside Israel, Sharon had warned that any act of terrorism against Israelis anywhere in the world would be the signal for an invasion of Lebanon: 'We have no choice. We cannot live under the threat of assassination and murder.' Using charts and maps, he detailed what he saw as the danger to Israel from 'the terrorists' across the border in Lebanon, and he said quite clearly, for the first time, that if Israel did go into Lebanon, its purpose would be the destruction of the 'terrorist organisations and their infrastructure.'

When the moment did come, it mattered little to Sharon that the excuse for the invasion had been provided by one of Arafat's enemies, the traitor Abou Nidal, a man condemned to death by the PLO. It was also of no concern to him that for all the talk of 144 truce violations in the previous year, not a single Israeli had been killed in Upper Galilee. The PLO, well aware of what Israel was planning, were doing all they could to avoid providing any pretext for an Israeli attack, and were scrupulously observing the ceasefire negotiated by Philip Habib. Of course, that could not go on once the Israeli jets began bombing targets all the way from the border up to Beirut itself, so the Palestinians unwittingly strengthened the hands of the hawks in the Israeli cabinet by firing into Israel from Beaufort Castle as soon as the Israeli action began. Indeed, one of their Katyusha rockets sliced off the side of a hotel in Kiryat Shmona where a Cabinet Minister, Yacov Meridor, happened to be spending the night. Not surprisingly, he was one of the large majority which voted in favour of the invasion when the issue was formally put to the cabinet, the lone voice in opposition being that of Mr Josef Burg, the Interior Minister, whose son was a prominent member of the 'Peace Now' movement. As it was, all the signs were that General Sharon would have gone ahead without cabinet backing, relying on the support of the Prime Minister alone, if it had looked as if his colleagues would go against him.

So, at 8 o'clock on Sunday, June 6th, the first of some eighty thousand soldiers who were to fight in Lebanon crossed the frontier at Metullah in Eastern Galilee and Rosh Haniqra on the Mediterranean. The stage was set for what turned out to be a classic, textbook tank and air assault on the conventional forces of Syria in the east of Lebanon, and a desperate, merciless pounding of civilian population centres in the west of the country, as the Israeli Defence Forces tried to get at the elusive Palestinians. As one United Nations officer there said: 'It was cannons against sparrows'.

At his command headquarters at Zefat in Galilee, General Sharon was joined by the Prime Minister, Mr Begin, walking with the aid of a stick following a hip injury. In those first few hours both waited anxiously for news of the Syrian reaction, which they believed would indicate the Soviet response to the Israeli action; if Syria opened up across the Golan Heights as a means of easing the pressure on its forces and the Palestinians in Lebanon, then Israel would have been the cause of a major new Middle East war, and would have had to send its army up to the gates of Damascus or even beyond to ensure success – a move which might have involved both the superpowers. General Sharon, with his deep personal dislike of the Syrians, might have welcomed this as a chance to finish off his old foes, but Mr Begin was more circumspect, and hoped that Israel would be allowed to concentrate on Lebanon alone.

What neither man had expected was that there would be no Kremlin response at all. In the event, the Russians seemed to have been caught off balance; they knew as well as anyone else that for months past the Israelis had had troops on the border ready to go into Lebanon, but at first it seemed they did not realise the scale of the invasion. All that came out of Moscow was a predictable Tass commentary describing the attack as 'the fifth Israeli war against the Arabs,' and saying that it had been done with the advance knowledge of the Americans. President Reagan became the only world leader to take any action: he personally appealed to Mr Begin to stop hostilities, and dispatched Philip Habib to the area to do what he could to mediate.

Syria had actually agreed to renew the mandate of the UN force on the Golan Heights only six days before, and so obviously had no aggressive intentions of its own. In fact, the Syrians, like many others, were not at all sure what the Israeli aims were, and so hesitated about where to concentrate their forces, or whether to allow them to become embroiled at all. President Assad did issue a few bold statements, promising that Syria would not allow the PLO to be destroyed, and saying he was putting all his troops at the disposal of Lebanon. In fact, the Syrian command was floundering. Their eventual excuse for failing to react promptly and efficiently was that they refused to fight a war at a time dictated by Israel – as feeble a get-out as any. All the signals from Syria were interpreted in Jerusalem as meaning that if Israel only wanted to create the twenty-five-mile security zone which General Sharon was talking about, then the Syrians in Lebanon would put up no more than token resistance, and would not play any part unless attacked. At the same time, the Syrian command made it plain that there were three places they would have to defend: Hasbaya, at the southern end of the Bekaa Valley, which guarded the main attack route up Syria's western flank; Jezzine, the mountain town which controlled access to the main Beirut-Damascus highway; and Beirut itself. In these first days, it rapidly became clear that Israel intended to take all three of Syria's 'no-go areas', yet still the Syrians did little. They sent their planes into action over Beirut, but they made no real attempt to stop the advance up the Bekaa Valley, where they had adequate forces to counter-attack in strength, and where they had built considerable fortifications.

At first, the only real problem for the Israelis was how to break through the UNIFIL lines at points held by Norwegian, Nepalese and Dutch troops. The Scandinavians on the road chosen by the Israelis were commanded by a captain who was also a pastor; they were lightly armed and could do little, so as the retreating Palestinians fired rockets at the Israeli column over the heads of the UN soldiers, they hastily dragged a white saloon car into place as a makeshift barricade, and dashed for their bunkers. As they ran, a shell landed, sending shrapnel flying in all directions, and killing an eighteen-year-old from Oslo. UN officers later identified the shell as one fired by the Palestinians – perhaps a diplomatic move, since the UN troops had to go on living in what was now Israeli-occupied territory. The Dutch battalion was stationed in the coastal sector, and somehow six Dutch soldiers found themselves alone on a road, facing a column of eleven Israeli Centurion tanks. They pulled concrete anti-tank blockades across the highway, then, like the Norwegians, took cover. This was strictly what they should have done, for General William Callaghan, the Irish commander of the force, had issued orders to his men to hold their fire and to take shelter. The Nepalese also received the same orders, but in typical Gurkha fashion, decided to follow Lord Nelson's example; a small detachment guarding Khardala bridge over the Litani River adamantly refused to move aside to allow an Israeli tank column through. 'Over our dead bodies,' they said in effect, standing firmly in line across the road. For twenty-four hours they stayed there, despite all the persuasions of the Israelis, until eventually, the Israeli column commander turned away, called up engineers, and took his tanks across a hastily constructed pontoon bridge over the Litani a little to the north. The incident nonetheless provided a graphic demonstration of what the UN men could have done, given the will, the leadership and the backing of New York.

The Israeli command had never worried overmuch about having to cross the UN lines, and carefully avoided what was known as 'the Marjayoun gap', an area not covered by any UN presence; this was probably because they were expected to use that route, and foresaw mines, tank traps and resistance from fixed anti-tank positions. Israel had for years past accused the UN forces of collusion with the Palestinians, and there had been cases of individual officers smuggling guns and explosives into Israel. Certain units were particularly disliked by the Israelis, as was shown when a Norwegian party returned to the border after taking the body of their slain comrade to Ben Gurion airport, for transport back to Oslo. The whole length of the frontier was marked by a twelve-foot-high wire fence, with occasional gates to allow access for the hundreds of Lebanese who worked in Israel; here the Israelis held the group up for twelve hours before grudgingly 'finding' the key to the frontier gate and allowing them back into Lebanon.

On this first night of the war, the most critical role was played by men of Israel's élite Golani Brigade, who were assigned a task which some of their own officers thought too difficult, too daring in conception, and too hastily planned. Their orders were to take Beaufort Castle, the old Crusader ruin which had become a symbol to both the Palestinians and the Israelis. Bombed, shelled and rocketed, still the Fateh men holding it stayed in place, using everything from mortars to 120mm cannons to shell the kibbutzim over the border in Israel just ten miles away. They boasted they could hold it for ever, and dared the Israelis to come and get them out. The Israelis did – yet it took eighteen hours from the time of the first bombing runs before the castle fell to the vastly superior Israeli assault team.

First the Israelis sent in their planes, the same F16s which had been used to demolish the Iraqi reactor outside Baghdad just a year before. The walls of Beaufort proved stronger than the defences of Osirak; every time there was a respite from the air-strikes, the PLO men were up on the ramparts again, pouring their shells into targets in Upper Galilee and harassing the advancing Israeli columns. So General Sharon decided that the best troops in the Israeli Army, the men of the Golani, would have to be sent in. According to Jacob Guterman, whose son Raz was the first soldier over the walls, the troops were sent into battle in too much of a hurry. Yet as usual, Sharon could put up the one convincing argument to which there could be no reply: his men succeeded.

The first group quietly forded the Litani River just after midnight, and using ropes and pitons, scaled the sheer face of the cliff leading up to the castle from the ravine at a bend in the river. Raz Guterman, first over, Major Guni Harnik, the commando leader, and the rest of them then flung stun grenades and sprayed machine gun fire around as they burst into the castle, taking the sleeping defenders by surprise. But the Fateh men were themselves an élite force; they quickly took up their prearranged defensive positions and fought step by step as the Israeli commandos advanced through the labyrinth of passageways and tunnels, winkling out the last Palestinians. In the end, every one of the defenders was killed, and by the morning, Sharon and Begin were able to land there by helicopter to underline the importance of the victory in front of the television cameras.

Sharon then returned to Jerusalem, while Begin met Major Sa'ad Haddad and made the fateful remark: 'Now Beaufort is yours' – words immediately taken to mean that Haddad's Free Lebanon strip along the border was to be massively expanded northwards. In Jerusalem that same day Sharon appeared before a meeting of the Knesset Foreign Affairs and Defence Committee, a group which was to give him increasing trouble over the weeks to come. He spoke with pride of the exploits of his men in capturing Beaufort, and told the members of the Knesset there that it had been 'a hundred per cent successful – not a single Israeli was lost.' When the general's remarks were reported on Israeli Radio, there was an immediate sense of shock among the men of the Golani Brigade: they knew, just as he did, that in fact six Israelis had been killed in the operation, including Guterman and Harnik, and that eighteen others had been wounded, including Ronnie Cohen, who had had to have both his legs amputated after stepping on a mine planted in one of the castle's walkways.

With Beaufort Castle silenced, the Israelis were able to move forward much more quickly and spread out northwards as soon as Nabatiyeh was taken. This once-prosperous market town, which had been the centre of the tobacco-growing region and home of the Regie, had become the headquarters in the central area for the PLO, who had commandeered offices and houses and, as a result, had regularly drawn Israeli fire onto the town. The Israelis had little trouble in taking the place, and the attack followed a pattern which was to be repeated as they advanced on Beirut: first Major Haddad's radio station warned the inhabitants to flee, or if they stayed, to hang white sheets out of the windows and white ribbons on their car aerials in token of surrender. Most did so, the only ones to hold out being some small groups of Pakistanis and Bangladeshis who were fighting with the PLO. The Pakistanis were volunteers and fought well, but the Bangladeshis had originally come to Lebanon as workers in a textile factory owned by a Palestinian and had then been 'conscripted' by the PLO.

Once the resistance was crushed, the Israelis who moved in had difficulty in distinguishing between damage caused by their assault and damage done months or years before; it was a much-fought-over town. But one boost for them was to find that they were in general welcomed by the mainly Shia residents of Nabatiyeh, who told them that the PLO had behaved like an occupying army for years past, never paying bills, and helping themselves to whatever they wanted. Heartened by all this, the Israelis began to think that perhaps the propaganda from Jerusalem might be right, and they really were liberators rather than conquerors. At the same time, however, there was still a fear among Israeli officers that things were not going quite as well as those back in Israel were trying to make out. They noted that few PLO men were caught at the roadblocks they set up; the vast majority seemed to have faded away once more, to man new defence lines further north.

Certainly the Palestinians had gone in a hurry. The Fateh offices overlooking the town hall were strewn with papers, medicine bottles and half-empty boxes of ammunition. In one room decorated with Fateh posters, a grenade still lay on a windowsill and someone had left behind a suitcase, which Israeli sappers cautiously examined for booby-traps: in fact, the case was found to contain pyjamas, a dressing gown, a wallet full of money and four clips for an AK47. Shoes, socks and uniforms were scattered about, and in the Fateh offices and the nearby Saika building, desk drawers were left open with papers spilling out, as though the PLO men had quickly seized the most important documents before escaping. All in all, the 'victory' Israel claimed in the town was a bit hollow, for Red Cross officials estimated that no more than a dozen PLO men had been killed or captured.

So complete was the guerrilla withdrawal that within twenty-four hours Major Haddad was able to tour the area to address the people of the town and tell them they were 'free at last'. This news was not greeted with much enthusiasm, and the Palestinian women and children among them were not encouraged when they heard that Haddad's 'heavies' had been to the lawyers of the town to tell them they should accept no cases from Palestinian clients. This was rightly taken as an indication that local people could do what they liked to evict squatters who had taken over their property or had set up tents or shanties on their land.

In the eastern sector, the Israelis, in pincer movements, had gone on to secure the Christian town of Marjayun and the Druze village of Hasbaya, where six months earlier residents had reluctantly allowed the PLO to take over a school to store guns and explosives. When the guerrillas had tried to exert their authority in the streets, however, a Druze council had met and sent men to burn down two Palestinian encampments. Understandably, when the Israelis arrived, they were treated like honoured guests, with people bringing them bowls of cherries from their homes.

As the Israelis moved further north, however, resistance began to become reasonably well organised. At Enharsha, thirteen miles above the Israeli border, a group of a hundred Palestinians lay in wait for a tank column. Rocket-propelled grenades were used in the ambush, but the fighters were no match for the gunners in the Israeli Merkava Chariot tanks; the defenders were decimated and the dead Palestinians flung into a hastily-dug mass grave by the side of the road. No effort was made to mark it. 'Why should we?' the Israeli colonel in command said. 'They put up a good fight. Now they are sleeping. We just dug a hole and put the bodies in, one alongside the other.'

On a line between Jezzine to the west and Rachaiya to the east, the Israelis proceeded to move tanks into the entrance to the Bekaa. They advanced in three lines across the Valley of Mimass, each column moving cautiously in single file because of the narrowness of the roads, with the lead tanks constantly harried by small groups of Syrian commandos dropped ahead of the advancing Israelis by helicopter. The Syrians succeeded in knocking out tanks using the Sagger anti-tank weapon, but the Israeli columns were not halted: up at the head of the Israeli advance was a team of specially trained engineers whose job it was to move any crippled tanks out of the way and to keep the column moving. One of the more heartening sights for the Israeli commanders was the success of their locally built Merkavas, which stood up well even to the Syrian T72s, the latest supplied by the Soviets. The only trouble with the Merkavas was their size: they were too wide to pass easily through the many villages lining the road running parallel to the Syrian border. However, their crews soon found that the front plates were quite strong enough to use as bulldozers, shoving aside the flimsy houses on the main streets, often with people still inside them.

While the tanks were advancing, the Israeli Air Force was taking out the Syrian missile system installed around Chtaura, denying the Syrian Air Force any protection and thus ensuring a clear run for the advancing Israeli armour. Yet the Syrians did commit their Air Force – and suffered their major defeat. More than sixty planes were sent up by Damascus to take on an Israeli air armada of some ninety F15s; twenty-five Syrian planes were shot down on that first day of aerial warfare, with no Israeli losses. The Israeli planes were faster and more manoeuvrable than the Migs, while the Sidewinder heat-seeking missiles and the radar-guided Sparrows all proved more effective than the Russian equipment. Most important of all, the Israelis had their Hawkeye command and radar planes flying high above the battle, and they were able to plot the movement of every Syrian jet from the moment it took off. The Syrians had to follow closely the orders given to them by ground controllers who tried to fight the battle for them, while the Israelis could rely on their individual judgment and daring.

The Syrians were out-gunned and out-fought: it was a battle of minds and electronics in which the Israelis outclassed the Syrians.

When the chance of a ceasefire came, President Assad seized it. He knew just how badly his forces had fared; but he also knew that he had to put an acceptable gloss on what happened for the sake of his people and the Arab world, since any admission of the decisive defeat which had been suffered would encourage dissidents at home and provide ammunition for his many critics in other Middle Eastern countries. The communiqué he eventually issued was a masterpiece of special pleading and obfuscation, a work of art even by Arab rhetorical standards. It said: 'We have always said, and constantly stressed, that our short-term aims of liberating occupied Arab territories and restoring the legitimate rights of the Palestinian Arab people were linked to the achievement of a strategic balance between Syria and the Zionist enemy. We recognised, and we said repeatedly, that given the present imbalance, a war would never achieve our objectives.' This theme – that the war had been forced on Syria at a time when it was not prepared for one and did not want one – was to be the main plank of the Syrian justification for what had happened. But there also had to be some explanation of the Syrian action – and inaction – in Lebanon. 'We did not go to Lebanon to fight Israel from there, and we did not decide the time and place of this war. The conditions necessary for the Arab war of liberation which will ensure the phased aims of the Arab nation, have not yet come about, and it is for those reasons that Arab Syria agreed to a ceasefire, which went into effect at 12.00 hours on June 11th.'

This was, of course, a fragile truce, and each side broke it when it suited them. The Syrians in particular seemed intent on seeing how far they could go with the Israelis, and regularly used Palestinian fighters who had been driven back behind the Syrian lines to test the Israeli positions. At Jib Janin, only twenty-two direct miles from Damascus itself, the Syrians allowed the Palestinians free rein, which always caused tension in this sector: the Palestinians would try to shoot up Israeli outposts with their small arms, Israeli forces would react with much heavier weapons, and the Syrians would then claim

Israel had broken the ceasefire, and use their artillery to reply. It was a game which both sides played, not only here, but all over the front.

In the area of Lebanon which they occupied, Israel spent much time and money in improving the road system. Huge supplies of tarmac were brought in and dumped in quarries, and young Israelis in their hundreds were drafted in as part of their national service to construct and improve roads in Eastern Lebanon. This was, of course, no labour of charity: the Israelis needed the roads to give them the mobility on which they depended, and they had done the same thing over the years in the south – not only in the area controlled by Major Haddad, but also in the no-man's-land of the Arkoub. At the same time, the Israelis imposed their own men on local authorities whenever they could, though in a number of cases Mukhtars and officials refused to move out of their offices or to allow the Israelis to take over.

In this eastern sector of Lebanon, a land of bare hillsides, a fertile, intensely cultivated valley floor, and small villages, the war between the Israelis and the Syrians was in general a conventional affair, in which the local people were involved only if they got in the way. If they did, no mercy was shown them. In the village of Mashghara, the small Syrian unit there retreated before the Israelis arrived, but the militiamen of the pro-Syrian Social Nationalist Party bravely but very foolishly resolved to stay and fight on their own, armed only with their Kalashnikovs. When the first Israeli vehicles arrived, the militiamen opened fire. The Israelis stopped, and the defenders thought for a few moments that they had held them off. Then the planes came over. The militiamen beside the road were all killed, and forty people in the tiny village were wounded. Later in the same village, the Israelis imposed a 6p.m. curfew because they suspected some of the boys of the village of sabotage. The old people understood, yet imagined that the Israelis had the same flexible sense of time as the Lebanese, so at 6.30 one elderly gentleman tottered down the street to call on a friend. He was shot dead, no doubt as a lesson to others.

Over on the Mediterranean coast, the picture was very different from the relatively clean campaign being fought along the Syrian border. In the west of Lebanon it was war with all its horror: a systematic destruction of the Palestinians and their strongholds, regardless of the cost in human, material or even public relations terms. Once the Israelis had broken through the UN lines at Naqoura, their first objective was the huge Palestinian refugee camp of Rashidiyeh, a sprawling maze of breeze-block shanties on the road into Tyre. Built in 1948 by UNWRA, and originally intended to house some 10,000 people, it had expanded steadily ever since, and by 1982 its official population stood at 15,200. However, that figure included only the people registered with UNWRA, and in fact many more crowded into the camp, which probably housed a total of more than 30,000 when the Israelis arrived. Five weeks after the Israeli invasion, when correspondents were first allowed to see the camp, no more than 4,000 women, children and old men were left. During those five secret weeks, Israel refused to allow Red Cross men, representatives of the local Lebanese authorities, or anyone else into the camp. Their very thin excuse was that visitors might get hurt by the mines which were still left about, and as if to support this claim, when journalists were finally allowed in, sappers were still rather ostentatiously blowing up caches of explosives and destroying arms dumps. Yet the huge damage caused in Rashidiyeh showed quite plainly that a deliberate operation had been launched simply to obliterate the camp, which had always been regarded by the Israelis as the main centre for operations into Upper Galilee and was the closest one to the Israeli frontier. The Israelis certainly found the expected military equipment there: two small motor boats armed with machine guns were in the tiny harbour nearby, there was a maze of underground tunnels, big stocks of arms and ammunition, and 252 bomb shelters. These last were probably the most important of all, as Rashidiyeh had been a regular target of the Israeli Air Force over the years.

When the Israelis first laid siege to the camp, as many people as possible went underground, and only the fighters stayed on the surface to try and hold off the Israeli Army. This they did for four days, while the Israeli troops stayed on the perimeter of the camp, realising it would be far too risky to try to go into the warren of tiny streets and alleyways. They called in air strike after air strike as the PLO men inside opened fire on them from different positions; gunboats lying offshore joined in, as well as heavy artillery further back; cluster bombs and cluster shells were used, effective from a military point of view, but taking no account of the thousands of women and children still in Rashidiyeh. Then, on the fourth day, Israeli planes dropped leaflets calling on the defenders to give up. According to many people there, the fighters shouted to people to stay in the bunkers, but many simply could not face it any longer, and emerged with their hands up or waving white towels or handkerchiefs. Mahmoud abou Kaid, a sixty-five-year-old Palestinian, was one who came out; he said that as soon as the Israelis saw the old people and children emerging from the camp, they held their fire and helped them to safety. Those who remained were not given a second chance. Israeli armoured vehicles began closing in from all sides, pouring concentrated fire into the concrete pillboxes and bunkers where the PLO men were still holding out. After seven days, the Palestinians were still at their posts, and Israeli infantrymen had to creep close under cover of darkness and drop grenades through apertures in the walls. In other places the desperate Palestinians leapt out of their bunkers in suicidal charges against the Israelis, who lost nine men in this cleaning-up process.

While Rashidiyeh was being cleared, the main Israeli force was sweeping north and launching a fierce attack on Tyre. There, the centre of the city was dealt a terrible hammering from air, land and sea, though much of it was pin-point bombing on specific targets which the Israelis believed were PLO offices or strong points, and through it all, the Phoenician and Roman ruins along the coast remained untouched. Once again, planes dropped leaflets urging people to flee, and about two thousand did go down to the beach, while the Israelis moved from building to building through the town, flushing out the last pockets of resistance. The centre of the town, particularly the area around the market, was badly smashed, but nothing there equalled the devastation caused further north in Sidon, Lebanon's third city. There, landing craft guarded by gunboats put troops and armour ashore on a beach in the Awali

Estuary, while the main square – Maidan Maarouf Saad, named after the Deputy whose assassination virtually started the Lebanese civil war – was blitzed by tanks and artillery.

Again, as they subjugated each community on their drive north, the Israelis used the same method repeatedly: first a concentrated pounding of the town, then leaflets and loudspeakers urging the townspeople to leave or surrender, and then a careful advance by the Israeli infantry. Mrs Carol Ghamloush, an Englishwoman married to a Lebanese, described the scene at Sidon: 'The Israelis told us in the leaflets and broadcasts that we had two hours to leave, so I dressed the children while my husband packed as much as we could take. Then we drove like the wind up to the mountains to take shelter with relatives. There was pandemonium on the streets as we left – people were crying, women screaming in terror, and the guerrillas running about everywhere. I think they were as frightened as we were.'

As the Israelis began their advance, the last people to get out saw the PLO fighters dashing from building to building in search of the best places to resist the Israelis. To no avail. In Sidon, the invaders were determined to avoid any more casualties for themselves, so they launched a massive barrage against the town, using cluster shells and phosphorus as well as high explosive. Much of the shelling appeared to be indiscriminate, with block after block of high-rise apartments and offices hit, and whole streets shattered. People who survived the first onslaught were often trapped in the débris of their homes, and hundreds of bodies were left where they lay, buried under hundreds of tons of rubble and concrete. A mass grave was bulldozed out in the central square of the town, and for a week new corpses were added daily, as the sickly-sweet stench of death led rescue workers to discover more corpses beneath the shattered buildings. So many had to be collected that eventually Red Cross workers simply sprayed the bodies with lime and left them, until people living nearby could stand the sight no longer and set them alight.

Lebanese authorities estimated that 10,000 had been killed in the first week of the invasion in the south, and 16,000 injured – a grossly exaggerated figure which was ridiculed by the

Israelis. Yet the Israeli casualty-lists were equally distorted: General Aharon Yariv announced in Tel Aviv that 10 people had died in Nabatiyeh, 50 in Tyre and about 400 in Sidon, with some 20,000 left homeless. Then, in a diatribe against 'the Western Press' for their 'malevolent' reporting, General Yariv came up with his own huge exaggerations: about 99,000 civilians had been killed in the years since the Lebanese civil war began in 1975, he said, with 250,000 wounded. In 1981, he went on, shelling by the Syrians of Christian areas of East Beirut and Zahle had resulted in the death of more than 400 civilians, while some 180,000 people had fled 'PLO terror' in Southern Lebanon. The general was hardly the man to counter 'exaggerations' by other people.

In a more realistic assessment, front-line officers estimated that the Israeli forces had killed about 1,000 PLO fighters on their drive north; many of them, as well as large numbers of civilians, died in one of the hardest-fought battles of the war, the fight for Ain Hilweh, the Palestinian camp north-east of Sidon. Just as in the case of Rashidiyeh, it was a month after the camp had been taken by the Israelis before journalists were allowed in, and by that time, the place had been razed to the ground. As in Rashidiyeh, small groups of survivors sat among the ruins, the women lethargically trying to cook on open fires, the children apathetic; many did not even look up as people spoke to them. From the wreckage it was clear that the bombs used against the camp were of the type which explode just above the surface, spreading their destruction over a wide area, and blasting down the thin walls of the refugee shacks. All that was left standing were a few cypresses and some radio antennae.

The battle of Ain Hilweh became one of the central, set-piece affairs in Operation Oranim (pine tree), as the army dubbed Mr Begin's 'Peace for Galilee' campaign. After the usual pounding, the leaflet raids and the broadcast appeals for surrender, the Israelis found that about two hundred and fifty guerrillas had taken over two mosques in the camp, which was packed with hundreds of civilians seeking refuge. Local notables tried to persuade the Palestinians either to surrender or to send the civilians out, and Arabic-speaking Israeli officers also did what they could, but the guerrillas refused to negotiate. 'We

will fight to the death,' they said. For six days the Israelis sat
outside trying to decide what to do; they then began the systematic destruction of the camp, with Israeli special forces moving in on the mosques behind a creeping artillery barrage. In
the end, the Israelis stormed the mosques, and the Palestinian
fighters there died as they said they would, fighting to the last.
What no-one ever disclosed was the number of civilians killed.
Palestinians and Israelis alike must share the blame for the
civilian death-toll, though the Israelis seemed to have a rather
more ruthless approach even than the PLO men: 'I regard all
Palestinians, except the women, as potential terrorists,' one
officer who had taken part in the battle said revealingly.

The destruction at Ain Hilweh was near-total, but the worst
destruction of all was at Damour, the market town nine miles
south of Beirut, which had earlier been fought over by Palestinians and Christians. Israeli paratroopers led the assault on
Damour, a stronghold of Ahmed Jabril's guerrilla group, and
a place where Libyan 'volunteers' were fighting beside the
Palestinians, manning the Sam Nine missiles, the mobile,
truck-mounted version of the shoulder-fired Sam Seven. These,
however, proved no more effective than the one-man Sevens
when the Israeli planes came over in waves to pound the town
before the troops went in. A paratroop officer who took part in
the final assault on Damour said: 'It was very difficult. The
Palestinians were fighting for their lives and they had nothing
to lose. It was sad – it's always sad when people have nothing to
lose.'

Almost every building in Damour was damaged. Ironically,
one of the few left untouched was in the main street; on it had
been scrawled in red the symbol of Fateh and the one word
'Victory'. The streets where vegetable stalls had once been
thronged by Beirutis, out for a Sunday excursion, were now
ploughed up by tank tracks; not a pane of glass could be found
intact in the town, and even the steel shutters over windows had
been blasted aside. The Israelis had a hard time at Damour and
were forced to send their planes back into the attack twenty-
four hours after they had announced that the town had been
taken. From Beirut, the Palestinian fighters at the southern
entrance to the city could see the Israelis in action around

Damour long after Israel radio had announced that everything there was quiet and under control: naturally, they drew their own conclusions about the accuracy of the Israeli broadcasts.

Still, the Israelis were slowly subjugating the towns and villages they had rushed through on their drive north, and as they did so, they rounded up thousands of 'suspects' – anyone with a Palestinian identity card who was between the ages of twelve and sixty seemed to be fair game. The Safa Citrus Corporation's packing sheds behind a high brick wall outside Tyre were taken over as an interrogation centre, as well as the beach near Sidon, and often Palestinians had to stand in the sun for up to forty-eight hours, awaiting their turn to be questioned by Israeli Intelligence officers. Usually the Israelis were helped in this task by local informers, many of whom wore masks to guard against the vengeance they feared would follow. In some cases, children as young as ten were taken in – the Israelis claimed that many had been caught in action against them, or in possession of weapons. 'The RPG kids,' as they were dubbed, became celebrities in Israel – anything to take peoples' minds off the far worse things going on. From the Safa interrogation centre, those identified as PLO members were shepherded aboard Egged buses brought up from Israel, and taken blindfold to the Ansar Prison Camp, a forbidding place on a windswept mountain top near Nabatiyeh.

The camp – those Israelis whose memories went back to Europe years before preferred to call it a 'centre' – was built in ten days, and initially housed six thousand captives. To keep them in and inquisitive visitors out, it was surrounded by twenty-foot-high earth ramparts, with guards at every hundred-yard mark, searchlights, barbed wire and all the other accoutrements of a prison cage. Steel watchtowers overlooked each section, and an armoured car regularly prowled the perimeter, with a soldier swivelling its machine gun menacingly. For some reason, presumably to make escape more difficult, strenuous efforts were made to conceal from the captives the destination to which they were being taken. As well as being blindfolded, guards on each bus ordered the prisoners to put their faces against the back of the seat in front as they reached a point two miles from Ansar; then their hands were bound behind their backs. No-one was allowed to raise his head until the buses were right inside the prison compound. Once there, the men were taken to a de-lousing station – something bitterly resented by many of the middle-class professional men also picked up in the dragnet – and were finally issued with blue serge uniforms. They were then formed into fifty-strong squads, and a Palestinian was placed in charge of each detachment and made responsible for liaison with the camp authorities; the Israelis allowed the prisoners in each group to choose their own leader, insisting only that he should be able to speak English, the *lingua franca* of the whole area. The prisoners were issued with the same rations as those given to the Israeli guards, and were allowed to cook for themselves; they lived in tents at first, but soon huts were built and even refrigerators installed – an indication to many of the men that they were in for a long stay. Exactly how long, no-one knew, for the Israelis refused to treat the Palestinians as prisoners of war: instead, they described them as 'administrative detainees', and would not even acknowledge that the Geneva Conventions applied to them. The Israeli attitude was that nothing should be done which could be construed as recognition of the PLO as a properly organised and legitimate force. For this reason, the Palestinians were treated quite differently from the 149 Syrians captured – 16 officers and 133 men. The Israelis justified their action by saying that many PLO men had been captured in civilian clothes; the real reason was that to most Israelis, brought up on the invective of Israeli leaders from Golda Meir ('There is no Palestine') to Menachem Begin ('beasts walking on two legs'), all Palestinians were terrorists.

The men in Ansar Camp often felt they had been abandoned by the PLO leaders, for in the way of the Middle East, they heard on the grapevine, accurately enough, that when the PLO were trying to strike a bargain over the return of the captured Israeli pilot, the only prisoner of the Israelis whom the PLO sought was Kozo Okamoto, the Japanese Red Army terrorist sentenced to life imprisonment in 1972 for the massacre at Ben Gurion airport in which twenty-four people were killed. Even Salah Ta'amri, the Fateh commander in the south and the husband of Princess Dina, the Egyptian previously married to

King Hussein, was not on the list of those the PLO wanted returned. Understandably the prisoners at Ansar felt neglected as well as dejected.

As the slow process of detailed interrogation went on, some of the prisoners were released and others sent to Israel to await trial. According to the Israelis, the Palestinians usually claimed they had joined the guerrilla organisations merely as a job, a means of making a living, though most of the foreign Arab nationals admitted volunteering for ideological reasons. Many of these were sent back to their countries of origin, a useful move from the Israeli point of view, as they would obviously be followed by their families, and there was little doubt that one of the quiet Israeli objectives – and one shared by many Lebanese – was to induce as many Palestinians as possible to leave Lebanon.

But this aim was also being achieved in a more sinister way: groups of Phalangist militiamen from the Beirut area began to drift into Southern Lebanon, often with jeeps mounted with machine guns. Even before the massacres at Sabra and Chatila, their appearance terrified the civilians, who had been left unprotected and living in pitiable conditions in the remnants of the camps. Everyone had tales, too, of people taken away in the middle of the night and never seen again, or of women told to warn their husbands not to show up if they wanted to stay alive. At Mieh Mieh, one of the smaller camps which had not been as badly damaged as the others, a mysterious fire broke out, destroying about a thousand of those houses which were still standing. In all, the UNWRA men estimated that some 62,800 Palestinians had lost their homes in the five camps in Southern Lebanon as a result of the Israeli invasion, while thousands more who had been integrated into the local communities, particularly in towns such as Nabatiyeh, had also been left without a roof over their heads.

And that was how both Israelis and Palestinians would have preferred things to stay. Despite continual International Red Cross pressure, it was months before the occupying authorities agreed even to allow tents to be erected for the homeless. The Israelis and Lebanese alike wanted the Palestinians out once and for all.

CHAPTER FOUR

Once it was clear that the Israeli invasion of Lebanon was something more than a punitive raid, or an occupation of the south alone – and that was a fact which emerged very quickly – then all the various parties involved began trying to work out their own strategy and war aims, and what they hoped to get out of the peace which was bound to follow. The result was a fascinating mosaic, in which each party to the conflict, even those ostensibly on the same side, had different objectives and varying ideas on how those should be achieved.

Even Israel lacked unity of purpose. There is no doubt that right from the start, General Sharon and General Eytan, with their less well-known but equally important colleague, General Joshua Saguy, the chief of intelligence, were determined to finish off the PLO once and for all; Mr Begin and Mr Shamir, the Foreign Minister, certainly knew that this was what the army wanted and went along with it. Other cabinet ministers, however, were only made aware of what was going on as it happened, so that there were serious rifts in the government, which were naturally reflected in divisions in the country.

On the other side, the differences were much more dramatic. The Palestinians had a simple aim – survival; yet even there, it was not just a simple matter of hanging on, of continuing to exist as fighters or as people. Rather, it was a question of individuals trying to stay alive, of leaders trying to maintain their position, organisations seeking to hold their influence, and for the PLO itself, it was a matter of trying to remain a force in the Arab world. The allies of the Palestinians, the Lebanese left, were more divided still: the Shia in the south, who had suffered so much from Israeli reprisals for Palestinian attacks into Upper Galilee, were quietly delighted to see the PLO beaten and thrown out of the area, while the Shia of

Beirut, organised into the militia group Amal and led by Mr Nabih Berri, fought long and hard beside the Palestinians to try to keep the Israelis out of the city. The Amal leaders in the capital realised that without the physical power of the Palestinians, they would soon be relegated to their old position as second-class citizens in the new Lebanon which would emerge – a Lebanon in which it was obvious that the Christians, under the leadership of the Phalange party, would once again be the dominant force. Not all the Shia felt this way, of course; there was a substantial proportion which had always remained loyal to the traditional southern leader, the Speaker of the National Assembly, Mr Kamal Assad, who had been supplanted by the more militant and charismatic Imam Moussa Sad'r in the 1970s; now this conservative, feudal element could come into its own again.

The Progressive Socialist Party led by Walid Jumblatt, which should have been the backbone of the National Movement, was equally divided, largely because of the weak, vacillating and ineffectual leadership of Jumblatt himself, a man not cut out for the position into which he had been forced. Walid Jumblatt was bound by the Lebanese feudal convention that a son must inherit his father's mantle and his responsibilities, and so had had to assume the leadership of the Jumblatti Druze of the Chouf area when his father, Kamal Jumblatt, had been assassinated in 1977; at the same time, he had had to take over as leader of the National Movement, the coalition of leftist parties cobbled together by his father in the Civil War. Walid Jumblatt was ill-fitted for this political role: a quiet man who preferred the good things of life to arguments in smoke-filled rooms, he would have been perfectly at home in a salon in Paris or on the campus of an English university. It was no pleasure to him to have to be accompanied by gun-toting guards, or to attend interminable meetings with people with whom he had very little in common. In a typically Lebanese contradiction, Walid Jumblatt, like his father before him, was a socialist millionaire, a vast feudal landowner and tribal chieftain. Yet it was plain that he would have preferred a much more modest position, and that, given the choice, he would have employed his wealth in quite a different way.

The faults, if faults they were, in Walid Jumblatt's character led him to make a number of tactical errors in the complicated politicking which went on during the three months of the Israeli war with the Palestinians in Lebanon. The result was that the rival Druze faction, the Yazbakis, led by the Emir Majid Arslan, gained a great deal of ground. Majid Arslan was one of the old school of Lebanese politicians who had been on the scene right from the foundation of the state in 1943 and had helped to work out the National Covenant which apportioned power among the various groups and communities. He therefore had a vested interest in seeing that the old agreements were kept. Like all the others, he had been a minister in a dozen or more cabinets, yet he still depended for his power on the support of his family followers. He was unwell now, but his son, the Emir Faycal Arslan, unlike Walid Jumblatt, was eager to succeed his father. The two Arslans early on made a realistic appraisal of the situation; they decided, quite rightly, that Israel was bound to win the war, that one of the Israeli objectives would be to install a 'friendly' government in Lebanon, and that they should therefore co-operate with those likely to take over. This was not quite as cynical as it might sound, for the Druze live in Israel and Syria as well as in Lebanon, and have traditionally put their religious loyalties above their national obligations – though equally, they have usually felt it right to go along with the dominant power in whichever place they live. Thus, Druze soldiers have formed a substantial and formidable part of the Israeli Border Police; they fought with the Syrian Army; and they served in the Lebanese Army, where the Chief of Staff is traditionally a Druze.

When the Israelis moved into the Chouf, Walid Jumblatt at first stayed at the family seat at Mukhtara, debating what to do, then moved to Beirut, still unsure of what policy to adopt towards the occupiers. The Arslans, on the other hand, had no doubts: they stayed in their mountain headquarters, they behaved 'correctly' towards the Israeli occupiers, they warmly welcomed delegations of Druze notables who came from Israel to attend various hastily arranged special events, and they kept in constant touch with 'the Lebanese legitimate authorities', a circumlocution which referred in the first place to the President,

Mr Elias Sarkis, but actually meant those surrounding him, and through them, the men who were bound to take over, the leaders of the Phalange.

Among the Palestinians, there were differences just as profound: at the simplest level, there were the dedicated revolutionaries typified by George Habash of the Popular Front for the Liberation of Palestine, who held the proper Marxist view that the best thing for the movement would be to fight to the end in Beirut and to go out in a blaze of glory. This idea, which was more current among the intellectuals of the party than among the fighters, rested on the assumption that by fighting to the death in Beirut, by turning the city into a 'Hanoi', such a powerful Palestinian legend would be born that the movement would endure from generation to generation, and that henceforth every Palestinian child would imbibe the story of Beirut, the need for vengeance, and the determination to return to Palestine, with his mother's milk. Habash and Nayef Hawatmeh of the Popular Democratic Front propounded this concept for a while, though it was noticeable that as the weeks went on, even they became less vociferous than at first: the bombs and shells took their toll even on the most profound revolutionary dialectic.

Other Palestinian leaders had different ideas. The two most senior men in Fateh, after Arafat, appeared to believe they could actually hold out in Beirut, and that if they resisted for long enough, outside influence would rescue them. It was not such a far-fetched notion, for Salah Khalaf and Khalil al Wazir knew more than most about the capabilities of their men and the means available to them. Salah Khalaf, Abou Iyyad, and al Wazir, Abou Jihad, had both been dealing for years with the fighting side of the organisation; Abou Iyyad had been the head of the Black September organisation, the clandestine group set up within Fateh to avenge the defeat in Jordan in 1970; Abou Jihad had always been in charge of the 'conventional' military wing of Fateh. Both knew the amount of ammunition available down to the last round, and as the stores which were to be found months later showed, there was no shortage even at the time the Palestinians finally did leave Beirut. Nor were the calculations of the two men concerning outside help too far from the mark:

every time Israel put in a new attack on the city, the more
people in America were alienated, and the easier it became for
the Reagan administration to put pressure on Jerusalem. Each
day that went by caused new anguish and shame to the Arab
countries, so that Saudi Arabia and even Egypt were constantly
being pushed into offering more and more political aid to the
Palestinians. In all probability, pressure from these two vital
allies would eventually have forced the United States to act
decisively to stop the carnage.

Arafat himself did not share this view. He had always hung
on to his position as leader both of Al Fateh and of the PLO by
three means: first, he was able to dispense patronage, in the
sense not only of appointing people to particular posts, but also
by way of pensions, indemnities for those wounded, or scholar-
ships for those wishing to study abroad. Second, he had control
of the apparatus of punishment – the Fateh military police, the
Armed Struggle Command – which could be used as a ruthless
instrument of repression as well as to protect the civilian
Palestinians. Arafat's third method of control was always to
rule by consent; he was a marvellous committee man, a chairman who never lost patience, who could listen to interminable
arguments with apparent interest, and who could detect infallibly on which side the balance lay. He was a consensus man
who now found himself forced into decisions. Rightly seeing
that he was now the focus, the lynch-pin on which the whole
Palestinian defence of Beirut rested, he became a far more
positive leader than he had been before.

Arafat's aim was the survival of the PLO as a force in Middle
Eastern politics – but the PLO which survived had to be *his*
PLO, an organisation much more of the centre than of the left, a
political entity ready to treat with Israel in spite of everything.
In his youth, Arafat had been a member of the Moslem
Brotherhood, that most conservative of all Arab political movements, and he had never shaken off many of the attitudes that
membership of the Brotherhood implied; now he was determined to avoid the 'radicalisation' of the Resistance Movement, something which many other leaders saw not only as
inevitable, but as highly desirable. So it was Arafat, and at first
Arafat almost alone, who insisted that negotiations should go

hand in hand with resistance, just as over the past years it had been Arafat who had sought to give the PLO a 'diplomatic' image, while allowing the 'militant' wing of his group to carry on their military adventures. Arafat had realised then that the terrorist attacks by the wild men of the movement served very well to maintain the focus of attention on the Palestinians, for all the bad publicity which resulted; meanwhile, he had carefully fostered his own image as the moderate, the father-figure, 'al Ikhtiar' – the old man – the one who would find the political solution and put an end to all the violence. Now he adopted the same tactics. He realised the value of a heroic defence of Beirut, not only in myth-making terms but also as a means of gaining time, and he realised too that he had to get all he could from the affair by his own diplomacy. He was guided in all this by Hani Hassan, who was his main political adviser, and who, with his brother Khaled Hassan, had a considerable influence on the movement; Khaled Hassan, who lived in Kuwait, constantly conveyed to Arafat an accurate assessment of the views of the moderate countries of the Gulf, and of their capabilities and willingness to take action. Hassan's information was useful knowledge to balance against the ideas of the radical Arab states, which were constantly being put forward by those Palestinians on the PLO Executive Committee who were their clients.

Another strand in the Palestinian warp in Beirut was represented by the military. For the first time, the professional soldiers of the PLO had real power and influence. In theory Khaled al Wazir held the equivalent of the post of Defence Minister in the Palestinian hierarchy, but all his experience had been with guerrilla fighting and clandestine operations, so that his views and advice did not carry the same weight as those of the men actually concerned with the defence of Beirut. The most senior of these on the Palestinian side was Brigadier Sa'ad Sayel, the Chief of Staff, who was the highest-ranking officer of the Jordanian Army to defect to the Palestinians in 1970. Trained in Jordan, Egypt and America, he was a professional soldier who was also a dedicated believer in the Palestinian cause. He was no politician, though he had been elected to the Central Committee; rather, he saw his role as that of commander of a garrison, working alongside the civilian authorities represented for him by Arafat and the leaders of the Lebanese left. Brigadier Sayel – Abou Walid – was a burly, moustached, always smiling man who inspired confidence in those around him; he was to die less than a month after leaving Beirut in an ambush in the Bekaa Valley. His memorial was a classic defence of an apparently open city, a defence which will be studied by revolutionaries and regular officers for many years to come.

It was fortunate for Arafat that Abou Walid had no political ambitions, for during the siege of Beirut he was the one man in complete control; if he had wished, he could have overridden the politicians at any time. As it was, he co-operated not only with them, but also with the leftist militias and with the Syrians, the other military force on hand. Originally, the Syrian 85th Brigade was stationed in Beirut, commanded by Brigadier Mohammed Halal, as well as a few detached units such as Rifaat Assad's 'Cavaliers'. The latter were widely known as 'The Pink Panthers' because of their lurid uniforms, and universally detested for their predatory habits; it was widely and correctly held that many of them had been freed from gaol on condition they joined this remarkable unit, and their main tasks were to 'liberate' cars, furniture, jewellery and anything else that their avaricious masters in Damascus deemed useful. The other Syrian unit in Beirut was an Intelligence section which occupied a building next to the Central Bank in Hamra; in normal times they played a shadowy role, more concerned with eliminating Syria's enemies than with gathering information, and in war-time they kept a low profile. It was significant that on the day the Israelis first tried to move into West Beirut along Corniche Mazraa, the Syrians all appeared in uniform for the first time. This was not out of bravado on their part, but because they were determined to be prisoners of war, not 'administrative detainees' like the Palestinians – or worse if the Israelis decided to treat them as spies. These Syrian Intelligence men, like so many of the odd Syrian units sent to Beirut, were widely held to be an unpleasant lot: they threw their weight about when Syria were running the show in West Beirut, then laid very low and did little to help when the Israelis were at the gates of the city.

In fact, the Syrian troops left in Beirut played very little part in the considerations of the politicians in Damascus. They were completely detached from their headquarters, and though they were still in radio contact, for everyday purposes they came under the command of Brigadier Sayel. In the same way, the PLA was in theory part of the brigadier's command, though in practice it operated very much as an independent group. The main PLA force was based in the shattered commercial centre of the city and around the port, holding that area of the Green Line which the Phalangists might choose as the most natural line of advance if they decided to switch from tacit to active support of the Israelis. Throughout the three months of the Israeli siege of Beirut, the PLA remained an effective, disciplined and smartly turned out force, in contrast to most other groups of the PLO, which were generally scruffy and fairly anarchic. Later, units of the PLA were the first to leave Beirut; this was because the Palestine command were anxious that when television cameras filmed Palestinian fighters on the way out, they should show soldiers in good heart and clean uniforms, not beaten men suffering from the privations of the blockade.

While Brigadier Sayel rushed about the city inspiring his men and personally supervising the organisation of the' defences, Arafat and the other PLO leaders were in constant rounds of talks, trying to hammer out common positions among themselves and with their Lebanese allies, and then to present a united front in their indirect discussions with the Israelis. This was one of the difficulties: not once did Philip Habib meet any Palestinian representative face to face, though at one time Hani Hassan tried to make a confrontation between Habib and Arafat one of the conditions of a Palestinian evacuation of the city; Habib rejected the notion outright, and after half-heartedly trying to keep it alive for a few days, Hassan had the sense to see that it was merely impeding the progress of the talks, and quietly dropped the idea.

Arafat at first shared the view of the radical wing of the PLO that the Palestinians could hold out in Beirut and force the Israelis to make a costly assault on the city. However, he was not happy at the prospect, and as the days of bombardment

went on, he became less sanguine still. It was as obvious to him
as it was to everyone else that the Israelis were prepared to be
quite ruthless and to sacrifice as many residents of Beirut as was
necessary to force the Palestinians out. As this realisation
gradually spread, Saeb Salam became one of the key figures in
the drama.

Salam by this time was eighty-two, another member of that
dwindling band of old-time politicians who had been there at
the founding of the independent Lebanese state. He had served
many times as Prime Minister and was almost the embodiment
of the Lebanese system, for just as other leaders had their
following in clans or tribes, or in some remote area of the
country, so Salam relied for his support on Beirut itself. At first,
he had inherited this power, for his father had been one of the
founders of the Makassed Association, the Sunni Moslem
philanthropic organisation which ran schools, hospitals, clinics
and clubs, and dispensed largesse to the needy, or more
regularly, the deserving. Later, Saeb Bek, as he was known, had
built on the foundations laid by his father by becoming the
perennial Deputy for the Sunnis of Beirut and thus extending
his patronage. He had added to his personal wealth in the early
'70s by levying taxes on the dozens of fruit-machine parlours
which were then the craze among the youth of the city – the
Beirut equivalent of Western amusement arcades – and had
also hitched his wagon firmly to the Saudi star, which not only
guaranteed him financial support, but was also useful now,
when powerful voices were needed to persuade the Americans
of what should be done. Mr Salam was often on the telephone to
King Fah'd, and much of his influence depended on that fact
being widely known. Like all Lebanese politicians, he was not
above using unorthodox means to secure his aims, and had
around him a côterie of very hard men to do his bidding.

At the time of the Israeli invasion, Mr Salam was well into
retirement, living quietly in his palace at Mousseitbeh and
leaving it to his son Tamam to carry on the family tradition,
while he merely held court, dispensed judgment and favours,
and made sure that the Sunnis of the city received everything to
which they were entitled, and a little more if possible. A very
short time after the invasion, however, Salam acquired a

central role in the affair. He was the one who could speak for the vast mass of the population of West Beirut, and who could deliver anything he promised on their behalf; he was also the one politician of stature in the city able to talk to the Palestinians and to the representatives of the 'other side', President Sarkis and the Foreign Minister, Mr Fuad Boutros, though it was usually left to the Prime Minister of the day, Mr Chafic Wazzan, to conduct the actual negotiations.

Wazzan himself was the one unlikely hero of the whole business. He could easily have gone to live in East Beirut, on the grounds that he had to be close to the President and to other members of the government. He refused to do so, and all through the siege stayed in his very vulnerable house in Raouche. Shells from Israeli gunboats frequently hit nearby, and on a number of occasions he and his family had to spend hours in the basement because of bombing in the area. Mr Wazzan, a fifty-six-year-old lawyer educated at the Arab University in Beirut and in Paris, was not a particularly brilliant man, nor even a star in the Lebanese political firmament, but he rose to the occasion. He had only two sanctions: he could threaten to resign, and he could refuse to attend meetings held in East Beirut. He used both tactics, but sparingly, and each time effectively.

In East Beirut, it was officially President Sarkis who met all the parties concerned, and who then dealt with Mr Habib, who was usually accompanied by the American Ambassador, Mr Robert Dillon, and more importantly, by Morris Draper, the best Arabist and the most experienced of the Middle Eastern diplomats in the State Department. President Sarkis had been elected six years earlier in a poll rigged by the Syrians, just as his successor would be chosen in a poll rigged by the Phalangists, with Israeli backing. A former governor of the Central Bank, Mr Sarkis was an unexciting, colourless man who had been chosen by the Syrians as one of the few available presidential candidates who had clean hands and would also do their bidding. Weak to the point of spinelessness, Sarkis took no initiatives of his own volition, made no speeches and issued no statements; he was a passive tool in the hands of men who were manipulating the authority of the presidency for their own purposes. His main adviser was Fuad Boutros, the Foreign Minister, who came close to being the direct representative of the Phalangists. Mr Boutros, a sixty-two-year-old lawyer and judge, was a dry stick, a man of far fewer words than the average politician, but was able cut through the verbiage of others and quickly get to the heart of any discussion. Early in the affair he had worked out the likely outcome, and to his credit, sought to speed up what he saw as the inevitable process of Palestinian defeat, Israeli victory and Phalangist take-over. He often appeared to be the advocate of the Phalangists; yet his strength lay in the fact that in different circumstances this Greek Catholic conservative might well have argued another case.

So the stage was set for the long and complicated negotiations: Arafat had to find a common position among the Palestinians; Salam and Chafic Wazzan had to reconcile the wishes of the Lebanese inhabitants of Beirut with the demands of the Palestinians and the force they and the Syrians in the city could muster; President Sarkis and his adviser Mr Boutros were, like it or not, the representatives of the Lebanese Christians; and Philip Habib and the other Americans had to represent not only the wishes of Washington, but also the conditions laid down by the Israelis. At the same time, all the Lebanese involved, in their different ways, were seeking to ensure the continued unity and liberty of their own country, though each one had a different idea of how that should be done.

The Israeli objectives were the only ones clearly spelt out, though even then only in piecemeal form. Originally, Israel had spoken merely of the need to establish a twenty-five-mile 'security zone' in the south, but that basic demand was rapidly expanded to include the withdrawal of the Syrians, the installation of a 'strong', *i.e.* Phalangist, government, and the conclusion of a peace treaty between Lebanon and Israel.

The Palestinians never did detail their war aims – not surprisingly, for it was a war they had not started, did not want and could not hope to win. Their initial position was that survival was all that mattered. Then gradually Arafat's pragmatism took over, and the continued existence of the PLO as the credible voice of the Palestinian people and a force in

Middle Eastern politics came to be seen as the overriding concern. For the National Movement, the Lebanese left, the first necessity was to act jointly with the Palestinians in the defence of Beirut; then, when it became clear after the first week or so that the Palestinians would eventually either be militarily defeated or would leave Beirut, the leftist alliance had to seek to ensure its own existence and to preserve as much of its former influence as possible.

The Lebanese right, the Phalangists, saw very clearly an opportunity to achieve all their own objectives without actually having to do any of the fighting. Bachir Gemayel, or rather, those around him, watched with glee as the Israelis organised the implementation of one of the main Phalangist demands: the expulsion of all 'foreigners' – Palestinians – from Lebanon. The Phalangists also realised that the only presidential candidate who would be approved by the Israelis would be Sheikh Bachir, so in one of the few hopeful moves of the whole affair, advisers such as Karim Pakradouni and the leaders of the Maronite League saw to it that the Phalangist militia were restrained from fighting actively on the side of the Israelis, much as many militia commanders would have liked to have done so. The very astute men in the Maronite 'think tanks' realised that not only would the Israelis expel the Palestinians and the Syrians from the country; they would also clear the way for the even more cherished dream of the restoration of the Christian ascendancy in Lebanon. The Maronite leaders therefore had the good sense to see that this would be done more easily and more effectively if the co-operation of the Moslem moderates, the vast bulk of the population of Beirut, could be assured.

The Americans, while passing on the messages from Jerusalem and occasionally putting forward ideas to resolve particular problems, were pursuing more fundamental aims: the State Department saw early on that the whole affair could be used as a springboard for a settlement much wider than that which was ostensibly being sought in Lebanon. There was at last, in the view of the American diplomats, the possibility of a general Middle East agreement, and without the participation of the Soviets. It was an accurate assessment, brilliantly ex-

ploited, and finally frustrated only by the extremism of the
Begin government.

The one and only purely Lebanese initiative during the
invasion was the attempted formation of 'a Cabinet of National
Salvation'. This was the brainchild of the Phalangists, with
American backing. The idea was to form a six-man government
which would include Bachir Gemayel and the leaders of the left,
Jumblatt and Berri, and the Sunnis, represented by Wazzan.
Such a government, the Americans and Phalangists thought,
could declare a state of emergency, which would then allow the
Lebanese Army to be deployed throughout Beirut. The fact
that such a move would be authorised by the principal leaders
of the National Movement, it was suggested, would ensure that
neither Amal nor the Mourabitoun would oppose the entry of
the army into the city, thus isolating the Palestinians. At the
same time, the Israeli presence around the perimeter would
deter the Palestinians from putting up any fight, and they
would retire into the camps to lick their wounds.

The participation of Walid Jumblatt was vital if this idea was
to be implemented, and when it was mooted in the middle of
June, he was still at his family home in Mukhtara, which was
occupied by the Israelis. All sorts of messages were sent to
Jumblatt, but at first he said he would have nothing to do with
it: he intended to stay in the Chouf, he said, and organise
'passive resistance' against the Israelis. As many unkindly
pointed out, passive resistance was about the only kind that Mr
Jumblatt might be good at. Eventually, Jumblatt was persuaded by his allies in the National Movement that his place
was in Beirut, and that if the 'National Salvation' government
was formed, then he should be part of it. Significantly, the
Israelis made sure that Jumblatt could travel freely and safely
from his home at Mukhtara, though he eventually arrived in
the capital in the car of Robert Barrett, the counsellor at the
American Embassy in Beirut.

With the cast assembled, those pulling the strings decided to
go ahead, and President Sarkis duly announced the establishment of a 'Committee of National Salvation' – one step down
from a cabinet, as it was felt that the existing cabinet should
remain in being and rubber-stamp the decisions it was hoped

the committee would make. Besides Gemayel, Jumblatt, Berri
and Wazzan, the committee also comprised Fuad Boutros,
there to back up Gemayel and ensure voting majorities for the
right if need be, and Nasri Maalouf, a little-known Deputy who
was the representative of the Chamounist faction among the
Christians. Still Jumblatt was reluctant to take part: he wanted
the committee expanded, he said, and asked that such moderates as former Prime Minister Rachid Karami, and Amin
Gemayel, the more reasonable brother of Bachir, should be
added to it. All the indications were that Jumblatt did not like
the prominent role assigned to him, and wanted to share any
blame or kudos. In fact, he eventually said as much: 'I do not
want to be the one to give the *coup-de-grâce* to the Palestine
resistance movement, or to be responsible for the destruction of
Beirut.' The short explanation seemed to be that Mr Jumblatt
did not want to take responsibility for anything. Eventually,
one or two meetings of the committee were held, and gave some
short-lived hope to the people of Beirut, who, perhaps naively,
were cheered to see that old antagonists like Jumblatt and
Gemayel found it possible to sit down together at the same
table. Many even noted with delight that in pictures taken of
Jumblatt and Bachir Gemayel sitting on a couch, Jumblatt
actually appeared to be smiling. On closer examination of the
photograph, Jumblatt looked more like a rabbit petrified with
fear in the presence of a stoat, and in private, when asked about
it all, he shrugged and said merely: 'Well, when the photographers are around, you have to smile.' Later that same night,
after a long dinner, the talk again turned to Gemayel, and this
time Jumblatt revealed his true feelings: 'I'll kill him,' he said.
'I'll kill him myself' – and he produced the small silver-handled
revolver he carried, and slapped it down on the table. The sight
of the gun which he had never used and which he disliked
carrying seemed to bring Walid back to his usual, more gentle
self; sheepishly he tucked it back into his waist-band, and the
brief demonstration of dislike was over.

On a practical level, the only useful result of the formation of
the Salvation Committee – apart from giving Beirutis a brief
period of euphoria – was that it led to a series of discreet
meetings between Palestinian and Lebanese officials. In par-

ticular, Arafat and Brigadier Sayel held a number of talks with Colonel Johnny Abdo, the head of Lebanese Military Intelligence, and other army officers, in which detailed plans were drawn up for a possible take-over of West Beirut by the army. These plans were eventually of considerable help when the Multi-national Force moved into Beirut, as well as when the Lebanese Army did eventually take over the city.

With the Salvation Committee out of the picture, Saeb Salam, Wazzan, Jumblatt and the rest of the politicians in West Beirut tried to work out a co-ordinated approach, and to find common ground with the Palestinians. Meanwhile Mr Habib found himself drawn into the minutiae of Lebanese politics and was forced to deal with matters which should never have been part of his brief: trying to get the Israelis to grant small concessions such as allowing particular shipments of aid through, or restoring the water supply, or simply avoiding bombing certain targets. Habib, whose grandparents had emigrated from a village in Southern Lebanon, though they were of Christian stock, was a man of infinite patience, as he had displayed on his earlier tours of the area, but many who dealt with him felt that he persevered too long, and that occasional outbursts of temper, or more forceful use of the power vested in him by the American administration, might have shortened the long agony of Beirut.

There was a strong suspicion in the early weeks of the conflict that Habib had no great desire to see things settled too quickly. He and the rest of the Americans were quite content to watch the Israelis cutting the PLO down to size, and all their soundings showed that their position was fully understood by the Arab countries. It was only as public opinion in America hardened and the reaction of the Arab states and the rest of the world began to change, that Habib felt any sense of urgency. By then, it was too late – the pattern had been set; from then on, everything had to go at a snail's pace, with interminable discussions bogged down in the most trivial details. Certainly, Habib was eventually remarkably successful, and it may be that his formula for negotiations succeeded where others might have failed. It would obviously have been a disaster if the talks had broken down at any stage and Habib himself had pulled

out, since it is difficult to imagine any other conduit which
would have allowed negotiations to proceed.

Habib sat Buddha-like through hours of Arab rhetoric from
all sides, patiently trying to bring the protagonists back to the
point, listening to views he had heard a dozen times before, and
only gently nudging people in the direction he wanted them to
go – in short, acting very much as Arafat did in the meetings of
his people. The lack of direct communication between Habib
and Arafat was the cause of many delays and misunderstand-
ings; Wazzan, for all his good intentions and personal probity,
was not the brightest of men, and the Americans, in particular,
felt that he often missed nuances, or failed to convey accurately
the sense of a meeting. Yet for all the set-backs, the hesitations,
and the apparent lack of agreement, the negotiations could
later be seen to have taken a steady course. The object of the
Israelis from the start was to get the Palestinians out of Beirut,
and this was the main thrust of all the discussions. The
Palestinians' first reaction was to delay this, and then to seek to
get what they could in return for an evacuation; while the
Lebanese left and the Sunni Moslems alike, once it became
clear that the Palestinians had to go, were seeking to safeguard
their own communities and the political future of their parties.

The Palestinians conceded very early on that they would
have to leave Beirut, and there can be no doubt that it was
Israeli pressure which brought them to that decision. After
weeks of bombing and shelling, Saeb Salam and the other
Moslem leaders made it plain to the PLO that they were not
prepared to see thousands more of their people slain in order to
satisfy the Palestinians' desire to create a legend. 'Sooner or
later you will have to go,' they told Arafat, 'so it is better for you
to recognise that fact and get what you can while you can.'
Where they miscalculated was in thinking that once the
Palestinians had agreed to leave, the Israelis would stop the
bombardment and work out an orderly Palestinian withdrawal, making some concessions in the usual give-and-take of
discussions. It did not happen like that. Instead, the Israelis
saw their bombs and shells as potent negotiating counters, and
continued to use them to the full long after Arafat had agreed
that he and his men would quit.

The first, and clearly unacceptable, Palestinian position, was that the PLO would withdraw from Beirut into the refugee camps around the city, while the Lebanese Army took over West Beirut; in response, the Israelis would withdraw about ten kilometres from Beirut and also reopen the Beirut-Damascus highway. This would not do: the Israelis could not be seen to be pulling back after being stopped by the Palestinians, and then bowing to American pressure. Equally, a Palestinian withdrawal to the camps, even if all heavy weapons were handed over to the Lebanese Army, would be merely a stop-gap solution, leaving the basic problem unchanged, in the Israeli view.

During a visit to Washington, Mr Begin was given a rough time by Senators, but apparently found in Mr Haig a man who agreed wholeheartedly with the Israeli position. Clearly a new solution had to be devised. First to come up with it was Mr Caspar Weinberger, the American Defence Secretary, who suggested that American troops could form part of a multinational force which would replace the Israelis in some areas and work alongside the Lebanese Army, a formula which was much later to be put into effect. Already, the 'no surrender' faction in the PLO was beginning to look for a way out in the face of the continued Israeli bombardment. Abou Iyyad, who had been talking tough at the beginning, now opened an escape hatch: 'The Americans are seeking our total capitulation', he said, 'but surrender is the red line we cannot cross. However, we are ready to accept Lebanese Government terms.' Thus was the way cleared for the cave-in which had to come.

CHAPTER FIVE

Life in Beirut during the blockade was noisy, dirty, dangerous and expensive. The blockade itself lasted for seven weeks, though the Israeli Army was at the gates of the city from June 13th onwards. At first, the Israelis allowed traffic to flow in both directions, and people were able to go back into West Beirut after crossing to the east, and vice versa. Then, from July 3rd, Israel imposed a total blockade of the city, a siege in the medieval sense, aimed at starving the inhabitants into surrender. It was a fearful time of hunger and thirst accompanied by shell fire and bombing, as the Israeli forces set about subjugating some 400,000 people in order to gain the surrender of the 10,000 or so fighters among them.

The encirclement of Beirut was completed on the weekend of June 12th, and took place just as the second ceasefire of the war went into effect. On June 11th, Israel and Syria had agreed to a ceasefire at noon the following day – this after Syrian forces had been mauled, the missiles in the Bekaa Valley destroyed, and a third of Syria's front line air force shot down. That ceasefire, however, did not apply to the conflict between Israelis and Palestinians: on the contrary, now that they were no longer fighting the Syrians as well, the Israelis were able to concentrate their fire on the PLO and on Saturday, June 12th, launched a massive series of air, land and sea strikes against them in the south and west of Beirut. At Khalde, Palestinians and men of Amal fought well, but were gradually driven back as Israeli artillery men kept up a steady barrage, with Israeli gunboats joining in. The Israeli Air Force set the pattern for the hundreds of further attacks they were to make during the next nine weeks, as they strafed the Kuwait Embassy district and Palestinian positions near the Arab University and in the Fakhani quarter. Then at 9 p.m. that Saturday, a ceasefire

between Israel and the Palestinians was observed. This had
been arranged by Philip Habib, who was then in Jerusalem,
and also oddly, by the one United Nations man in Beirut, Samir
Sanbar, who passed the messages to the PLO and dealt directly
with the Palestinians. On this occasion, the PLO agreed to a
ceasefire 'on the basis of the UN resolutions'. It was the only
time the UN took a direct hand in negotiations, and it was the
one time the PLO were approached directly by any negotiator –
from then on, Habib always worked through the Lebanese
Prime Minister, Mr Wazzan, or the former Prime Minister,
Saeb Salam.

With the truce still holding, Sunday, June 13th, was a quiet
day in Beirut and its surroundings; it was also a busy time for
the Israelis. During the day, their tanks rolled into Souk el
Gharb and Shemlan, though no-one took much notice and
there was no resistance. In the evening, just as quietly, the
Israelis moved into Baabda. As Abou Iyyad observed, General
Sharon had acted just as he had in 1973: it was during a formal
truce in the war with Egypt that Israel had moved its troops
forward to complete the encirclement of the Egyptian Third
Army.

Baabda was the seat of the Lebanese presidency, a firmly
Christian area with open roads leading into East Beirut; by
moving in there, the Israelis linked up with the Phalangist
forces and completed the ring around the city. General Eytan
summed it up: 'We have achieved the total isolation of the
terrorists on land, sea and air,' he said. 'We have established
continuity with the Christian quarters in the north of the city.'
The General also noted that his orders were not to take Beirut,
but to 'destroy the terrorist infrastructure.' In the meantime, he
said, the PLO would not be able to reinforce its defences with
Syrian help.

General Sharon himself went to Baabda, and after having his
photograph taken while sitting behind the desk of the Lebanese
gendarmerie commander, went off for a quiet word with Bachir
Gemayel. Sharon felt the Phalangists had not been as helpful as
they should have been, and demanded more co-operation. After
all, he pointed out, Israel had supplied almost everything they
had wanted; now was the time to make the payment. Gemayel

gave evasive answers; even then, his eyes were fixed firmly on the Lebanese presidential elections, and he knew that his chances would be ruined if he sent his men into action on the side of the Israelis.

There is no doubt that the people of Baabda were pleased to see the Israelis, for they believed that their arrival heralded the end of the Palestinian 'occupation' of their country. Like so many Christians, they chose to blame the Palestinians for all their troubles, making them the scapegoats for the ills which had beset Lebanon for so long, many of which were of their own making. But the mixture of jubilation and curiosity shown by the people of East Beirut quickly died down. Soon Israeli soldiers and tanks were a familiar sight in East Beirut and in most other parts of the Christian areas of Lebanon, and slowly, by their obtrusive presence and high-handed ways, the initial mood of welcome cooled into grudging acceptance, and then into the kind of quiet hostility which every occupying force must bring out in the hearts of local people. The Maronite owner of a Jounieh restaurant, for instance, was not amused when Israeli customers asked him for 'some typical dishes, something very Palestinian.' Nor did the Lebanese take much heart from the extra business brought in by the Israelis; certainly the soldiers paid for what they wanted, but they paid in shekels, the Israeli currency worthless outside Israel, with its steady 100-plus per cent inflation rate. Still, no Lebanese would turn away money of any kind, so a Lebanese-Shekel exchange rate was soon fixed – and changed daily – and Lebanese traders could be seen queueing up outside the mobile banks which the Israeli authorities sent north to cater for the needs of their troops.

In Israel, there was some crowing at the quick and easy success of the army in completing the encirclement of Beirut. There was also some disinformation: Yasser Arafat, the Israelis claimed, had taken refuge in a foreign embassy in Beirut, an embassy identified by the Israelis. This 'leak' to the Israeli press was in fact part disinformation and part an example of Israel's usually good, but sometimes incomplete intelligence on what was going on in Beirut. What had actually happened was that Arafat had called at the Soviet Embassy just off the

Corniche Mazraa to see Mr Alexander Soldatov, the ambassador. After an hour or so, Arafat had left. Apparently the Israelis
had learned that he had entered the Embassy, but had failed to
notice him leave – or perhaps had chosen not to do so.

The Israelis were now tightening the noose around the city.
They pressed forward at Khalde, but found the opposition
there too tough; their tanks moved out into Upper Maten to
hold the Syrians there; and they moved into Shweifat to
threaten a Palestinian stronghold at the Science Faculty building of the Arab University and to position their guns overlooking the Palestinian refugee camp of Bourj Brajneh, next to
Beirut airport. Once those moves had been completed, Israel
agreed to a new truce, though formally it said it was merely
adhering to the earlier one. In fact, Habib had asked for a
forty-eight-hour respite in which to try and get negotiations
moving again.

The truce did not last. The Israelis resumed their shelling
of the southern outskirts of Beirut, with gunboats joining in.
It was on the coastal road at Khalde that Israel encountered
some of the toughest opposition of the whole war, though the
irony was that most of the defences there were manned not by
Palestinians, but by men from Amal. These Shia Moslems
usually came originally from Southern Lebanon, and so had
little reason to love the Palestinians, whose presence there
had prompted so many Israeli attacks. Yet once the Israelis
launched their full-scale invasion of Lebanon, old differences
were forgotten. The Amal militiamen fought side by side with
the Palestinians, and in a number of sectors manned the line
alone. At Khalde it was Amal which held the main road, while
the Palestinians were spread out inland, around the main
coastal runway of the airport. It was a surprise to many to find
Amal so well organised: they all wore uniform, had plenty of
weapons and ammunition, had a proper chain of command,
signals and so on. Much of this had been quietly handed over to
them when the Iranian force which had once formed part of
UNFIL pulled out; a number of Iranian soldiers and officers
had also remained behind and had taken part in organising and
training the Amal men. At Khalde, the commander was a
Lebanese, a man originally trained in the Lebanese Army.

With his men, he lived in one of the old beach-side restaurants which had been taken over. An articulate, civilised, French-speaking man, he told me during one bombardment: 'I don't like these damned gunboats any more than you do, and to tell you the truth, I'm not too fond of the Palestinians, either. But when Lebanon is invaded, I'll fight alongside the devil if necessary.'

It was one of the oddities of the time that Lebanese of all Moslem groups, who had been cursing the Palestinians almost as virulently as the Christians, not only joined forces with them to fend off the Israeli attack, but also came to evince a grudging but growing admiration for them. As the days turned into weeks and months, the people of West Beirut – which still included a surprisingly large number of Christians – found themselves identifying more and more with the Palestinians and the other defenders of the city. After all, these unshaven, ill-dressed, sloppy groups were doing what no Arab army had succeeded in doing: they were standing up to the Israelis, and stopping them.

People also began to notice, perhaps for the first time, that the Palestinians were far more reasonable and considerate of the local population than some others among them. There was plenty of trouble inside the city during the siege of Beirut, but it was rarely caused by the Palestinians. It was the 'Hamra cowboys', the young men in rather well-cut khaki fatigues and cowboy hats, and carrying fearsome assortments of rockets and RPGs as well as the obligatory Kalashnikovs, who caused the real problems. Usually, these were men from one of the prolifer-ating local militias, or from the Mourabitoun, the Sunni Mos-lem militia of Ibrahim Kleilat. Gunfights often erupted when opposing groups tried to take over an apartment in which to house some of 'their' refugees, or to seize a building so that they could use it as a storehouse for ammunition, or for looted property, or for new offices to give added prestige to their particular movement. As the arguments escalated beyond the verbal stage, trucks with machine guns mounted on them would start blasting away at each other from opposite ends of a block. Once, this happened around the Commodore Hotel, home to the hundreds of journalists in West Beirut, and suddenly machine gun bullets whipped over the top of the swimming pool, cutting leaves and branches off the trees there and dropping them onto the heads of the few hardy or foolish souls sitting outside. Another time, the only restaurant still open, Myrtom House, the Austrian establishment run by Johannes Matchek, was the target of their attentions. On each occasion, it was the Palestinians who had to sort it all out. First, their local commanders would try and mediate: then, if they failed, PASC or Fateh detachments would be called in. That was usually enough, for the Palestinians were still the single most powerful organisation in West Beirut, with greater fire power and heavier weapons than anyone else.

The Palestinians also had more supplies than the other groups. In addition to weapons and ammunition, they had stockpiled food in various stores and warehouses around the town and in the labyrinth of tunnels built under the refugee camps, as well as fuel oil, bottled gas, spare uniforms, radio sets and everything else an army would need. It was the Palestinians who provided the Commodore Hotel with extra diesel oil when the generators there were in danger of shutting down. Youssef Nazzal, the young owner who had made the Commodore the international press centre during the Civil War, quietly pointed out to his Palestinian contacts that if the generators were stopped, the telexes would not work, and without telexes journalists could not do their job, in which case everyone would go off and report the war from East Beirut. The Palestinians took the point: in this war, the journalists were more use to them than a regular battalion of infantry – not because the Press corps in West Beirut were putting out propaganda, but simply because they were describing day by day what they saw and heard. Journalists with the Israeli forces could only photograph clean, well-uniformed young Israeli soldiers firing at West Beirut, and report the threats and statements issued by General Sharon or General Eytan. In West Beirut, the photographers could produce pictures of the results of that shelling – ruined buildings, maimed children, grieving mothers; the reporters could describe everyday life in a modern city where water and electricity were cut off and food was prevented from getting in. The Israelis could not win; throughout the world they were coming to be seen, not as the one civilised force in the barbarian Middle East, but as aggressors much worse than any others, people willing to sacrifice the whole civilian population of a city in order to destroy a tiny group of their enemies, a nation ready to use its own overwhelming force in a manner which should have gone out with the Dark Ages.

With Beirut encircled, the Israelis gradually turned their attention to other areas. They moved out into the mountains to the north-east of the capital, apparently with the intention of putting more pressure on the Syrians, whose troops in the Bekaa Valley could be threatened if the Israelis seized the Anti-Lebanon range hilltops. The Israelis' prime objective, however, was the Beirut-Damascus road. With their forces in Baabda at the western end and at Qab Elias near Chtaura, Israeli guns and tanks could already easily prevent Syrian reinforcements moving in from their own country, or those in West Beirut from getting out. But that was not enough: for by risking occasional Israeli shelling or strafing from the air, some supplies and men could still get through.

What may finally have persuaded the Israelis to act was the arrival of a group of Iranian volunteers. Ayatollah Khomeini had warned that he intended to send units to Lebanon, whether or not the countries through which they had to travel gave their permission – something which sent shudders down the spines of Iraqi and Syrian leaders alike. Eventually a group of several hundred Iranians did cross Syria into Lebanon. They got as far as Bhamdoun when Israel attacked. All day the Israeli jets kept up their bombing of Syrian positions, the planes flying in pairs, with hardly any anti-aircraft fire to deter them. Rich refugees from West Beirut staying at resort hotels in Broumana sipped their drinks as they watched the Israeli planes wheel in, drop their bomb loads, and turn away to refuel and re-arm as others took their place. At night, helicopter gunships kept up the offensive, dropping flares and shooting up anything that moved on the ground, confident that with their excellent communications, tightly co-ordinated timing and good discipline, no Israeli troops would move in before the scheduled time. Israeli APCs moved about the perimeter of the fighting, broadcasting messages to the Syrian troops – messages which were to become

the standard Israeli prelude to an attack in Beirut and anywhere else where they expected resistance: 'Surrender or die;
get out while you can; soon we are coming in.'

This time, the Syrians took no notice, except to open fire as
best as they could on the cruising Israeli armoured vehicles. It
looked as if there was going to be a battle. In the event, it was a
minor one. The constant pounding from the air by the Israelis
had taken its toll, to such an extent that although the Syrians
fought back, they could put up little serious opposition when
the Israeli tanks moved in. At such close quarters what was
needed was individual dash, swift exploitation of a situation,
even foolhardiness. All these things the Israelis had, while the
Syrians were still trying to put into practice ponderous Russian
military tactics which called for numbers rather than daring,
and set-piece battles instead of quick breakthroughs. Less from
lack of bravery or will to fight than through poor strategy and
inferior armour, the Syrians were quickly and decisively
beaten. Bhamdoun was taken by the Israelis, who thus gained
total control of the highway into Beirut from Syria.

After the fighting, President Assad sent a message of con-
gratulations to his troops which amounted to an admission of
defeat and a recognition that for all practical purposes the war
was over. 'You have fought gallantly . . .' he said, with a strong
emphasis on the past tense, and a clear implication that nothing
more could be done. Though the first and only formal ceasefire
between Israel and Syria had gone into effect at noon on June
11th, it was the ceasefire of June 25th which actually marked
the end of any real hostilities between Israel and Syria. After
that, Israel only once took any large-scale action against the
Syrians, and that was more a punishment for allowing Palestinian action and a deterrent against similar moves in the future,
than a continuation of the war.

The actual purpose of this particular ceasefire was to end a
massive Israeli bombardment of West Beirut, the heaviest up to
that time, in which Israeli artillery, tanks, planes and ships
shelled targets along the coast from Minet el Hosn to Ouzai. At
the same time, Shweifat and Aramoun were battered by Israeli
guns at almost point-blank range, and Israeli planes bombed
the already devastated Palestinian districts around the Arab

University, along Corniche Mazraa, and in Fakhani. So bad
was the damage caused and so intense the bombardment that
rescue workers could not reach the bodies of people killed, or
free those still living who were trapped in the débris. One
reason for the ceasefire, it was said, was to allow fire and
ambulancemen to do their work. But it was also noted by many
that the truce coincided with the upheaval in the American
cabinet caused by the resignation of the Secretary of State, Mr
Haig, and his replacement by a man much closer to the Arab
camp, Mr Shultz.

With the new ceasefire holding for a few days, the Israelis
turned to other means to keep up the pressure on the Palestinians and the people of West Beirut. Just as they had done before
their assaults on the southern towns, so now in Beirut the
Israeli planes dropped pamphlets urging the population to flee.
On this first 'leaflet raid', the planes dropped their messages
mainly over the Palestinian areas of the city. The pink sheets of
paper fluttering down in the sunlight made a pretty sight after
the havoc wrought by Israeli jets, but the message they contained carried no good cheer. Written in Arabic, the leaflets
read:

> To the residents: The Israeli Defence Force is continuing its war
> against the terrorists and has not yet used its full force. It is
> concerned not to hurt innocent civilians or anyone who does not
> fight against it. Residents of Beirut: Use the ceasefire to save your
> lives. You have the following alternatives: Through the IDF forces
> on the Beirut-Damascus highway, or Northward in the direction of
> Tripoli. Save your life and the lives of your loved ones. Signed: The
> command of the Israeli Defence Forces.

The Israeli message had its intended effect. Hundreds of cars
queued up to get into East Beirut, many with bundles of
clothing and other household items stacked high on the roofs,
and packed with whole families anxious to escape the street-
fighting they feared was coming. So great was the crush at the
Galerie Semaan crossing-point on Sunday, June 27th, that
many people, lulled by the calm there and the absence of any
shelling, decided that they would stay at home after all, and
turned back into West Beirut. Next day came what many saw

as a final warning. Again the jets came over to drop leaflets and this time they said: 'Flee for your lives.' On blue paper now, the sheets looked silver as they floated slowly down in the last rays of the setting sun. (At this stage, the Israelis usually sent their jets over at sunset, so that they could fly in out of the west and so make life more difficult for the anti-aircraft gunners. Later, when they had tested the Palestinian air defences thoroughly for weeks and realised how ineffectual they were, they attacked at any time of the day or night.) On this occasion, the leaflets were dropped over the centre of the city, in the Hamra area. They read:

> Thousands of your brothers have taken the opportunity given to them and have left Beirut and are now living in peace and safety. The ceasefire is granting an indispensable opportunity to the residents of West Beirut to save their lives and the lives of their loved ones. You who are still present in Beirut today: remember that time is running out. The later you leave it the more you expose your life and the lives of your loved ones to danger.

Again, many people rushed to their cars, convinced that an attack was imminent. The trouble was that for many, it was impossible to go. For one thing, they feared that if they did, their apartments would be occupied by some of the thousands of refugees from the south who had poured into Beirut – for in Lebanon, as in most Middle Eastern countries, people were apt to put all their money into their homes, goods and furnishings, so that to leave their apartments meant abandoning all they had worked for all their lives. Others living in Beirut had no choice: the Phalangists announced that while all Lebanese would be allowed into East Beirut, Palestinians and Syrians would be turned back. Others again who had relatives in the north of the country hesitated to go there because of reports of fighting in Tripoli between Syrians and local militias, and interfactional quarrels. Some were too old and infirm to leave, and finally, many felt a strong determination not to be ordered around by the Israelis and were ready and willing to stick it out in their own homes in their own city, come what may. This was reinforced by appeals to the inhabitants from both Sunni and Shia leaders not to abandon West Beirut.

In the end, only about 4,000 inhabitants of Beirut decided to leave as a result of the leaflets dropped by the Israelis – hardly a significant number out of the 400,000 who stayed on. Each day the truce lasted, more people did go, but the panic exodus of the first days was not repeated, and even Mr Begin's message when he spoke in the Knesset – 'Leave by car, leave on foot, but leave' – failed to shake the resolve of those who remained. Similarly, when Israeli radio in its Arabic service began broadcasting appeals to the Palestinians to lay down their arms, the result was nil. Only one Palestinian of any rank defected to the Israelis during the war: he was a Fateh officer in Sidon who, after the Israeli occupation, claimed he had long been opposed to the PLO's military adventures against Israel, and believed only in political efforts to regain the homeland. He said he had saved many Lebanese from ill-treatment at the hands of PLO men. There was obviously a high degree of self-interest in his claims, and Israel gave him publicity merely for propaganda reasons. The only others to side with the Israelis were informers who may have been Israeli agents all along, or who were bribed or frightened into helping the invaders. With hoods over their heads, they sat beside Israeli interrogating officers at a table set up on the beach at Sidon; as Palestinian prisoners were brought forward one by one, the hooded men either nodded or shook their heads; a nod meant at least further interrogation; a shake of the head was a passport to eventual freedom.

With the ceasefire still holding, Israel now began to apply a new form of pressure on West Beirut: the Israeli jets stopped their leaflet raids, and instead gave a foretaste of things to come. Now, when they came out of the sun, they screamed low over the Palestinian areas of West Beirut, then went into steep climbing turns to avoid any anti-aircraft fire, releasing hot-air flares to divert Sam Seven missiles – the small shoulder-fired ground-to-air missiles which were the only ones the Palestinians had. So July began, with mock-raids by the Israeli planes by day, and the same planes flying over every night, dropping flares and generally maintaining the pressure on the already nervous population. It was an effective tactic, which kept the Palestinian gunners constantly on the alert; because they were nervous, short of sleep and jumpy, they were then liable to fire

off at shadows, thus enabling the Israelis to claim that the
Palestinians had broken the ceasefire and they had merely been
forced to retaliate.

In fact, Israeli artillery did open up on targets on the
southern outskirts of the city, shelling Bourj Brajneh and adjac-
ent areas. At the same time, there was a series of tough statements from Israeli leaders, notably the Israeli Chief of Staff,
General Eytan, who warned: 'If the terrorists do not get out of
Beirut, they will have to be destroyed. They must leave so that
there will be no need for an operation harder than the one now
going on.' Mr Begin, too, accused the Palestinians of 'taking
hundreds of thousands of civilians hostage' – a strange claim, as
the Palestinians and their allies manning the crossing points
into East Beirut never closed them or turned anyone back.
Finally, General Sharon himself visited East Beirut and gave an
impromptu Press conference on being spotted by journalists in
the Hotel Alexandre in Achrafiyeh – the Alexandre being the
East Beirut equivalent of the Commodore in West Beirut,
though a pale shadow of that remarkable establishment.
General Sharon added to the disquiet by his apparent reason-
ableness: 'We believe in co-existence with the Palestinian
people . . . We are not fighting the Palestinian people.' However, he pointedly refused to say that his men would not go into
West Beirut, and further doubts were raised about Israel's
intentions when General Eytan said that though he believed a
political solution was close, 'military means may have to be
used to step up the pressure.'

So almost a month of occupation by the Israeli forces came to
an end in Lebanon, with the capital now besieged and threats of
worse to come. Already things were bad enough: the electricity
supply was on for only four hours a day, in each area, so people
had to rely on generators if they lived in expensive apartments
or hotels, and on candles and bottled gas lamps everywhere
else. There was free passage between the eastern and western
halves of the city for those willing to brave the Phalangist
militia checkpoints and the Israelis, but each day there were
traffic jams in one direction or another – eastbound if there had
been heavy shelling or bombing, westbound if a few days of
relative quiet had persuaded people it was safe enough to return

to take a look at their homes or businesses. The night sky was regularly lit up by Israeli flares even when there was no shelling or bombing, and Israeli planes were active every day, making sure there were sonic booms even if they did not carry out any offensive action, so as to keep the people of West Beirut in a state of tension.

Yet after a month, Palestinians and Lebanese alike had learnt to live with it all. They took to the shelters when the artillery opened up or the bombs came near, and they emerged afterwards to pick up the pieces. Banks were open for a few hours most days; there was plenty of food in the shops; petrol was in short supply, but could be found – and for the youngsters, the space invader arcades were all equipped with small generators, so that they could keep going during all the daylight hours.

Beirut, as usual, was learning to live with the siege, and that was something that could not be allowed.

CHAPTER SIX

The turn of the screw came on July 3rd, after a day of heavy artillery duels between Palestinian and Israeli gunners, and increased psychological pressure by the Israelis. Using loud-hailers, the Israeli soldiers at the Galerie Semaan crossing point urged the people just down the road to leave, while Israeli radio warned that measures were about to be taken to tighten the noose around Beirut. The threats were swiftly made good: the crossing points between East and West Beirut were closed to anyone and anything trying to enter the besieged western sector. The siege had turned into a blockade.

Hardly anyone noticed at first. The shelling which had begun the previous day intensified and went on all night, so that when dawn came, the whole of the southern suburbs of Beirut were covered in a pall of dust and smoke. Standing on the top of an eleven-storey building close to the Museum crossing point, one could watch the shells crashing into Bourj Brajneh refugee camp next to the airport, the most recently built of the camps and one that housed as many Shia refugees from Southern Lebanon as it did Palestinians. Earlier, I had watched the same spectacle from up the hill at Baabda, where Israeli artillery spotters had set up their binoculars, telescopes and maps in St Anthony's school, with a field telephone at hand to direct the fire of the artillerymen positioned in the hills a kilometre or so behind them. Every now and again they would ask for phosphorus to be used, so that they could identify the hits more accurately – the phosphorus shells sent up clouds of white smoke as they landed, as well as setting fire to buildings and any people in them. Now, at the Museum, one saw the same thing from a different angle, and at the same time, one could watch the traffic below, which was all going in one direction. Friendly Fateh men lugged a theodolite up to the roof so that we could watch the Israeli soldiers at the first checkpoint in East Beirut. They looked very busy: all the arrivals from the west were shunted along to be searched by Phalangist militiamen, while the Israelis dealt with the few people trying to get back into West Beirut. The only ones they allowed through were Lebanese Army men in uniform, gendarmes or policemen. And one policeman who did make it across held out his hands ruefully as soon as he arrived: the Israelis had taken away from him even the one bottle of mineral water he had been carrying.

Only then did people realise the significance of the new Israeli move: they had cut the water and electricity supplies to the west. Mr Mahmoud Ammar, the Minister of Electric and Water Resources, described how it had been done: an Israeli Army engineer squad, led by an officer, had gone to the water distribution centre in Achrafiyeh, in East Beirut, on Sunday afternoon. The Israeli officer had with him all the plans of the installation, and he and his men knew exactly what to do. They had turned a wheel, and then removed the wheel itself; and as simply as that, half a modern city had been deprived of water. Mr Ammar explained that it had been possible to cut off the supply because West Beirut was lower down than Achrafayeh and was supplied by gravity. By closing the one valve, not only had West Beirut been deprived of water, but also some low-lying areas of the Christian East, mainly Furn el Chebbak, Badaro Street, Ain Rumaneh and Hay el Siryan; clearly some of the residents of the East were expected to make sacrifices to force the Palestinians out. It was the same with the electricity supply: on the same Sunday afternoon, Israeli engineers had gone to the main centre of Karantina, and thrown the switch; then to make sure that the supply would stay cut off, Israeli engineers also blew up high-tension cables at Hazmiyeh.

The reason Mr Ammar, one of the lesser-known Lebanese Ministers, took it on himself to explain what happened was because the Israelis had denied any responsibility. When the blockade had begun on Saturday, they had given a metaphorical shrug of the shoulders and implied it was all being done by the Phalangists. Mr Ammar's statement explicitly denied this: it was the Israelis who did it all, he said categorically.

And it was the Israelis who enforced the blockade, though

often through their Phalangist surrogates, who were the men who actually manned the roadblocks and turned back lorry-loads of food, and even searched the few people allowed to go into West Beirut to make sure they were not carrying anything with them. At the same time, the Israelis kept up their intensive bombardments of the west, with shells and captured Katyusha rockets pouring in steadily. There was some movement on the ground too, with Israeli tanks moving forward in the Shweifat area and towards the airport from the Khalde front. It was not a major advance, but more a form of military pressure calculated to reinforce the economic pressure – and it was not without loss: the Palestinians claimed to have knocked out six tanks, and though this was an exaggeration, the Israelis certainly did suffer some casualties and damage.

As usual, once they had achieved their objectives, the Israelis agreed to a new ceasefire. This latest one went into effect at 4.30 p.m. on Monday, July 5th, largely in response to pressure from America, and from Mr Habib. Again, it was short-lived: the Israelis lit up the night sky with flares which Palestinian gunners could not resist trying to shoot out; once again, conditions were created in which Israel could claim that the ceasefire had been breached. Sure enough, only a day later, a new bombardment of West Beirut began, with shells thudding in at a rate of three or four every minute, smashing into buildings already damaged by previous strafing, spreading new rubble over the streets of the Fakhani and Arab University districts, and sending people scurrying down to the shelters once more.

The following morning there was a huge pall of smoke over the city: a rope warehouse in the Talat al Khayat district had been hit, and had burnt throughout the night. The reason, it emerged, was that 'The Voice of Lebanon' radio, the broadcasting station of the Phalangists, had claimed the previous evening that the Palestinians had installed 'Stalin organs', the multiple rocket-launchers, somewhere in the district. Immediately afterwards, Israeli 155mm cluster shells had landed there, starting the fire at the warehouse in Hachem al Khalil Street.

At this time, Israel was consistently denying reports from

West Beirut that it was using cluster bombs and cluster shells –
weapons which had been supplied to it by America on the strict
understanding that they were to be used only 'for defensive
purposes'. This time, the people of Talat al Khayat were
determined to disprove the Israeli claims. At the warehouse, a
man who gave his name only as 'Mahmoud' and said he had
been trained in the Lebanese Army, showed an unexploded
155mm shell which he had carefully dismantled. Some of the
150 'bomblets' it contained were laid out in neat rows on the
bonnet of a car; others were left still packed inside the shell
casing to show how it all worked. There then occurred one of
the more bizarre episodes of the siege: a diminutive member of
the Mourabitoun came along, looking very angry indeed. 'Why
are you taking his picture?' he demanded of Jill Brown, the
photographer with me. 'Why do you want his picture, what are
you doing?' Patiently, I explained that it was proof that the
Israelis were indeed using prohibited weapons. 'You should not
do it,' said the Mourabitoun man. 'Anyway, you are very tall
and I am very short and you make me very nervous.' The
conversation was becoming surrealistic; then all became clear:
our diminutive friend was cross because, he said, *he* was the one
who had dismantled the shell, and not 'Mahmoud', who was
claiming the credit. 'I am very brave,' the Mourabitoun man
said. 'You see this badge?' He pointed to a Cedar emblem sewn
onto his trousers. 'I took that from a Phalangist I killed in the
Civil War. I am not frightened of anything.' And with that he
picked up one of the bomblets from the shell and began tossing
it idly from hand to hand. 'Now you're making *me* very nervous,' I said, edging carefully away.

Yet the incident did show that the Israelis were quite deliberately using cluster shells on densely populated areas, and for
specific reasons. If it had been true that the Palestinians had
installed a Stalin organ somewhere in Talat al Khayat – and the
local people swore that they had not – then cluster shells, which
are basically anti-personnel weapons, would have been more
effective than high-explosive shells, which would have had to be
remarkably accurate to achieve any success. The use of the
cluster shells in the area – at least twenty fell – was militarily
sensible, though it showed a total disregard for possible civilian

casualties. It was a pattern which was to be repeated many times over.

Day after day now, the shelling went on, with the Palestinian quarters on the southern outskirts of the city bearing the brunt. The Palestinian offices at Fakhani were hit time after time, yet remarkably, no-one was ever killed there: as soon as the planes came over, people either took to the basements, or sheltered under the stairs on the ground floors, which were protected by sand-bags.

At the PLO information office, Mahmoud Labadi, the chief spokesman, and his assistants, moved out of their fourth-floor offices and set up shop in the shattered hallway on the ground floor. All day they sat there, on kitchen chairs 'borrowed' from neighbouring buildings, entertaining the dozens of journalists who turned up and pouring glasses of black tea. The PLO insisted on correspondents renewing their passes every week – the more cynical suggested that it was because they could then be sure of seeing reporters at least once in seven days. In fact, Labadi, once noted for his taciturnity and total lack of information, did a remarkable job throughout the siege: he was always available, and although he rarely had anything new to say to those who saw him regularly, he was always ready with the same well-polished speech for newcomers, always willing to do television interviews or to supply guides to take people to the scene of the latest incident.

These guides, Mahmoud, Aziz, Mohammed and the rest, were young professional men or graduates, who spoke at least one or two languages besides Arabic; they contributed greatly to the image of the PLO which came across so strongly during the blockade: that of a moderate organisation under savage attack from an overwhelming power. They were also remarkably efficient young men. When I once wanted to visit the old central area of West Beirut, the commercial district destroyed in the Civil War, I was politely but firmly turned back by the commander of the Palestine Liberation Army unit in charge there. I asked Mahmoud for help, so with his pistol stuck in his waist-band as usual, this rather scruffy young man laboriously but doggedly worked his way right up the chain of command of the PLA in Beirut until he reached the CO, a Brigadier sitting in lonely splendour in a suite in the Menendez Hotel in Phoenicia Street, headquarters of the Beirut contingent. With permission granted, we then worked our way down the command ladder again, until we wound up with the officer who had first refused us access. Now he was all smiles and helpfulness as he warned us not to put our heads above the earth ramparts thrown up to block streets, in case the Phalangists less than a hundred yards away decided to fire. We did, they did, but the burst went over our heads.

The constant shelling, the growing shortages, the ever-present fear and insecurity affected everyone. In offices where men and women worked together it was noticeable that people touched each other a lot; often men would put their arms round girls and hug them in a totally asexual way. Similarly, the girls would often hold the men's hands or stroke their heads in passing. Everyone needed reassurance wherever they could get it, and many of the people staying on in West Beirut were without their spouses or families. They found that fear was no aphrodisiac; for men and women alike, it was comfort that was needed, someone to say 'Don't worry, it will be all right', even when they knew it probably would not be.

Yet even the daily horrors of Beirut brought good to some people. On one occasion, a group of armed men went to the Zarif prison and ordered the warders there to open the gates. The prison officers wisely obeyed, and 187 convicts walked to the dangerous freedom outside, among them murderers and rapists, including Ibrahim Tarraf, a killer known as the Landru of Lebanon, who had shot two people, cut them up and disposed of the remains in various dustbins. Another prisoner who vanished was Aymane Zahreddine, convicted of the murder of no less than nine people. With so many other dangers to consider, no-one was particularly concerned, and in fact the authorities themselves – such as they were – freed men from another prison in a particularly vulnerable area.

Throughout June there had been a series of car bombs in the city, at Ain Mreisseh, near the Phoenicia Hotel, outside the French News Agency, near the Green Line, and in various other places. Now, amid the growing chaos of the siege, the Palestinians produced the perpetrators, four men who admitted they were responsible. One was caught when his car was stopped in a routine check at a Palestinian road block and found to be packed with explosives; the others were traced through the registration numbers of cars, or engine numbers discovered on the débris after explosions. The four men, Said Shaar, Hussein Jaber, Yahya Simhat and Hussein al Sayyed, all came from Southern Lebanon, and one of them, Hussein Jaber, said he was a member of Major Sa'ad Haddad's militia. All of them claimed they had been forced to carry out their acts of sabotage by threats against themselves or their families.

The four men were paraded at a news conference, all looking very much the worse for their experience; they had obviously been beaten up, although they made no complaint about this to the Press, and in fact spoke without prompting of the way they had been recruited by men of Major Haddad's group or by the Phalangists, but at the behest of an Israeli Intelligence officer, a man they knew only as Abu Jabal. After the Press conference, conducted by Abu Haitham, head of the PLO security department, the men were taken away, and journalists were told they would be given 'a field trial'. Next day, three of them were shot in the crater caused by the biggest bomb they had set off, one which had contained at least 300 kilos of explosive and had been placed near the Phoenicia Hotel, causing large numbers of casualties. Their bodies were then taken away for burial, and in the crater a small placard was left. In Arabic, it read: 'So die all traitors.'

As the days passed, the pressure was unremitting, with Israeli guns pounding the city from the hills above West Beirut, planes bombing where they chose with absolute impunity, and the gunboats continuing to hammer the coastal areas inaccurately, but nonetheless with devastating effect. The tired inhabitants each had their own scale by which to measure the severity of what was going on, but by common consent, some days were worse than others. The weekend of July 10th was particularly bad, and though as usual it was West Beirut which bore the brunt of it all, the East did not escape unscathed. Palestinian rockets hit the Presidential Palace at Baabda, no doubt aiming for the Israeli tank park nearby. With blithe disregard of the warning given, the Israelis left their vehicles where they were,

packed side by side below the palace. Very shortly, the
Palestinian gunners found the range, and a number of Israeli
vehicles were destroyed. Only then was this particular vehicle
park abandoned and the cars and lorries dispersed.

On the Sunday, the bombardment went on for sixteen hours
without pause, and was particularly heavy around the airport,
where the Israelis made a number of probing attacks. Shells fell
on the airport itself, and wounded some of the thirty or so
Lebanese gendarmes, who, in a remarkable display of devotion
to duty and courage, remained at their posts throughout the
whole period. Lebanese security men working for Middle East
Airlines also stayed at the airport the whole time, despite the
mortars falling there and the destruction of planes on the
tarmac. In the end, their ordeal was made pointless, for when
the Israelis finally occupied the airport buildings, they smashed
down every door, rifled every cupboard, and scattered the
contents of every drawer. The soldiers then stole anything that
took their fancy, while the commanders organised the removal
of some of the sophisticated computer equipment used by
MEA. Two officers flew off in a light plane which had not been
damaged, and took it home to Tel Aviv. They were the only
ones court-martialled.

The Sunday bombardment, July 11th, was much less of a
one-sided affair than usual, mainly because Syrian forces remaining in Beirut joined in. They still had about forty 122mm
and 130mm field guns, as well as Katyusha rocket-launchers
and Stalin organs. The Syrian field guns opened up on Christian areas which had previously been untouched, notably at
Dora, north of Beirut, the site of the main oil storage depot, and
at Dbayeh. Shells exploded close to the Alexandre Hotel in East
Beirut, where a member of the British Diplomatic Wireless
Service from the evacuated Embassy was injured while watching it all from the rooftop. One man who escaped was General
Eytan: during a tour of inspection of the area around Baabda he
stopped to talk to the crew of a gun firing into Bourj Brajneh; a
mere two minutes after he had left the place, shellfire from West
Beirut knocked out the gun and its crew.

In West Beirut, this was the worst day so far. The streets
were deserted except for ambulances. Four hospitals were hit,

and according to doctors at the American University Hospital, the biggest in the city, the main problem was to find space to stack the dead bodies until they could be identified by relatives. After the battle, in which it was estimated that some 10,000 shells and rockets were exchanged, the toll was nearly 200 dead in West Beirut in the single day. Every street showed new scars; at the Museum crossing point, the road was littered with débris; the Argentine Embassy and the French ambassador's residence had taken new hits, and every one of the tall buildings opposite the racecourse showed fresh signs of damage. At first, it seemed that the Israelis had been shooting there just for the sake of it; in fact, the Palestinians and their Lebanese allies had moved rocket-launchers right up to the Green Line, as the boundary was known. In the garden behind one building, Fateh men proudly showed off Grad launchers they had been using the previous night – weapons of terrifying inaccuracy, the elevation given by turning a knurled screw, the direction by manually pointing the thing in the direction it was to shoot. Given those conditions, it was remarkable that the gunners ever managed to put the rockets where they were intended to go. Somehow, amazingly, they often did.

At 9.30 p.m. on the Sunday, a new ceasefire went into effect, and people wearily emerged from the shelters in which they had spent the whole day. In the basements, families had staked out little patches for themselves with blankets, mattresses and pillows, often with kerosene lamps or candles. Usually, the father had his Kalashnikov with him, though in many places Palestinian guards insisted that all weapons should be stacked at the door – they knew only too well how quarrels can erupt in conditions of stress and forced proximity, and they also knew that in Lebanon noisy arguments can all too often turn into shooting matches. While they sheltered from the bombing, people spent the time listening to the small transistor radios which were standard items of equipment for everyone, right down to the poorest. Everyone knew by heart the frequencies and times of news broadcasts, though when the shelling was actually going on, the Phalangist 'Voice of Lebanon' was always the one listened to most. On this station, announcers always broke into programmes to give the most up-to-date news in both Arabic and French. Their information was usually good, and always fast, thanks to their system of 'stringers' all over the capital, informants would phone in to give details whenever anything happened in their areas. The Phalangist radio station identification was always a delight, with different announcers adding their own individual comments; a typical one ran: 'This is the Voice of Lebanon, the voice of liberty, the voice of dignity – and of good music too'. It seemed something of an anti-climax.

Once a ceasefire was announced, everyone would wait cautiously for a while to see if it took hold, the men lounging about the entrance to the shelters while the women tidied up and organised the children. Then, when it looked reasonably safe, out they would go, and in minutes the resilience of the Lebanese would be seen as lamps were lit on balconies, food was put on the stoves, and people called across from one house to another to hear the latest news and to make sure that friends and neighbours had survived the day. 'Hamdullah al salamah,' they called to each other: 'Thank God you are safe and well.'

With the new truce holding for a while, the daily battle was to survive the blockade, and here again, Lebanese enterprise at one time threatened to undermine all the Israelis efforts. It was the telephone which made it possible. For a time, telephone contact between the eastern and western halves of the city was difficult, if not impossible, largely because a main cable had been deliberately cut; eventually, this was repaired by a few of the unsung heroes of the siege, the technicians who somehow always managed to keep some kind of service going, often at considerable personal risk. With the lines restored, merchants in West Beirut who for years had been dealing with colleagues in the east proposed secret deals, and soon lorry-loads of fruit and vegetables began getting through.

At first, this was done in two ways: in East Beirut, merchants paid out an average of LL 3,000.00 a truck for anything sent in. The money was paid to Phalangist guards along the Green Line, who would take down one of the sand-bagged walls blocking off the small side streets. At the other end, more money changed hands, and again, while the first line of sand-bags was

being hastily rebuilt, a new breach was being made in the
second. The very brave drivers who brought the goods in were
handsomely paid for the risks they took; the merchants made a
good profit despite the heavy bribes they had to pay out; and
the retailers – usually street vendors – did equally well. The
people of West Beirut were delighted to see fruit and vegetables
back on sale, though only the comparatively well-to-do could
afford to buy. When the first barrow-loads came in, prices were
three, four and five times the normal; later, prices levelled off as
more got through, but even so they never went below double the
usual price. In a typically Lebanese way, the laws of supply and
demand could be seen in action, as daily prices reflected the
amount on offer and the willingness or ability of people to pay
the prices asked.

A second way into West Beirut was both more hazardous and
more rewarding: it was the route up from the south, which
entered the city through the regularly shelled Bourj Brajneh
camp. This was used mainly by people bringing petrol into the
city, the scarcest and most precious commodity of all. At first,
people stocked the boots of their cars with plastic jerrycans full
of Israeli imported petrol, and bluffed or bribed their way past
checkpoints. These early consignments sold for LL 350.00 for
20 litres, almost ten times the normal price. Then, as these
useful, necessary and very bold profiteers gained confidence,
40-gallon drums were loaded onto pick-up trucks and brought
in. However, over-confidence eventually set in, and people
stopped taking proper precautions, or perhaps did not pay out
enough money; also, there seemed to have been a change of
Israeli personnel at the checkpoints, with Military Police
brought in to replace the infantry soldiers previously stationed
there. Whatever the reason, a number of trucks were turned
back in the most brutal way. Three pick-ups travelling through
Schweifat to Hay al Sellom were stopped by Israeli guards; the
drivers were told to get out at gun-point, then the soldiers fired
their Uzzi machine pistols at the tyres of the lorries, before
setting their petrol tanks ablaze. It was an effective way of
discouraging others from attempting that route, though it made
a marked contrast to the behaviour of some other Israelis, since
many traders from Upper Galilee were doing deals with

Lebanese merchants, knowing full well that their goods would eventually wind up in West Beirut.

Certainly much of the fruit which went into Beirut from the south of the country was from Israel itself. One tell-tale sign was the water melons: those grown in Lebanon are uniformly green, while the Israeli variety have green and yellow stripes. Similarly, the different aubergines could be spotted instantly, as those from Israel were bigger and fatter than the thin, long varieties grown in Lebanon. Michel Khoury, Governor of the Central Bank, was worried at what he described as Israeli 'dumping' in the south, and feared that Lebanese farmers would be forced out of business by the more highly developed and sophisticated Israeli growers. In Beirut the people knew very well where everything was coming from, and cared very little: all they were concerned about was to get fresh food for themselves and their children.

In spite of the enterprise of the blockade runners, it was getting increasingly difficult to maintain basic supplies. The main trouble was the lack of fuel. The shortage of petrol meant that even the rudimentary garbage-disposal system which had been in operation had to be abandoned, since the refuse lorries were immobilised. There were even days when ambulances could not go out, and the distribution of emergency rations by voluntary organisations such as the Haigazian College had to be suspended for lack of petrol for the trucks. Even worse was the shortage of diesel oil, which threatened the supply of bread. If that had run out, the Israelis might have won, since the Lebanese regard their flat Arab loaves as a staple of life and might have rebelled if they had not been able to obtain fresh every day. Fortunately, most bakeries somehow managed to keep going, and long lines of people could be seen waiting outside every day, refusing to move even when the shelling crept closer. On a few occasions, arguments over who was first in the queue led to full-scale shoot-outs in Hamra and other areas, and later, armed militiamen were posted outside every bakery to maintain order and settle disputes. The system worked very well, and the PLO saw to it that bakeries were supplied with fuel from their own large stocks.

Flour remained a major worry. West Beirut needed a total of

180 tons a day in normal times, and even after the exodus of so many people, the requirement was still considerable. All this was pointed out to the Israelis time after time, and time after time they either agreed and said lorries would be allowed through, then stopped them at the port, or else claimed that the whole matter had to be decided back in Jerusalem. So exasperated did John de Salis, the Chief International Red Cross delegate, become that he went up to Baabda one day to meet Colonel Paul Kadar and show him the effect of the Israeli blockade.

De Salis took with him a bottle of vintage brandy, some smoked salmon and some caviar as gifts for the Israeli officer, who had been a former Consul-general of his country in America. The message was plain, but de Salis spelt it out all the same: 'If you have money or a gun you can get anything in Beirut.' The Red Cross, he said, was concerned with those who had neither, but they could do nothing alone – they had to have the help of the Israelis. Colonel Kadar, a decent man in a difficult situation, took the point and promised to consult 'headquarters' on the specific points raised: permission for flour to be sent into West Beirut and, above all, for fuel oil.

Apart from the lack of water, it was the shortage of diesel which caused the biggest problem, for everything depended on the individual electricity generators. Most places were equipped with a generator of their own, for there had been a shortage of electricity in Lebanon for years and everyone with any foresight had bought one. The places most at risk were the hospitals, and the bigger they were, the greater the danger, for it was at the main hospitals that blood and plasma were stored, and any loss of refrigeration would result in the entire collection being lost.

Right at the beginning of the invasion, the Palestinian Red Crescent had put into operation a contingency plan it had drawn up years before to counter this threat. This was largely the brainchild of Dr Rio Spirgi, a Swiss who had previously worked for the ICRC, but who had left because of what he called that organisation's 'top-heavy bureaucracy and lack of determination' in 'political' situations. Dr Spirgi had been with the Red Crescent in Beirut for some two years, and as well as performing operations when necessary, had gradually assumed the position of chief of planning and right-hand man to Dr Fathi Arafat, brother of Yasser Arafat and head of the organisation. With Dr Emil Makhlouf, these three formed the core of the committee which administered the Red Crescent throughout the siege. They met at Dr Makhlouf's office in Hamra each day after Dr Arafat had done his rounds, to assess the situation and to prepare for what was to come.

Their first moves in putting into effect the plan drawn up by Dr Spirgi were the most important and successful. In effect, they called for the dispersal of all hospitals around West Beirut. When the invasion began, the main hospital in West Beirut was, as it remained, the American University Hospital, which catered for anyone – anyone, that is, who was able to pay. As well as applying and teaching American medical and surgical techniques, the AUB had also adopted American financing methods, and had to be satisfied that payment would be forthcoming before treatment was begun. Now, one of the strengths of the PLO was that it had always seen to the welfare of its wounded and disabled people, making sure they had treatment, pensions and anything else they needed. So, at the start of the war, Dr Arafat met the AUB administrators and gave them a categorical assurance that all bills for treatment to Palestinian fighters or civilians would be met in full by the PLO. This was a promise that was faithfully kept. Somehow, even after the Palestinians had left Beirut, the last bills were duly paid at the hospital.

The strictly Palestinian hospitals available to the PLO were the Akka, at Bir Hassan near the Kuwait Embassy; the Gaza, inside Sabra camp; and the Jerusalem. The other big hospital was the Barbir, run by the Sunni Moslem Makassed organisation, the philanthropic group headed by Saeb Salam. However, all these were in highly vulnerable areas, so Dr Spirgi's plan was to have a large number of small hospitals around the town. Eventually, some twenty-five were set up, in schools, hotels and any public or private buildings which could be found or requisitioned. The idea was that these emergency centres would be able to provide immediate medical attention whenever there were large numbers of casualties; then, all those capable of being moved would be sent out to other make-shift hospitals not overwhelmed with casualties at that time; and in a third stage, the wounded would once again be distributed around the various centres for continuing treatment. It was a system which worked very well.

During the war, only one of the emergency centres was hit. This was at the Triumph Hotel, which was struck by a shell and briefly set on fire when the Bristol Hotel immediately opposite was chosen as a target by Israeli gunners during an intensive bombardment of the city. The Triumph was in fact the show-piece hospital of the Red Crescent, not because it was the biggest or best, but because it was readily accessible. It was there that the Red Crescent established their public relations office, and it was there the television teams and cameramen were taken after each bombardment when they wanted pictures of the wounded. The Triumph contained women's and children's wards as well as men's wards where the fighters were taken, and some of the most harrowing pictures to come out of the whole period were taken there.

Most desperate of all was the huge hospital for geriatrics and the insane in the middle of Sabra camp. It was hit during six separate bombardments. After the first time, most of the fifteen hundred staff left, and as many as possible of the patients were sent to their families or to other hospitals. But some five hundred remained, many of them severely mentally disturbed children. About twenty dedicated members of the staff braved the near-daily bombing of Sabra camp to tend the remaining inmates, though their task was made almost impossible; because of the position of the hospital, supplies could be taken there only rarely, and stocks soon ran out; there was only one cook to prepare the basic meals which were all that could be served; no laundry was possible, so very soon the children were kept naked in a ward, with the most disturbed among them having to be tied to their beds with bandages to stop them hurting themselves when the shelling or bombing started again. It was a scene straight out of Hogarth: urine and excreta on the floor, an all-pervading smell, demented adults wandering about aimlessly, harassed, fatalistic staff trying desperately to cope in dreadful conditions, themselves as frightened as their charges after weeks of terror. On the top floor, visitors were shown the shattered children's ward, once a model of its kind, offering the best treatment available in the country; now it was littered with glass and débris, with the children's Fisher Price toys still lying where they had left them. Staff who gladly spared the time to show people around gazed sadly on, then quietly pointed to the Red Crosses painted on the building, and the flag hanging limply outside.

The Lebanese Red Cross, the ICRC and several other agencies all did what they could, and Richard Grove-Hills, the Oxfam representative, did much to get supplies to the hospital. But no-one could find anywhere to put the children, in particular, where they could be given care and all kept together. Then, towards the end of the affair, Mother Theresa appeared on the scene. The more cynical feared that she was about to exploit the situation for publicity for herself and her Order; like all groups depending on charity, the Nobel-prize-winning nun from India needed to be in the news if donations were to continue to come in. She may have had that in mind; if so, it did not matter, for she was the one who got things done. John de Salis, the ICRC man who was himself no slouch when it came to organising relief, summed it up when he said: 'It's a remarkable experience to meet an efficient saint.'

Mother Theresa went to the hospital, dropped briefly to her knees to pray, then went around hugging the children and issuing a series of orders to the ICRC men, to the Lebanese Red Cross, the PLO guides, the hospital administrator and anyone else around. To the amazement of everyone, it all worked; a school was found in a relatively safe area where the children could be housed; food was produced; nuns from Mother Theresa's own Order arrived to help with the nursing, and everything down to nappy pins was thought of. Within three days Mother Theresa had achieved what relief organisations had failed to do for two months.

Before Mother Theresa appeared, life was getting progressively worse for the people in the city; it was the water situation which was causing most problems. The absence of mains water was not the total disaster it might have been in another city, as many people in West Beirut had always depended on wells,

rather than the municipal supply which was erratic and sometimes undrinkable. Now that the wells were supplying the
whole city, the water-table was dropping daily. The result was
a swift increase in the level of salinity; the one UN water
engineer in West Beirut found that the level was eight times
that considered permissible by international agencies. Soon the
water was brackish at best, and Red Crescent and relief
organisation doctors were going around the makeshift homes of
the refugees to warn mothers of families of the danger of
drinking the water as it was. Without thinking, they began
advising people to boil it all before use. Women looked at them
in amazement. 'You tell us to boil water, but we have none,'
said one. 'And when we do get some, God willing, we shall have
nothing to boil it with. Do not waste our time.'

The refugees were all over the town now, living in half-
finished buildings or in any unoccupied places they or their
armed friends could break into. The ground floor of the Reuters
Office in the Union Building at Sanayeh housed dozens; a huge
camp grew up in the forecourt of the Concorde Cinema; others
lived in the shells of buildings under construction; one family of
eight took up residence in the cab of an abandoned lorry. The
women were constantly busy, desperately cleaning, searching
for food, cooking, washing clothes when water was available,
and somehow, catering for their families. The children played,
queued for water, stole vegetables from carts when they could.
For the men, there was little to do, and gradually they grew
more apathetic, sitting gazing into space, occasionally rousing
themselves to argue with neighbours, and occasionally,
in desperation, begging from visitors. It was a demean-
ing and degrading existence about which they could do nothing.

Somehow, all the refugees were looked after to varying
degrees. The PLO made sure they got basic UNWRA rations,
supplying them from a huge store which had been established
in the city. Israel tried to score some propaganda points when
the Palestinians placed this depot under armed guard, though
without much success, since the guards were to prevent anyone
getting in to steal supplies. They were also there to prevent the
UNWRA officials from moving stocks out: some remarkably
unthinking official had proposed using some of the goods stored

in West Beirut to supply other areas of the country, particularly villages in the south under Israeli control. Not surprisingly, the Palestinians in West Beirut were determined to hold onto all there was.

For reasons rooted in the culture of the Palestinians and the Lebanese, a division of responsibilities arose without discussion among the refugees and the residents of the city alike: always it was the duty of the women and children to get the water. At first, the long lines of people at each stand-pipe or well collected water in any receptacle they could find – bottles, saucepans, buckets. Gradually, more order was introduced, with those who could afford to buying two-gallon plastic jerrycans, and the PLO supplying them to the poorer people. In this way, everyone was given a fair and equal ration. The men, for their part, stood in line at the bakeries. An odd but noticeable fact was that there were never quarrels in the queues for water, while violence often flared outside the bread shops. It was remarkable, too, that the Lebanese, even in these circumstances, could not curb their natural entrepreneurial instincts. Even on the worst days, somehow, somewhere, people always managed to buy large quantities of bread and to re-sell it at a higher price from the bonnets of parked cars to others unwilling to stand in line for an hour or more. Once again, those without money suffered: to keep their place in a bread queue or a water line, people had to stand patiently even while shells were falling nearby. The children, usually laughing and playing about as they waited, went silent as the shells or bombs came nearer: but they stayed.

The lack of water led to the development of some odd skills. People began to boast proudly of how little water they needed to wash with. By common consent, the minimum required for a shower was one litre: the method was to pour water over one's head from an old Sohat mineral bottle while standing in a small basin. Soap was then applied, one stepped out of the basin, and the water caught there was used to rinse off the lather. It was surprisingly effective. Mineral water itself was still available right up to the last days: some 40,000 cases had been delivered just before the siege began, and supplies lasted to the end. But instead of being LL 2.00 at the most, it finished up at LL 18.00 a litre.

The main method of cooking in Beirut was by bottled gas, and these bulky containers were difficult to find. Eventually, however, lorry-loads somehow found their way across the line and the bottles were put on sale at LL 50.00 and LL 60.00 each, instead of the regulation LL 20.00. In the few hotels that were still open, hardly any shortages were noticeable, as big stocks had been laid in early on. At the Commodore, the journalists who were almost the only clients jokingly complained about their monotonous diet, which consisted of smoked salmon every night – the hotel had received a big consignment just before the invasion. The Commodore also had good stocks of meat, so though the accompaniment each night was usually rice, the food was good. At the Bristol, too, an almost full menu was always available, and at the slightly more down-market Mayflower, used mainly by foreign volunteer relief workers, Munir Samaha, the owner – a Christian living in West Beirut – was able to provide basic meals the whole time, though eventually the well ran dry and water to the rooms had to be cut off.

For most of the war, two restaurants were open, Hans Matchek's Myrtom House and the Relais de Normande, run by Corinne, a Belgian lady. Both had operated throughout the civil war as well, and both agreed that things had never been as difficult as they were during the Israeli siege. In Hamra and other streets in the centre of the town, small cafés selling shwarma managed to cook on most days, and the local grocery shops seemed to have stocks as big as those of the supermarkets, so that everyone with something to sell made money during the war in West Beirut.

The people who really made a fortune during the siege were the taxi-drivers catering specifically to the journalists. According to their colleagues, the American TV networks seemed to have inexhaustible supplies of money to spend on taxis, and set the pace with grossly inflated daily rates which were then taken as the norm. Certainly the drivers often earned their money. One of them was killed when he took a group of TV men to the front at Khalde, just south of Beirut – at least, according to his family. The man's brothers, more angry than sorrowing, turned up at the Commodore to demand compensation from the TV men who had been with their brother. After much haggling and some hard words, as well as the production of a number of guns by the Kurdish family, a settlement was reached at $5,000 for the car and $35,000 for the man. Payment was made and the TV crew were allowed to go, and did. The only trouble was that a number of witnesses later claimed to have seen the supposedly dead driver alive, well, drinking coffee, and with a broad grin on his face . . .

CHAPTER SEVEN

West Beirut was increasingly cut off now. Traffic from east to west remained prohibited for all but special categories, and the only people travelling regularly between the two halves of the city were police, diplomats and journalists.

The contrast between the two sides of the city became daily more noticeable: in West Beirut, huge piles of rubbish littered every street corner, with buzzing clouds of flies forming a miasma over them by day, and rats and cats competing for any edible scraps by night. At dusk, the streets filled with smoke as people went out with a few drops of precious kerosene to set the rubbish alight; by now, even the minimal service available before the invasion had been halted by the municipal authorities, since petrol could no longer be found for the rubbish lorries. The centre of West Beirut, around the Hamra area, was more crowded than ever before, with hundreds of people packed into every available space.

The character of the Hamra area changed, too. Long ago, before the Civil War, it had been the most fashionable street in the city. Since 1976, it had become much less chic, with the shops consciously changing their merchandise to appeal to a wider and poorer clientèle, but still it had retained a lively air and a certain elegance. Now, it was as if Chatila and Sabra had come to Hamra: Palestinian and poor Lebanese women, children trailing at their skirts, could always be found there on their mysterious errands; Palestinian men armed with Kalashnikovs and rocket-launchers swaggered along the pavements, most of them wearing over-tight trousers, many holding hands, and often with a couple of grenades slung suggestively low at the back of their belts. They became known as the Hamra cowboys, and whether by chance or by the business flair which only the Lebanese possess, an enterprising street trader soon set up a

stall selling wide sombrero-like cowboy hats. The poseurs of
Hamra bought them – black ones, of course.

The contrast between the street life of Hamra and the rest of
West Beirut was remarkable: Corniche Mazraa, once as busy
as Hamra though more functional and down-market, was never
a place to linger. Situated on the edge of Fakhani and other
Palestinian areas, it was regularly shelled and bombed, and the
Soviet embassy on a corner there was hit half a dozen times.
Although people still lived and worked there and the shops
were often open, it was never regarded as a safe zone and so
never attracted the strolling life of Hamra. Further out, it
turned into a moonscape of shattered, deserted buildings.
Occasionally, one came across a family still eking out a pre-
carious existence in the ruins of their home, often supplied and
supported by groups of fighters holding positions nearby.

After weeks of bombardment, the pine forest on the way out
to the airport was as grim a picture as any: the trees had all been
cut off or burnt out, and only the calcined trunks were left:
stark, blackened stumps ten or twelve feet high, pointing
accusingly at the sky. At the Martyrs' Cemetery where all the
Palestinian fighters were buried, men worked quietly every day
preparing the new graves they were certain would soon be
needed; even there, the shells came in, headstones were over-
turned, newly buried bodies were thrown out of their graves to
be buried again.

And yet even in the midst of all this horror, the old feuds and
rivalries between the various Lebanese and Palestinian factions
still flared up, and in each area order had to be maintained by
the firepower of the strongest group there. In the Kantari
district where I was living, it was Jumblatt's Progressive
Socialist Party which was in control. The commander of their
militia had suffered some damage to his throat which had been
successfully repaired by the implant of a kind of small micro-
phone in his voice-pipe. It was a strange, surreal but reassuring
experience when shooting broke out around the building in the
middle of the night to hear the man's Dalek-like tones ordering
everyone to hold their fire, then gratingly settling the dispute
through his own inbuilt loudspeaker.

Much less reassuring was to see the effect all this was having

on the children of the city. On one occasion I was forced to take
shelter in a house near the Galerie Semaan crossing while two
rival groups used Kalashnikovs and machine guns to decide
who had precedence. There, a young Christian woman from
Southern Lebanon, alone in the house with her eighteen-
month-old son, told me how she had been bombed out of her
village, bombed out of Nabatiyeh, bombed out of Sabra camp,
until she had finally wound up in this breeze-block shack in one
of the most exposed and dangerous places in the city. As she
told her story, the bursts of firing went on outside; she appeared
to take no notice, but her son Khaled, lying on a bed, quietly
beat his head on a pillow in time to the bursts of gunfire and
moaned softly to himself.

This time, the feast of Id al Fitr, usually a joyous occasion,
with new clothes for the children, jewellery for the women, and
feasting for everyone, was a sombre affair. The shelling of
Beirut went on in a desultory, intermittent way, until on July
21st, news came of five Israeli soldiers killed in an ambush
near Lake Qaroun in Eastern Lebanon. At the same time, six
others were wounded in an attack near Tyre, and more still
around Beirut. Immediately, the Israeli artillery went into
action in earnest, punishing the people of West Beirut for what
had happened far over in the east of the country – an archaic
form of 'eye for an eye' logic in which Israel often indulged. At
the end of the third week in July, Israeli planes were back in
action over Beirut and heavy fighting was still in progress in the
Bekaa Valley, with Israel claiming it had opened up on Syrian
positions for two hours 'to teach the Syrians a lesson.'

The message, apparently, was that the Israelis would not
tolerate hit-and-run raids by Palestinians based behind the
Syrian lines, or serving with the Syrian Army. The Israelis
held, quite rightly, that any raids from areas controlled by Syria
could only be made with the permission and active help of
the Syrian Army. In fact, over the years, any Palestinian
action from Syria had to be sanctioned by Syrian Military
Intelligence, whose officers actually went so far as to issue
passes to Palestinian guerrillas enabling them to move
through Syrian lines. Just the same system had been introduced in the Bekaa Valley, so that on this occasion at least the

Israelis were right in their 'collective punishment' of the Syrians.

In the Bekaa, Israel once again demonstrated its total air superiority. The Russians, aghast at the destruction of the Sam Six missile defence system they had installed for the Syrians, had put in place a number of Sam Eight ground-to-air missile batteries, the latest in the Soviet Air Defence arsenal, which had been sited and installed under the supervision of Russian technicians. Israeli reconnaissance flights quickly spotted the new batteries, and on July 24th the Israelis decided to take them out. Once again, pilotless drones were first flown over, and as usual, the Syrians could not resist shooting down these flying electronic sensors. The Israelis knew all they needed to know about the new missiles; they sent their planes over and in minutes took them all out, using 'smart' bombs – bombs directed onto their target along laser beams – to ensure accuracy. This time, however, the Israelis did not get away scot-free: one Israeli Phantom was shot down by a Syrian battery operating from just inside the Syrian border, with the loss of its two-man crew. For once, the Israelis were prevailed upon not to take revenge by hitting the batteries inside Syria proper, as they threatened to do, since even Mr Begin saw the force of the American argument that at this stage such a move would be the sort of serious escalation which Washington could not countenance.

Back in Beirut, the Israeli planes had returned to the attack for the first time in a month, bombing the now 'traditional' targets around the Arab University, in Bir Hassan and in the refugee camps. The geriatric and mental hospital in Sabra was hit once again in these raids.

For seven days this series of attacks went on, with gunboats and artillery joining in. Now the Israelis adopted a new tactic: in the past, the jets had always made at least one warning pass over the city before coming in on their bombing runs. Now, they swept straight in from the sea, dropping their bombs on their first sortie. The result, naturally, was many more civilian casualties. New targets were hit, too: the gunboats concentrated on the Raouche district along the seafront, once the home of many ambassadors and their staffs. The apartments of the Irish, Austrian and Dutch ambassadors were hit, though all

were by this time safely in East Beirut. The Canadian, Mr
Theodore Arcand, was the last ambassador to leave, staying in
his apartment in Raouche until it too was made uninhabitable
and turning over the ground floor of his embassy in Hamra to
refugees. Even then, Mr Arcand made daily return trips to
West Beirut, usually with his wife, in spite of the fact that his
government had ordered him to move to the east. Single-
handedly, he did more for the morale of the small remaining
number of expatriates living in West Beirut than all the other
ambassadors put together, most of whom had left very early on
in the affair, taking their cue from the Americans, who had
pulled out on June 29th.

The Americans did at least send round a printed note telling
their nationals they were going, as did the French and Germans. But the first time any British people knew that their
embassy was going was when staff at the seafront building were
seen dashing out, suitcases in hand. Nothing more was heard
from them in West Beirut until the ambassador's office in
Antelias was tracked down on the top floor of the Bourri
Supermarket. When the ambassador, David Roberts, did make
one of his rare return trips to the west of the city, he was
accompanied by two British guards, and all three wore ident-
ical dark-blue safari suits. Mr Roberts was made 'Sir David' in
the 1933 New Year Honours list.

It was getting towards the end of July now, and after two
months of constant warfare, punctuated only by brief spells of
comparative peace which left the nerves as frayed as ever, the
fatigue could be seen on people's faces. Many found themselves
unable to concentrate, so that reading any but the lightest of
books was impossible. One highly respectable middle-aged
businessman bought himself a large collection of pornographic
literature, as he found this occupied his mind sufficiently, while
making no demands on his intellect.

The Palestinian fighters were in better heart than most, for
they had a clear idea of what they were doing, they were well fed
and looked after, and above all, they remained motivated by the
burning determination to regain their homeland – that fierce
desire instilled in every Palestinian child at his mother's knee.
Even the contradictory statements and messages issued by

their leaders seemed to have little effect on their morale: the fighters, like all the other Palestinians, were highly political animals, and they saw all the politicking as a means to an end, a corollary to what they themselves were doing. They were quite happy to listen to all the differing statements, believing firmly that it was part of the overall strategy of the revolution, in which the part they played was just as important. The Israelis took a different view: they – or at least the Minister of Defence and his henchmen – believed that by keeping up the pressure on West Beirut, they could eventually break the will both of the residents and of the Palestinians. They almost succeeded with the first aim, but never got anywhere near with the second.

As the Israelis kept up the daily and nightly pressure on Beirut, with constant air raids and artillery attacks, the night sky lit by flares and obscured again by smoke from burning buildings, the prospect of an Israeli assault on the city seemed hourly more probable. The Palestinians also believed it was coming, and statements by their Chief of Staff, Brigadier Sa'ad Sayel, claiming that Beirut was 'impregnable' seemed very like whistling in the dark. The 'concrete and steel' barricades he boasted of could be seen by those inside the beleaguered city for what they were: somewhat pitiful heaps of earth on all the main streets, piles of sand hastily bulldozed into position, which seemed likely to do little more than briefly obscure the view of the advancing tank commanders.

Nonetheless, these same heaps of earth had been laced with mines, and every road now had holes dug in it, ready to receive more; many had already been cordoned off and turned into minefields. One of the few English people left in West Beirut, Mrs Sunnie Mann, was walking her dogs near Chatila camp in true British fashion, when she saw Palestinian fighters busily employed in the road ahead of her. When she asked what they were doing, they explained cheerfully that they were planting mines. 'But I always walk my dogs here,' she complained. 'No problem,' they replied. 'These are only anti-tank mines; you can walk over them with no trouble.' And when Mrs Mann still looked dubious, the Palestinians jumped on one of the mines to show that it was harmless to the weight of a human.

The ceasefire which everyone had been praying for finally

came on July 28th, ending seven days of some of the most intensive exchanges of the war. This time Christian areas had suffered as well as the western part of the city: Grad missiles had been fired at Jounieh during the day, causing panic among bathers on the beaches there, and a woman had been severely injured when she had been trampled underfoot by others desperately trying to get away. In East Beirut a mortar barrage had caused further damage and casualties – but there had been nothing in the East to compare with the intensity of the bombardment in the West. On the day before the ceasefire, the Israelis kept up the shelling for thirteen hours without a break, and hardly any part of the city escaped unscathed. Arafat himself was caught in the barrage as he drove along Corniche Mazraa. With his guards he hastily took shelter in a small nylon-processing factory nearby, hardly the safest of places. On emerging, he drove off again and ran straight into a small gun-battle between competing factions. Abu Haitham, his personal guard, hastily snatched off Arafat's distinctive peaked cap, which he had adopted at the beginning of the war instead of the more familiar keffiyah, and pushed the PLO leader down onto the floor of the car. As Abu Haitham well knew, there were plenty of armed men in Beirut who would have wept no tears if Arafat had been 'accidentally' shot.

When the ceasefire did come that day, it was in a most cynical way. It was 9 p.m. before Mr Habib, ensconced in his eyrie up at Baabda, finally succeeded in getting the Israelis to agree to a ceasefire; just before that time, the Israelis sent a message asking for 'an extension' – in other words, an extension of the time in which they could go on lobbing shells into the western half of the city. The reason, they said, was that they needed an hour or so more in which 'to silence the source of fire' coming in to their positions. In fact, they had known the ceasefire was to go into effect at that time, and had arranged to move up troops and tanks as soon as the deadline was reached; however, something went wrong, and when 9 p.m. arrived they were not ready – so they asked for the extension. Eventually, it was agreed that the truce should start at 10.30. In the intervening hour and a half, the Israelis poured in everything they had, and when the ceasefire finally came, they kept up a desultory

fire for another thirty minutes as they moved their units forward near the airport – just as they had always intended to do.

This ceasefire was one of the shorter-lived ones. Within
forty-eight hours it had been broken, with Israel putting the
blame on the Palestinians, who they claimed had opened fire on
their positions with light weapons, wounding two soldiers. As
the Beirut newspapers noted, this seemed poor justification for
the massive retaliatory bombardment launched by the Israelis,
which was as heavy as any that had gone before.

Another ceasefire followed, and then in less than forty-eight
hours, another bombardment, but this time by air. This turned
out to be the longest continuous air raid of the war, and the
longest ever to be flown by the Israeli Air Force. For fifteen
hours on that Sunday, the Israeli planes came over in waves,
systematically pounding a succession of different targets. First
it was the Fakhani district and around Bir Hassan, the Arab
University, and the other Palestinian areas: the wrecked,
rubble-strewn camps, the lonely gun positions, the shattered
Corniche Mazraa. Then gradually the planes moved closer and
closer to the city centre, the Hamra district. Targets in Rue
Verdun were hit, and in Raouche on the other side. Buildings
used by the few Syrian units left in Beirut came in for particularly heavy bombardment, although no-one could work up
much sympathy for the Syrian Intelligence units or 'The Pink
Panthers', the hotch-potch of villains put into uniform by
Rifaat Assad to carry out his own often criminal plans in Beirut.

Down near the seafront, Katherine Leroy, the diminutive
French photographer who in her lifetime has seen more combat
than all the United States Marines put together, took up her
usual station on top of a tall building used by some of the
Syrians. As before, they made her welcome; then when the
bombs started dropping, they all trooped off. Hours later, when
they came back, she asked them why they had gone, since it was
not usual for them to leave their positions during raids. 'Well,
you see,' they said airily, 'we have moved fifteen tons of
ammunition into the basement here, so we thought we had
better go to the next building.'

The air raids and bombardment on this day – August 1st,
subsequently known as 'Black Sunday' – left 165 dead and 400

or more wounded. The Israelis, however, described this massive pounding as 'a localised affair'. They used it to move their
troops forward again, this time to occupy the airport, which
had lain between the opposing forces: the group of very brave
Lebanese gendarmes who had remained in the terminal buildings the whole time – perhaps uselessly but nevertheless a vital
symbol of the authority of the state – finally had to withdraw.

It was, without doubt, the worst day of the whole long series,
a shattering experience which left one drained, exhausted,
emotionally bereft. It said much for the resilience of the people
that within half an hour of the ceasefire, which came into effect
at about 5.15 p.m., the children were once again out on the
streets, queues were forming for water, and people were moving
about their own areas visiting each other to see how things had
gone. This time, though, they found that it was not only the
Palestinian areas and the stretch of coast which might be used
for Israeli landings which had been hit. Even the solidly Sunni
Moslem and residential area of Mousseitbeh, where Saeb
Salam had his home and offices, received dozens of shells and
bombs; Salam's own building was hit and his files and records
strewn over the street.

That weekend at the end of July seemed as bad as any could
be, but there were dire warnings that more was in store.
General Drori, the Israeli northern commander, announced
that if people chose to stay in West Beirut, they would have to
bear the consequences; and Major Sa'ad Haddad appealed to
the people via his 'Voice of Hope' radio to leave the capital and
make way for its 'liberation'. Many of the 400,000 or so still in
West Beirut would have liked to have done so; after two months
of war, they had had enough; they were tired, often dirty, some
were hungry, all were frightened. The trouble was, most had
nowhere to go. The Palestinians could not leave even if they had
wanted to; those Lebanese who were still there either had no
friends or relatives in the east they could live with, or no money
to live on if they went there; others were afraid to leave their
apartments, in case they were occupied and looted.

As each day passed, the centre of West Beirut was becoming
more and more crowded, as refugees came in from the ever-
contracting outskirts. It was the law of the gun in West Beirut

too, with each faction defending its own area and its own people, and the PLO, as the strongest group, trying to keep the lid on it all. There were many nasty incidents: David Zenian went home one day to find a group of armed men breaking in the door of a vacant garage below his apartment. They claimed to be taking the place over in order to house some refugees: fair enough. What they actually used the garage for was to store some thousands of cases of looted Sohat mineral water which they sold a few cases at a time to keep the price up, while the poor supporters of this particular political party scrabbled in the streets for a few drops of water from broken pipes – the water and electricity were briefly restored at the end of July, then cut off again after a couple of days.

Then on August 4th came what everyone had been expecting: the Israeli attack on West Beirut. It began just after midnight, and was later dismissed by the Israelis as just one more of those little local affairs of which they had spoken earlier. In fact, it was a strong, co-ordinated attack which was meant to cut West Beirut in two, with an Israeli column moving in and taking up position on Corniche Mazraa, thus isolating the camps from the rest of the city. The plan was that other Israeli units would then move in from the south, around the airport and at Bir Hassan, to clean out the camps, while Palestinian fighters were prevented from getting out by the Israelis on the Corniche. At the same time, other units would move in through the port to take over Ras Beirut and engage the militiamen in that area.

In East Beirut, the Israelis made little secret of their intentions: photographers were quietly tipped off that they should be down at the Museum crossing point at midnight to get some good pictures. Another Israeli officer told one journalist: 'See you in the Commodore this evening.' All of them were quite clear that this was the big push, and that it would take only a few hours to get through the Palestinian defences, establish new positions, and mop up. It was a sad failure of Israeli Intelligence, for in the event the Israeli troops were given a very bloody nose and were forced to pull back – one of the few times this had ever happened to Israelis in combat.

The day began with massive artillery barrages in two areas,

the Mazraa and Fakhani districts, and the old commercial centre of Beirut. The latter had been shattered during the civil war and left uninhabited, home only to units of the Palestine Liberation Army. These had their headquarters in the Menendez Hotel in Phoenicia Street, and their strongholds in the charred and empty shell of the Holiday Inn and in the unfinished Murr Tower, overlooking the whole quarter.

For something like six hours the Israeli gunners pounded a rectangle from the Green Line to the top of Hamra, the rolling curtain of fire going systematically back and forth all night, smashing into buildings, churches, mosques and homes. The refugees living in the Kantari sector, mostly Shia from Southern Lebanon, crowded into basements and shelters, families staking out living areas with blankets and pillows, candles or small gas lamps lighting each little group, while the men stood at the entrances to the shelters, Kalashnikovs at the ready. The PLA men took shelter too, leaving only one or two men crouched behind well sand-bagged observation points, ready to give warning by field telephone if the Israelis should move. As dawn broke, the whole of Kantari was covered in smoke and dust. Silent family groups could be seen through the haze, walking swiftly in to the centre of the town, refugees now who had no more than half a mile to go.

Across the city, on the other front, it soon became clear that the real attack was taking place directly opposite the Museum, while another was launched from Khalde towards the Lebanese Army barracks at Bir Hassan. The Fuad Chehab barracks, as they were known, lay just behind the golf course, and had been empty since they were abandoned by the army in 1975. The only Israeli success of the day was to move in there. At the Museum, the barrage was followed by an advance by six Israeli tanks which lumbered straight down the road, carefully negotiating the sand barricades in their way. At first, they met no opposition worth speaking of, and the Israeli tank commanders saw no-one in the road ahead of them. Then, as they reached an intersection, it all happened: rocket-propelled grenades fired from only yards away smashed into the tank tracks, immediately disabling two; B7 and B10 rockets, high-explosive, armour-piercing and deadly, found the weakest points in the tanks, while machine gunners sprayed the roads to deter any infantrymen from trying to clear out the defenders and let the tanks through.

Two tanks were knocked out in the first engagement, but significantly, not the two at the head of the column: they were allowed to proceed to the next crossroads, where they met the same fate as the first ones. Through it all, Palestinian gunners kept up a steady barrage on the Israeli troops waiting just a few hundred yards back, and an old T34 tank owned by the Mourabitoun fired round after round until its red-hot gun opened up at the muzzle like the petals of a flower.

The Israeli troops at the Museum had now had enough. The two surviving tanks pulled back, and the infantrymen hurriedly took shelter behind the earthworks erected by the Palestinians, leaving their dead still lying in the roadway. By their own admission, the Israelis lost nineteen killed in this engagement – a huge casualty figure for them. In return they gained only the area on the eastern side of the Museum which had previously been no-man's-land. To make matters worse, though the Israeli's did not know it at the time, the men who had beaten them were Syrians: Brigadier Sayel, the man responsible for organising this classic defence of an obvious attack route into a built-up area, had quietly brought in a couple of units of the PLA to man the vital anti-tank weapons in the side streets. He wanted to be sure that the lead tanks would be allowed through, and he rightly feared that the Palestinians alone would not have the discipline to hold their fire until the correct moment. So it was Syrian officers with PLA men who played the most vital role – though it was PLO fighters who caused such devastation to the Israeli infantry, often racing directly across Corniche Mazraa, firing from the hip, in a determined effort to stop any direct Israeli attack.

Only in the area between Khalde and the airport did the Israelis have any success. There, the country was more open, allowing them to deploy their tanks as they wished and to move up with little opposition. Again, the PLO plan was not to try to stop them in open country, but to reserve their main defence for when the Israelis moved forward into the Bir Hassan area or into Sabra camp.

The Israeli reverses as usual were the prelude to a savage retaliatory bombardment. This time it was often difficult to see what targets they were aiming at. Certainly, during the night, the shelling of the port had been indiscriminate, the Israeli gunners simply laying down a rolling curtain of fire in the hope of interdicting any movement of troops or supplies and of hitting some PLA positions. Now in daylight some targets were evidently chosen, but many shells seemed to have been fired at random. One apparently stray tank-round hit a room in the Commodore Hotel. At the Bristol Hotel, however, the Israelis were obviously aiming carefully: three rounds hit the building, and as I sheltered in the basement with other guests and hotel staff, I counted at least twenty others within a fifty-yard radius.

The reason for the shelling of the Bristol Hotel appeared to be the fact that up to a day or two before, a recoilless rifle mounted on a jeep, and frequently photographed, had been stationed outside the hotel, while a heavy gun had been positioned just a hundred yards behind it. As it happened, both had been removed by this time, but the Israeli artillerymen presumably thought that the presence of both weapons was an indication that the hotel was used by important people. Perhaps the most important man there was the owner of the Summerland Hotel, who had already suffered a similar bombardment on his own establishment, the newest and most luxurious in Beirut. Also present in the basement that day were two professors from Georgetown University in Washington. They occupied themselves composing cables to President Reagan and polishing up the reports they would make when they got back to the States – if they got back to the States. Being at the receiving end of an Israeli bombardment did wonders for the often abstruse academic prose. The Bristol Hotel was set alight, and two floors burnt out before staff managed to stop the blaze, using saucepans full of water to supplement the fire-extinguishers available. In the meantime, the Triumph Hotel just opposite, one of the emergency casualty stations, had been hit and a man killed there.

The shelling went on throughout the day, and though occasionally the Israeli gunners did seem to be aiming at selected targets in the vicinity, it seemed to be in essence another

Chafic al Wazzan, the Lebanese
Prime Minister.

Yasser Arafat, leader of the PLO.

Kamal Jumblatt, leader of the
Progressive Socialist Party and
spokesman of the leftist coalition.

Saeb Salam, the former Lebanese
Prime Minister who was a vital
intermediary in the negotiations.

Menachem Begin, the Israeli
Prime Minister.

'Arik' Sharon, the Israeli Defence
Minister and architect of the
invasion.

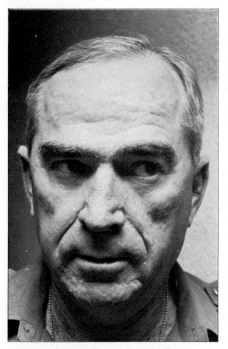

General Rafael Eytan, the Israeli
Chief of Staff.

Philip Habib, the ever-patient,
ever-present American envoy.

Above Mohammed Ali Mourra and his wife pick through the wreckage of their apartment in the 'safe' Hamra area of Beirut. With their two children, they left the flat a minute before the phosphorus shell hit it and set it ablaze. **Below** Men had to leave their guns at the entrance when they went into the shelters. A 16-year-old Palestinian rescue worker sees that the rule is obeyed.

Above Nowhere was safe in West Beirut during the siege, but the worst-hit area of all was the Fakhani district, where many Palestinian offices were located. Here, an apartment still burns hours after a bomb had demolished the building. *Below* For weeks Israel denied that it was using cluster bombs and shells on residential areas, so 'Mahmoud' carefully dismantled one which landed in the Talat al Khayat area.

An Israeli tank at Baabda menaces a Palestinian strong-point in the
Arab University only half a mile away.

This war did not stop for the Shabbat, the Israeli holy day, so devout soldiers had to say their prayers wherever they found themselves.

Above Lebanese and Palestinians alike became refugees, and found shelter where they could. This family lived in a half-finished building, a cable-reel for a kitchen table, tins to store the precious water.
Below Somehow, a living had to be made, life had to go on. An old woman living in the open in Sanayeh Gardens set up a stall to sell whatever she could find, while a boy never parted from his most precious possession, the bicycle which had carried him to safety.

Umm Amna, five times a refugee, faced an uncertain future stoically; her 15-year-old friend Leila was less phlegmatic: 'We will remember, and we will repay,' she said.

'punishment' bombardment – this time for Israel's lack of success in pushing through the ground attacks it had planned. The Central Bank was hit, and a number of other buildings at the end of Hamra, including the offices of *An Nahar* and *L'Orient*, the leading Arabic and French language newspapers. The first shells to land nearby fortunately fell on a car park behind the National Bank, and the staff of the newspapers and the foreign correspondents who had their offices there had enough experience to know that more were likely to follow. They quickly went down to the machine room in the basement, where the printers positioned the rolls of paper so as to form additional barricades. They were only just in time: minutes after the last members of the staff had gone downstairs – or so everyone thought – two phosphorus shells crashed through the fourth and fifth floors, wrecking the offices there.

One shell went through the United Press International bureau, where a number of foreign correspondents worked. One of them, Thaddeus Jacowski of the Polish news agency, had admitted earlier that the sustained shelling after so many weeks of war had made him 'rather nervous'. As a result, he said, he had been taking a little whisky – all day. By the time the shells started coming in, Thaddeus was very drunk indeed, so when everyone else went to the basement, it seemed like a good idea to him to jump the queue for the Telex. He sat himself down at the machine and began sending. A moment later, the two shells crashed through the building, one passing no more than four feet away from where he was sitting. This set the office alight, so Thaddeus took off his shirt and tried to beat out the flames; failing, he walked downstairs and out into the street, where shells were still falling. George Semerdjian, the *An Nahar* photographer, went to look for him; he later explained that the Pole was so drunk he thought he might have jumped out of the window.

At this time, Israel still had not admitted that it was using phosphorus shells, so it was something of an irony that it was a phosphorus shell which landed on the UPI office. By a further irony, the picture being transmitted when the office was hit was a photograph of a woman with 90 per cent phosphorus burns, which Jill Brown had taken at the Triumph Hospital earlier in the day. When the shell went through and stopped the machine, the picture itself was sprayed with phosphorus.

A number of other buildings around the top of Hamra were hit as well as the newspaper offices, and here the only possible target was the headquarters of Syrian Intelligence in Beirut, which was housed in a block next to the Central Bank. One shell did hit that building, but on a corner used by a travel agency, and not at the side used by the Syrians – a particularly unpleasant lot, whose main function in life appeared to be to harass the local people and to carry out Rifaat Assad's private tasks, which often involved finding good cars and shipping them off to Damascus. At the back of that building was another used as a dormitory or barracks by a group of university students who had joined Fateh, and in a vacant space nearby was a mobile gun used by the National Socialist Party. Hardly targets meriting a sustained fifteen-minute bombardment.

Few people were killed in that particular district that day, since most of the buildings there were substantial old blocks of apartments with soundly constructed cellars. Some inhabitants, however, were forced to take more risks than others. One Lebanese family moved from their own small building into the basement of a bigger place nearby, taking with them children, dogs, cats, a budgerigar and their Seychelloise maid. While the shelling was in progress they decided they needed some blankets, so the maid was dispatched to get them. Off she went, a lonely figure in the deserted street, where shrapnel was still falling. Later, a fire broke out in one block, and a team of men set to work filling buckets from the one water tank still available. They were somewhat surprised when the owner remonstrated with them for leaving the tap running while the buckets were passed up and down the chain. Even under such conditions, it seemed, a certain group of Lebanese could not shake off their old attitudes – attitudes which had done so much to provoke the Civil War seven years earlier, and which had played a part in bringing the city to its current desperate plight.

As darkness fell that Wednesday, the shelling eased off a little, though random rounds were still coming in. Next day people were out early, picking through the débris of their homes in search of relatives or of family goods buried under the tons of rubble. That morning no-one was quite sure what had happened or what would happen, for one of the few reliable sources of information, *An Nahar* and *L'Orient*, did not appear. The previous day had been their 50th anniversary, and in spite of the war Francois Akl, the editor, had been planning a special issue. But there had only been enough fuel left to run the big generator – vital for receiving news agency tapes as well as for operating the machines – for another few days; so after the shelling, the printers and staff had held a meeting, and at last they had decided that enough was enough. Many of them had been sleeping on the premises for weeks, eating makeshift meals organised for them by Irene Mosalli, wife of one of the paper's senior staff men. Even though it was the 50th anniversary, they had decided they needed a break; reluctantly Mr Akl had agreed, and for the first time in all those fifty years, no paper appeared.

Within a day, however, officials of the PLO called on the newspaper executives promising to supply as much fuel oil as was needed; they realised the importance of the continued appearance of independent, accurate and respected newspapers, frequently quoted in other publications outside Lebanon. The owner-publisher, Ghassan Tueni, who was also the Lebanese ambassador to the United Nations in New York, was hastily consulted by Telex. His reply was brief and firm: on no account should the papers accept help from the PLO. He understood and appreciated the motives of the PLO, but he was determined not to take anything which might in the future be construed as having had an influence on the paper's editorial policy. Mr Tueni had always fought to keep his newspapers free of any outside pressures, and even now, he was determined to keep that up. Better to close down than to render the papers susceptible to pressure, or if none existed, then to be *seen* as being susceptible to pressure.

On the day following the attempted Israeli push into West Beirut, things returned to what passed for normal in the city – sporadic shelling, overflights by Israeli planes, and a massive new exodus of people from the Moslem areas. Even now, old habits died hard: at the Galerie Semaan crossing point, the only one open for cars, rival factions shot it out as an argument flared up between officials of the different parties, while just up the hill, Israeli soldiers looked on in amazement.

Then on Friday, August 6th, came a new development. The Israelis made a determined effort to wipe out the Palestinian leadership – and showed a remarkable ruthlessness in the way they did so. The basement of a tall apartment block at Sanayeh had been fitted out as a conference room by the PLO, and was used for meetings of the executive and for conferences with Lebanese ministers and officials. On this day, Arafat, Salah Khalaf and Khalil al Wazir were among a number of senior Palestinians holding discussions with Marwan Hamadeh, the Lebanese minister whose main task was liaison with the Palestinians, and a number of other Lebanese officials. They began their meeting at about 12.30, and at 2 p.m. a single Israeli plane flew straight in from the sea and dropped a laser-guided bomb directly on the building.

This was no ordinary bomb; by "chance," I was only a hundred yards away when it was dropped, and I was amazed at the massive damage caused after the relatively light sound of the explosion. It was clear that this was something new. The block had not been damaged in the usual way, with débris flung across the street and walls ripped away; rather, the building had collapsed in on itself. Palestinian rescue workers who were quickly on the scene described it as an implosion, and spoke of 'a vacuum bomb' which sucked out all the air in a structure, causing it to fall inwards. In fact, the bomb used was later more accurately described as a percussion bomb, designed to penetrate the roof of a building and to explode when it reached the ground floor.

Clearly, the Israelis knew what they were doing on this raid: they obviously had firm intelligence that the basement was used for top-level meetings and that one was in progress that day. Unfortunately for them, the meeting had broken up some fifteen minutes before the bomb hit, so that the victims were the families living in the block, most of them Palestinians and refugees from the outer fringes of Beirut. More than a hundred were killed, among them members of the family of the man called Abu Haoul, the head of Yasser Arafat's squad of special guards, and of the PLO security apparatus. To compound it all, just as all the rescue workers arrived and began work, a massive car bomb went off nearby, killing many more people. For ten days afterwards, rescue workers went on trying to reach the well-shored-up basement of the building in the hope that someone might have been left alive there. No-one was ever found.

This attempt to decimate the Palestinian leadership, for that was clearly what it was, showed both the strength and weakness of Israeli intelligence in Lebanon. It was obvious that the Israelis had agents in West Beirut, and that those agents were in touch with Israel. Early on in the war, the Palestinian operations room was bombed within thirty-six hours of moving from its previous location, and was hit again twenty-four hours after moving once more. For some reason, it was left alone when it moved to a third building, this time in the Zarif district, probably because the Israelis preferred to know exactly where it was; they could then send troops directly there when they moved into the city, or bomb it at some such crucial moment.

There were stories, probably apocryphal, of Palestinian officers in Southern Lebanon being saluted by Israelis who arrived there, or of shepherds suddenly appearing in Israeli Army uniforms. Less dramatic but more likely, the Israelis almost certainly had large numbers of informants being run by agents in Beirut. Hundreds of people in Sanayeh would have seen Palestinian leaders arriving regularly for conferences in the building there, so that an Israeli agent could easily organise a watch on it, and send a radio message back to headquarters when a meeting began. The Palestinians did no radio monitoring worth speaking of, and had no directional equipment with which to pin-point transmitters. As it was, it would have been almost impossible, for Israeli agents normally use a device that reduces a long encoded message to a single one- or two-second bleep, impossible to locate in the time available. However it was done, it was clear it was done – and not only on the occasion when the Sanayeh building was hit. Time and again the Israelis showed themselves well aware of Palestinian movements, and within hours had plotted new dispositions. There was, however, no evidence at all that the Israelis had any informant in the higher ranks of the PLO, as was sometimes suggested.

Rather, all the indications were that the Israelis were relying on
the observations of large numbers of people in their pay in
Beirut, as well as on intelligence gathered by the Phalangists,
who had a considerable network in the city.

The destruction of the Sanayeh building, with its huge loss of
life, had a considerable effect on the Palestinian leaders. Even
they, it appeared, had not appreciated just how ruthless the
Israelis could be, nor how determined they were to eliminate
the PLO command. They were even more concerned because
they knew so many of the families who were killed, either
because they were dependents of their own bodyguards or
officials, or because they had seen them whenever they had
attended meetings in the building.

While the pounding of Beirut continued, the Palestinians
were slowly giving in to all the Israeli demands for their
withdrawal from Beirut, though Israel kept adding to its list of
requirements. In these first weeks of August, the Israelis began
objecting to the deployment of any multi-national force before
all the PLO had left the capital – something which both the
PLO and the Moslem leaders of West Beirut saw as absolutely
essential. This requirement on the part of the PLO and Moslems showed clearly that they had a better grasp of possible
risks, and the capacity for hatred and willingness to commit
atrocities of the Phalangists, than did the Americans and the
others arranging matters. Yet in spite of the steady daily
progress towards agreement, Israel kept up its military pressure, and in these last violent days of the war, embarked on an
even more extreme 'eye for an eye' policy. Thus, an attack on an
Israeli patrol near Aley drew not only Israeli air strikes there,
but artillery shelling of West Beirut; sniping from rooftops near
the Museum crossing point was answered by the destruction of
two buildings; and eventually, in what turned out to be a final,
massive pounding of the city, General Sharon sent his planes in
to give a last demonstration of what Israel could do when it
chose to.

It was on Thursday, August 12th, that Beirut suffered its
most concentrated air attack. It began at dawn after a night of
steady shelling, and it went on for eleven hours, with the jets
carrying out their strikes at the rate of one every four minutes.

Throughout the day it was impossible to hold a conversation: the scream of planes going into their steep, attacking dives drowned all attempts to speak, and the non-stop crunch of exploding bombs and shells punctuated every sentence. Standing in a street near Hamra, I found it almost impossible to hear as Dr Paul Morris, a British doctor working with the Palestine Red Crescent, explained how he was clearing all but the most desperate cases out of his makeshift hospital, ready for the influx he knew would come – few casualties were brought in during the day-long raids, as rescue workers could not move about and ambulances could not negotiate the blocked streets.

Hardly a district escaped the Israeli attack. The Barbir hospital near the Museum was hit for the second time, and staff and patients had to be evacuated under fire. The mental hospital in Sabra, where five hundred patients, children and old people were still living in the care of only seventeen staff, was further damaged. The few remaining Syrian positions in the city were selected as special targets, since Israel was now pushing its new demand that all Syrian forces should leave Lebanon. A former Syrian strong-point at the Bain Militaire on the sea-front, now occupied by a small unit of the Lebanese Army, was repeatedly strafed; so too was another Syrian position not far from the British Embassy. Chafic Wazzan, the Prime Minister, threatened to break off all negotiations unless the raids stopped, and Bassam abou Sharif, the Palestinian spokesman, said that the PLO had given all the concessions which Israel had demanded. 'Yet still they do this to us,' he said, as the bombs fell not far from where he was speaking. 'They want to destroy the city and kill us all.'

It certainly looked like it that day. But then at 5 p.m. Mr Habib once again worked a miracle, and a ceasefire was declared. This time, it had taken the direct intervention of President Reagan to stop the carnage. He had telephoned Mr Begin and threatened that the Habib mission would be broken off and other sanctions taken unless the aerial pounding of the city was halted. For once, the Americans talked tough, and the Israelis appeared to believe they meant what they said. In his first telephone call to Mr Begin, the President spoke of 'the outrage and shock' he felt at what was going on. In a partial

transcript released by the White House in a clear effort to show
that America had not sanctioned the air raids, Mr Reagan was
quoted as telling Begin: 'I want the bombing to stop, and to
stop now.' When the Israeli Prime Minister said it would,
Reagan snapped: 'It had better.'

Of course it did not – not at that particular time. Before the
bombing could stop Mr Begin felt it necessary to call a special
cabinet meeting, where there were sharp exchanges between
General Sharon and some of his colleagues; while the arguments continued, so did the air raids. It was not until the Israeli
cabinet had concluded its meeting at the Knesset in Jerusalem
that the order was given to the Air Force to end their attacks. By
that time, some two hundred people had died in Beirut, with
another three hundred injured; eight hundred houses had been
destroyed, most of them in the Sabra and Bourj Brajneh camps,
which Israel appeared to want to raze before any lasting
ceasefire went into operation; hundreds of apartments in the
city centre and the Raouche area had been hit; and everywhere,
people were once again on the move, desperately searching for
some shelter for the night and for the next days.

Even with an apparently effective ceasefire in force, stray
shells still landed. One 155mm round hit an apartment just
opposite the Commodore Hotel just as all the guests ventured
out to eat dinner at tables around the empty pool, with their
chairs pushed close up against the plate-glass windows of the
foyer to take advantage of the protection against shrapnel
offered by the overhang of the roof. The shell whirled through
the apartment, failed to explode, and wound up, intact, on the
bed of an elderly gentleman living there; had it gone off, dozens
of people would have been killed, many cut to death.

That day, Thursday, August 12th, though no-one realised it
at the time, marked the virtual end of the war. Still ahead were
more air strikes on Syrian positions in the Bekaa and around
Aley; some shoot-outs here and there; and the eventual entry of
the Israelis into West Beirut, with all the horrific consequences
of that move. But as the people of West Beirut picked themselves up once again and braced themselves for the worst, they
found instead that over the next days things actually began to
get better. For the Lebanese, the war was over.

CHAPTER EIGHT

It was on July 3rd that Yasser Arafat formally and in writing agreed that he and his men would leave Beirut. He did so in a short message addressed to Mr Habib which was clearly intended to leave scope for much bargaining; but it did say quite categorically that the Palestinians were prepared to go, as Israel insisted. The hope was that, as a result, the Israelis would stop the bombardments, lift the blockade of the city, and that negotiations could proceed in a reasonably calm way. The Israelis, however, were having none of it. They refused to lift the blockade, they kept up the military pressure and they rejected in advance the Palestinian proposals, which were intended only as a first position. These were that the PLO should be allowed to keep an office in Beirut, as they did in other countries, with one of the acknowledged leaders staying to head it; that units of the Palestine Liberation Army should be attached to the Lebanese Army, again as in other countries – two brigades of 1,000 men each was the first suggestion – and should be stationed outside Beirut; and that those Palestinians left behind should be given the full protection of the Lebanese law – that is, accorded Lebanese citizenship.

All this Israel rejected. There was to be no PLO presence in Lebanon, no deployment of any Palestinian units with the Lebanese Army; everyone had to leave. This uncompromising position the Israelis maintained until the end. Despite the criticism prompted by their actions, they achieved almost everything they set out to do by way of the physical dispersal and destruction of the Palestinians; but they signally failed to achieve their political objectives.

Then came one of the most significant and important moves of the whole negotiating process. In a carefully worded statement, President Reagan announced that he was ready to send

American troops to form part of a multi-national force in Beirut. Speaking in Los Angeles, Mr Reagan said: 'The government of Lebanon told us that a multi-national force might be essential for temporary peace-keeping in Beirut, and informally proposed that the US consider making a contribution to that force. The Lebanese government has not made a formal proposal, but I have agreed in principle to contribute a small contingent of US personnel subject to certain conditions.'

Those conditions were that a formal request for American troops should be issued by the Lebanese government, and that all the parties concerned should agree to that deployment. An indication of the amount of preparation which had already gone on was given in quiet background briefings for American correspondents in Washington. In these briefings it was emphasised that the troops would be in Beirut for only a short time and that the numbers involved would be no more than 1,000. It was also specified that a Marine detachment would provide the men needed, and that if the American troops came under fire they would immediately withdraw – something which did not endear the administration to Marine officers imbued with the gung-ho spirit of Guadalcanal and all the other names on their long roll of honour.

Reagan's announcement that he was ready to send men was the first major policy step after the resignation of Al Haig on June 25th, which came soon after the Washington visit by Mr Begin. In his resignation speech, Haig clearly indicated that he believed President Reagan had departed from the foreign policy line previously agreed: the inference was that Haig's own support for Israel, strained though it was by the savagery of the attack on Beirut, was no longer in tune with the thinking of the President. Mr Reagan himself, it was felt, was coming more and more under the influence of Mr Weinberger, a more moderate man than Mr Haig, with the result that the Secretary of State had to go.

There is little doubt that Mr Haig did not resign voluntarily, and that Weinberger, William Clarke, the National Security Adviser, and the rest had pushed him out after a battle which had been going on behind the scenes in the White House ever since his appointment. According to many American diplomats and also a number of Arabs who had been in Washington earlier in the year, Haig had basically agreed to the Israeli invasion of Lebanon, adopting the thesis that the destruction of the PLO would clear the way for an overall settlement in the Middle East, with local West Bank figures agreeing to accept limited autonomy along the lines of the Camp David accords. Equally, Haig had accepted the argument that by destroying the power of the PLO in Lebanon, that country would be able to resolve its internal conflicts, that it would form a strong central government, and that Bachir Gemayel would then feel secure enough to sign a peace treaty with Israel.

No-one suggested that Mr Haig condoned the severity of the Israeli bombardments or approved the Israelis' sledgehammer tactics; in fact, because of his known sympathies for Israel, he was one of the leading and most influential voices urging moderation. At the same time, Haig was a soldier who understood the old military adage about not making omelettes without breaking eggs. He could stand the carnage shown nightly on American television screens, while those around him, perhaps more accurately assessing American reaction, refused to do so. President Reagan, the epitome of the great American middle-class, middle-brow, slightly right-of-centre Mr Average, found himself totally out of tune with his Secretary of State, a Dr Strangelove figure in a White House that had never been entirely at ease with foreign affairs and was now increasingly perturbed by what was going on in the Middle East.

Mr Haig's departure was hastened by the messages sent by Philip Habib, who argued strongly that some American commitment was needed as a reassurance to both sides in the conflict. At one point Habib threatened to quit unless he got the declaration he was seeking, which at that time would have been more modest than the President's offer to send troops. Haig was prepared to tough it out, with the Palestinians, with world opinion, with American domestic reaction, and with his own envoy, but the messages to the White House from the Arabists in the State Department and from the CIA were enough to tip the balance: both warned that Saudi Arabia would act if America failed to modify its apparent support of Israel.

This was a persuasive argument with Reagan's immediate entourage, a California Mafia which knew little of foreign affairs but which did understand very well the power of Saudi oil and Saudi money, and the likely response of American voters. Added to which, Reagan read more into the changes in the Saudi leadership caused by the death of King Khaled than may actually have been there. All in all, Reagan was very ready to do as his advisers suggested: to ditch Haig and signal by his choice of the new Secretary of State a shift in American policy to Arabs and Israelis alike. Thus, George Shultz was picked, not only because of his undoubted ability and his previous loyal service to the Republican cause, but also because of his earlier position on the Board of the Bechtel Corporation, with its close links with Saudi Arabia. Such a choice would be seen throughout the Middle East as an indication of the new direction proposed for American policy.

Shultz endorsed the 'maximum option' which had been proposed by the Arab lobby in the State Department: that promising American troops for Beirut. It was a risky move so early in his incumbency of the department, particularly as it immediately alarmed a number of pro-Israeli senators, and set all the alarm bells jangling in Israel itself. There, the government showed itself less than tactful by its eulogy of Haig, 'an outstanding statesman and a loyal friend,' while giving an extremely lukewarm welcome to Shultz. Arab countries predictably approved the change, with the PLO describing the former Secretary of State as 'an accomplice of General Sharon.'

Fortunately perhaps for American even-handedness, as soon as the announcement of American willingness to send troops to Beirut was made, it was promptly rejected by the PLO, which under the terms of the offer, would have to agree to the deployment of the Marines. In fact, this prompt refusal by the PLO, made by a member of the PLO delegation at the UN in New York, was simply an illustration of the poor communications between the PLO in Beirut and their offices around the world. The New York man took it on himself to greet the idea of sending American troops to Beirut to supervise a Palestinian evacuation as 'ridiculous', while in Beirut, Bassam abou Sharif, a member of the politbureau of the Popular Front who was increasingly the spokesman for the whole PLO, gave a cautious welcome to the proposal, which he said would be acceptable if the Americans were part of a multi-national force.

The idea of a multi-national force had always appealed to the Moslems of West Beirut, who saw very clearly the possible dangers if either the Israelis or the Phalangist militia, or both, were allowed a free hand in the city. Accordingly, the Prime Minister, Mr Wazzan, was told very firmly by the Moslem leaders – Salam, Takieddin Solh, Selim al Hoss and the rest – that he must ensure that the force was in position before the Palestinians withdrew. The Sunni Moslem leaders feared that during any interregnum between the withdrawal of the Palestinians and the arrival of international peace-keepers, the Phalangists would take the opportunity of settling old scores; they also knew that without the numbers and the firepower of the PLO, their people were quite incapable of standing up to the Phalangists, who were stronger even than the Lebanese Army itself. Nor did the Moslems like the alternative proposed: that the Lebanese Army should be deployed before the arrival of the Americans and the rest. They had no faith in the abilities or neutrality of the Army.

Though the Moslem leaders eventually won the day and the international force was deployed before the Palestinians left, its over-swift withdrawal would show that they had been right in everything they feared. The eventual Israeli move into West Beirut, the swift, well-planned subjugation of Amal and the Mourabitoun, the only armed and organised groups who might have delayed a Phalangist onslaught long enough for the world to intervene, and the final horrors of Sabra and Chatila – all these proved that the Beirut politicians understood more about their fellow-countrymen and about the Israelis than the highly-paid theoreticians in Washington. Perhaps they missed one significant point: Bachir Gemayel was the one leader unreservedly and consistently opposed to the arrival of American troops. Skilfully playing on American fears, he asked what the US would do if a Communist squad in West Beirut fired an RPG at an American jeep and killed four soldiers. The Americans, he said, would become like the UNIFIL forces: powerless to act, yet the target of Palestinian attacks. Only the Lebanese Army, he claimed, was suited to take over Beirut.

His arguments fell on deaf ears in America, where President Reagan was becoming increasingly exasperated by what he saw as Israeli intransigence. The nightly television newscasts had as much effect on the President as they did on anyone else, and since Mr Reagan knew that Philip Habib was succeeding in arranging the evacuation of the PLO, the continuing onslaught appeared to him to be nothing more than gratuitous violence. So there were some tough messages from the White House to Jerusalem, culminating in the telephone call in which Reagan demanded a ceasefire. Never had relations between America and Israel been so bad.

The trouble was that the Palestinians mistook American anger with Israel for American blessing of their position, and American willingness to move closer to the PLO. Not for the first time, the Palestinians grossly overplayed their hand, with Hani Hassan trying to arrange a meeting between Arafat and Habib in return for PLO agreement to leave Beirut. Habib himself did not even bother to ask guidance from Washington – he rejected the suggestion out of hand; and to show how attuned he was to the thinking of the administration, his move was mirrored in Washington when officials refused to receive Hani's brother, Khaled al Hassan, as part of a delegation dispatched by the Arab League.

Yet Palestinian efforts, though they were over-pitched, did have some effect. It was appreciated by Habib, and through him by the administration, that the PLO had to be given some sort of a fig leaf to cover the nakedness which would follow the dispersal of their fighting forces; so in mid-July, while Israel was applying the pressure both by military means and by the threat of even greater violence, President Reagan sent a signal that America was ready to do something for the PLO. His administration, he said, was engaged in a thorough reappraisal of its whole Middle East policy; as that policy had previously rested firmly on the premise that Israel was America's one sure ally in the area, almost a surrogate, any change in policy would be bound to benefit the Arabs at the expense of Jerusalem. This fact seemed to be appreciated in Saudi Arabia, but was not properly understood by the PLO, who singularly failed to take advantage of the opportunity offered.

As usual, the PLO were pinning their faith on others doing things on their behalf: this time, it was a visit to Washington by Prince Sa'ud, the Saudi Arabian Foreign Minister, and Mr Abdel Halim Khaddam, his Syrian counterpart. The PLO saw the visit as their salvation, although oddly enough, the Israelis too attached huge importance to it, devoting most of a five-hour cabinet meeting to considering possible scenarios. In the event, this two-man Arab League delegation to Washington achieved nothing: the only suggestion they were able to make which the Americans found at all interesting – and it was not a new one – was that the Palestinians should be moved out of Beirut to Northern Lebanon while their eventual destination was being worked out. This, it was thought, would be an effective means of ending the siege of the capital. No doubt it would have been if the Israelis had agreed, but the situation did not arise, for not surprisingly, Lebanese leaders from the north, Deputies, notables and religious figures, all objected strongly to the transfer of the problem from Beirut to their region. Similarly, the Palestinians themselves showed little enthusiasm for a move which would probably have entailed a journey through Christian-held territory, and which would have ended with them being dumped in an unfamiliar place, with only personal weapons, and without their families.

Yet the idea had a reasonable purpose behind it, for one of the stumbling blocks in the negotiations was the difficulty of finding somewhere for the PLO to go. The Arab brothers of the Palestinians, almost without exception, showed a marked reluctance to welcome those they had supported so vociferously from afar. The reason was obvious: few Arab régimes could boast sufficient stability to withstand the influence exerted by some thousands of armed men.

Syria was a classic case, for it would have to take the largest number of Palestinians, and was most susceptible of all to unrest. For years, President Assad had been discreetly waging a war against his opponents, who were led by the Moslem Brotherhood but drew support from the solid Sunni middle class represented by the merchants of Homs or Hama. He had

succeeded in containing the insurrection against his minority
Alawi régime only by the most draconian security measures,
culminating in the bloody rampage through Hama by men of
the Special Forces led by Rifaat Assad, the President's brother.
The memory of that massacre was still fresh in people's minds,
so it was easy to see how the opposition in Syria might greet the
arrival of some thousands of Sunni Moslem Palestinians, all
experienced guerrillas with recent experience of street fighting,
as a gift from on high and a signal to start the revolt all over
again. It was no surprise, then, that Syria prevaricated over
taking in the Palestinians, and refused to be swayed even by the
prospect of the usual huge application of Saudi money. It was
only when President Siddam Hussein, always on the lookout for
a way to attract Arab attention, announced that Iraq would be
willing to take any number of Palestinian fighters, that President Assad quickly agreed to take his share: the Syrians would
rather have the Palestinians where they could see them and
control them, than allow them to be used by their old enemy
Iraq.

While negotiations on this vexed question were in progress
all over the Middle East, Yasser Arafat was still doing what he
could to extract political mileage out of the situation. One of the
more bizarre episodes was the visit to West Beirut of Congressman Paul McCloskey, accompanied by some members of an
American 'fact-finding delegation'. The leader of the six-man
mission, Representative Nick Rahall, joined his colleagues
when they visited the city, but Elliott Levitas, a senior and
staunchly pro-Israel member of the team, would not even risk
meeting Arafat. He thus missed what at first seemed like a
triumph for the visiting Congressmen, for in a note to them
which they hailed as a 'breakthrough', Arafat solemnly wrote:
'Chairman Arafat accepts all UN resolutions relevant to the
Palestinian question.' McCloskey immediately and sensibly
asked if that included Resolution 242, which implies Palestinian recognition of Israel, and Arafat replied that it did,
provided it was taken with all other resolutions. Mr McCloskey
then returned to East Beirut, waving his scrap of paper, and
proclaiming that this was a development which enabled the
United States to open direct negotiations with the PLO, since

Arafat had agreed, in his view, to recognise Israel's right to exist. 'I intend to go back, and I hope my colleagues will join with me, in recommending to Secretary Schultz that we now open negotiations with the PLO,' Mr McCloskey said, in the fractured American habitually spoken by Congressmen.

The delegation leader, Nick Rahall, was more circumspect and better informed. He pointed out that Arafat had not specifically and separately agreed that Israel had a right to exist, but had accepted 242 along with all other resolutions – those of the General Assembly as well as the Security Council. Mr Rahall observed that instead of singling out Resolution 242, as the Americans wanted him to do, Arafat had insisted on lumping it with all others. 'He would not unilaterally accept the State of Israel, as he wants that to be simultaneous with all other resolutions, which recognise the right of both Israel and the Palestinians to exist. Arafat has said all this before, though not as clearly as this,' the Congressman noted, and recalled that Arafat's acceptance of Prince Fah'd's eight-point plan at the Fez Arab summit had implicitly recognised Israel. Mr Rahall was obviously more experienced in foreign affairs and better briefed than Mr McCloskey, who in Jerusalem next day, was forced publicly to go back on all he had said and to endorse the general American line that there had to be explicit and clear recognition of Israel by the PLO before the United States could enter into any dialogue with the Palestinians.

The whole thing was a storm in a tea-cup, and seemed to stem from Arafat's own desire to try to move things forward and secure face-to-face negotiations with the Americans as the reward for agreeing to leave Beirut – something which Hani Hassan had been trying to achieve by behind-the-scenes diplomacy. Since the more subtle Hassan had already failed to make any progress, there was little hope that Arafat himself, never a particularly adroit negotiator, could succeed, but nonetheless the temptation offered by the naivety and credulity of some of the American Congressmen had been too much for him to resist.

Altogether, it was an interesting if fruitless afternoon for the Americans, who were frankly amazed at the extent of the devastation they saw as they were carefully driven through some of the worst-hit Palestinian areas to their meeting with Arafat. There was one memorable moment, too, when one of the best-dressed and most striking-looking of the women secretaries noticed the stares she was attracting from the Palestinian militiamen, who were not used to such apparitions. Shuddering visibly at the rough-looking types on the streets, she turned to one of her companions and in a breathy voice, said: 'Lord sakes, have you ever been looked at by anything quite as horrible ever before in your life!'

With a ceasefire giving a respite from the constant bombardments of the third week of July, the end of the month brought clear political progress towards a settlement of the affair and a firm commitment from the PLO to leave West Beirut. This was emphasised when a six-member committee of the Arab League, including Farouk Kaddoumi of the PLO, met in Jeddah. The committee unanimously adopted a number of points, the second of which laid down that the PLO had agreed to move its forces from West Beirut, and was now only seeking guarantees from the Lebanese government about protection of the camps after the fighters left, and the safety of the guerrillas during the evacuation. In addition to this, the committee called for a multi-national force to be sent to Beirut, though apparently by this time the Palestinians were willing to entrust their fate and that of their dependants to the Lebanese Army alone.

All the indications were that the PLO was resigned to going, and that only the details still had to be arranged. However, that did not stop Israel launching on August 1st its most concentrated attacks of the whole war, provoking new expressions of displeasure from President Reagan, and a boycott by Mr Wazzan of scheduled meetings at Baabda. Mr Habib now had his own plan for the evacuation of the fighters, which called for withdrawal by land and sea over a period of two weeks, and deployment of the multi-national force a few days after the guerrillas had begun to leave. This last was the sticking point – not so much for the Palestinians as for the people of Beirut who would remain behind. They were still convinced that without the Palestinian fighters to defend them, they would be at the mercy of the Phalangists, and they noted with alarm that Israel continued to object to the deployment of UN observers in the city. With a certain prescience, the left-wing newspaper *Ash Sharq* said in a headline: 'Israel's reservations about the observers hides an intention to commit new massacres.' The refusal by Israel to allow the UN observers called for by the Security Council, prompted the Soviets to convene a new meeting to consider what action should be taken to force Israel to comply with the previous resolutions, which had implied that sanctions would be imposed unless Israel withdrew to the lines it had occupied around Beirut before it had captured the airport and surrounding area during the fighting on the first weekend in August. America had not voted on that resolution, but President Reagan had seemed to endorse it by 'appealing' to Mr Begin to order his troops to move back. Naturally, there had been no response.

All this gave the opportunity for Moscow to play a more active role, though even now the Russians did not seem to know quite what to do, for throughout the crisis they had merely reacted to events, and had never sought to take the initiative. Now, they were plainly worried at the prospect of American troops being deployed in Lebanon, and gave a vague warning that if that were done, all their policies in the Middle East would be framed in the light of that move, a woolly construction which appeared to mean that the Soviets might have to put some of their own troops into Syria to balance an American presence in Lebanon, in just the same way that the Soviet fleet in the Mediterranean had been moved to match the dispatch from Italy of units of the American Sixth Fleet. There was in fact little the Soviets could do except huff and puff, for they had clearly lost the technological battle with the Americans, and had been seen by the Arabs as impotent allies in a crisis.

The total defeat of Soviet weaponry was the most serious consequence of the war for Moscow. The Syrian Sam Six missile screen in the Bekaa Valley had been installed according to directions drawn up by Soviet technicians, and after the batteries had been put in place, in June, 1981, two senior Russian officers had toured the area around Chtaura with their Syrian counterparts, advising on slight modifications of the positions, which had been made the same day. The missiles were linked to a computer inside Syria, which was serviced and maintained by Russians, and though Syrian specialists manned the whole complex, all of them had been trained in the Soviet Union and were under constant supervision by Russian officers. There could be no question of Syrian incompetence. The Syrian Air Force pilots were also Soviet-trained, and though observers noted that they did not press home their attacks with the same determination as the Israeli Air Force, this was more a matter of Soviet tactics than reflection on their courage, since the clear lesson was that American electronic counter-measures, adapted by the Israelis, were totally effective in diverting the Russian air-to-air missiles, just as they had deflected the ground-to-air Sam Sixes. On the ground, too, the Soviet tanks showed themselves to be no match for the Israeli Centurions, or even for the locally produced Merkavas. The whole thing added up to a complete triumph for Western technology, a humiliation for the Soviets, and a serious loss of Russian influence throughout the Middle East.

Not only were the Soviets beaten on the ground, they never made any real efforts to give diplomatic help to their client states or friends in the area, and they were fumbling in their handling of the crisis in international forums. The Soviets, it seemed, were more concerned with their own security than that of their allies. They sent a very high-powered Air Defence team to Damascus, which led the Syrians to believe that they were to be given the benefit of the latest Russian expertise and technology. In fact, the Soviet group spent all its time assessing what had happened and transmitting the information to Moscow, where experts could then apply the lessons learned to the situation in Europe, a much more important theatre from the Soviet point of view. The Syrians were given some new Sam Eight batteries, but this appeared to be more in the nature of an experiment, a cynical battle-field test, than a real effort to help a hard-pressed ally. In the event, the Israelis had no more trouble in taking out the Sam Eights than they had with the Sixes.

By contrast, the French were effective and useful in their dealings in Lebanon, which they regarded as having a special relationship with France by virtue of old colonial ties. The French ambassador, Paul Marc Henry, was regularly used by the PLO as a channel of communication when their distrust of

the Americans became acute. There were times when Hani
Hassan and the other negotiators saw Philip Habib as little
more than an Israeli stooge, and it was at such times that they
turned to the French to float new ideas for them, to pass quiet
words to certain more sympathetic quarters in Washington, or
to drum up support at the United Nations. The French, for
their part, were unfailing in their support, and early on sent two
of their senior Quai d'Orsay men to Lebanon in a public show
of solidarity. Indeed, M. Francois Gutman, the director of the
French Foreign Ministry, went out of his way to add that as well
as 'listening to all sides' – the usual anodyne diplomatic phrase
– he and his colleague, M. Bruno Delay, were there to demonstrate French determination to do all they could 'to avert a
massacre' in Beirut.

As early as the beginning of July the two French special
envoys assured the Palestinians – they had no hesitations about
meeting PLO leaders – that France was ready to send troops to
Lebanon if they were needed, or would immediately sanction
the transfer of the French units serving with UNIFIL from the
south of the country to the capital. M. Gutman also floated the
possibility that France might recognise the PLO as the representative of the Palestinian people, though at that stage he did
not believe they could claim a 'monopoly'. More appropriately
and more hearteningly for the Palestinians, M. Gutman also
said that even if the PLO were destroyed, the fact of Palestine
would remain. It was a lesson the French were quick to learn,
but the Israelis never did.

The Arab states had always seen the Palestine question as
being at the core of the whole long-running Middle East crisis;
but that did not necessarily mean that they believed in auto-
matic support for the PLO, or even for Arafat. Each separate
state had its own axe to grind, as well as its own contribution to
make to the overall Arab strategy. Saudi Arabia was of course
the most important country concerned, both for its influence in
the Middle East and the pressure it could exert in the rest of the
world. The Saudis had placed themselves firmly in the Western
bloc, refusing even to have diplomatic relations with Russia –
though they were not above using the links established by
Kuwait when they found it useful to do so.

Successive Saudi leaders shared President Sadat's belief that
in the Middle East, 'America held 90 per cent of the cards.'
King Feisal, in his time, had been the most dedicated anti-
Zionist of them all, convinced of the basic iniquity and evil of all
Israelis. His successors were less fanatical, and Fah'd, both
when he was Crown Prince and day-to-day administrator, and
when he succeeded King Khaled and became in title what he
had already been for years past, took a more pragmatic view of
things. The Saudis, under Fah'd, were quite prepared to accept
reality, and that meant coming to terms with the existence of
the State of Israel. What annoyed the Saudis more than
anything were the divisions in the PLO and the vacillations of
the leaders, as well as the public manner in which the Palestinians debated their affairs; the Saudi way had always been to
reach agreement in private, to make no announcement, but
quietly to apply the decisions reached. So when Arafat, during
one of his regular trips to the Kingdom – usually with begging
bowl in hand – suggested early in 1981 that it was time the
Saudis took a more active role, Prince Fah'd asked in some
exasperation what the PLO wanted and was even more exasperated when Arafat could not come up with a clear answer.
The Prince sent Arafat away with a firm instruction to work out
exactly what the PLO policy was, to make it practical and
practicable, and only then to return.

Chastened by such tough talk from someone who had always
been one of his main supporters, Arafat returned to Beirut and
held a series of meetings with the leaders of the PLO, and with
such influential 'laymen' in the Palestinian community as Said
Akl, who actually wrote what later became known as 'The
Fah'd Plan'. In the seventh of its eight points, this plan
recognised the right of all States in the area to live within secure
and recognised borders – in effect giving Palestinian recognition to Israel. Arafat personally endorsed this, and was thus
committed to backing the proposals when they became the
main item on the agenda at the Fez Arab summit at the end of
the year.

The plan was a disaster as far as that meeting was concerned,
and almost as bad for the PLO, with some of Arafat's closest
aides turning against their leader. Farouk Kaddoumi, most

moderate of all the members of the top echelon, formally voted against Arafat when it was discussed, not because he disagreed with any of the provisions of the plan, but because he realised better than the others that it would tear the Arab world apart at a time when unity was needed more than ever.

Kaddoumi turned out to be right. President Assad refused even to attend the summit, and those who did turn up were bitter in their denunciations of what they called 'this sell-out' by Saudi Arabia. Prince Fah'd was not used to such talk, and came close to storming out, but instead, the whole conference decided to go home and do nothing. The trouble always was over Syria, for President Assad felt that in all the negotiations, the rights of his country were being ignored. He wanted the Golan back – or something in exchange for it – just as much as the Palestinians wanted a homeland. Given that position, there was no way in which Assad could support ideas, which if adopted, would have settled the Palestinian problem and committed the Arabs to peace with Israel, leaving Syria more alone and isolated than ever. So Syria wrecked that first Fez summit, and sent the Saudis seething back to Riyadh.

Prince Fah'd and his colleagues did not like being so publicly rejected. The Saudis, however, had moved out of their passive diplomacy period, the time when they merely reacted and never initiated and relied entirely on their millions to further their aims. Now, under Prince Fah'd, Saudi Arabia was much more of a force in the Arab world, with clear aims consistently pursued.

First among these was to remove the cause of all the trouble, the lack of a homeland for the Palestinians. This was not merely a theoretical objective either: the Saudis of the day believed just as firmly as King Feisal had in the legitimate rights of the Palestinians, and they saw the Israelis as interlopers and usurpers of Arab land. If they did not have quite such a blinkered approach or such a strong personal dislike of the Israelis as their illustrious predecessor, this was because the new generation of Saudi rulers were more worldly men, conscious of the interplay of interests. This, however, did not make them any less determined.

Second in the Saudi list of priorities was the readmission of

Egypt to the Arab family. The Saudis, like the Egyptians, always saw an alliance between their two countries as a natural development, and one which would benefit not only the two states concerned, but would also lend stability to the whole area. They believed that Saudi money and oil, harnessed to Egyptian manpower, technical ability and expertise, could be the balance wheel of the whole region. Though they objected bitterly to what President Sadat had done in making what amounted to a separate peace with Israel, they understood his motives. Now, however, Sadat was gone, and President Hosni Mubarak had taken his place. Mubarak, unsullied by any taint of the Camp David accords, and carefully keeping his distance from Israel while faithfully carrying out all the Egyptian promises made, would be an acceptable figure to all Arab states if he could be induced to break with Israel, or if – a more likely and attractive prospect – the other Arab countries could be presented with a situation in which there would be nothing wrong in the Egyptian-Israeli relationship. In other words, the second strand of Saudi policy depended entirely on the first: the settlement of the Palestinian issue, in the Saudi view, would come only if all the Arab countries were united both in making it a priority, and on the means to bring it about. This in turn led to the third objective of Saudi foreign policy: to promote unanimity among the Arabs, as hard a task as any that could be imagined.

The result of all this during the Israeli invasion of Lebanon seemed to be a return to the old Saudi way of merely reacting, rather than doing anything positive. Certainly, the Saudis were quick to condemn what was happening, but at first they did nothing else. The reason was that their assessment of the situation was as faulty as anyone else's: they believed that the Israelis were intent only on clearing the PLO out of Southern Lebanon and 'punishing' them for the attack on Shlomo Argov, and for past shelling and raids into Upper Galilee from Lebanon. It was only when they realised the full extent of the Israeli objectives that the Saudis became really alarmed. Before that, they had been privately content to see the PLO cut down to size, for like many others, they found the Palestinians troublesome clients, bickering among themselves, divided, yet always there and always capable of bringing ruin on the rest of the Arab world. A quick military defeat for the PLO, the Saudis thought, might concentrate the minds of the Palestinian leaders, and induce them to be more malleable, and more ready to settle for the second best which the Saudis believed was all that was possible. Similarly, Saudi Arabia had not been at all sorry to see the Syrians taught another sharp lesson by the Israelis: the Saudis did not like the close Syrian relationship with the Soviet Union, or President Assad's attempts to forge his own radical block in opposition to the moderate Saudi grouping. A swift but not total Syrian reverse would have been no bad thing, in the Saudi view.

When things went too far, King Fah'd began to play an active role. It was a Saudi initiative which eventually forced the Arab League to call a special meeting of foreign ministers, and to set up the carefully chosen 'committee of six' to deal with the conflict in Lebanon. Several times the King was on the telephone to President Reagan, using language very similar to that which Mr Reagan used to Mr Begin on occasion. For King Fah'd was now getting first-hand reports from Beirut, not only from Arafat, who was regularly in touch, but also from Mr Salam, who was more realistic and more trusted by the Saudis. Salam had always been a Saudi protégé: he was a good Moslem and a man the Saudis saw as a bastion against the spread of revolutionary ideas in a country they had long regarded as one of their main holiday homes. The Saudis realised quite early on that the PLO would have to leave Beirut, largely because Mr Salam reported accurately on the feelings of the Sunni community in the city. The result was that as early as the beginning of July, King Fah'd was trying to prepare for the post-invasion period.

As part of that process, King Fah'd summond Bachir Gemayel to Taif, ostensibly to a meeting of the Arab League committee, actually to be told a few truths by the Saudis. It was noticeable that Bachir returned to East Beirut – ferried from Cyprus in a Lebanese Army helicopter – in a very bad temper indeed. Reports at the time said Gemayel was angry because of Saudi insistence that international observers or a multi-national force should be deployed in West Beirut at the same time as the Lebanese Army went in there. The Saudis certainly had said that, since they had been reflecting the fears of massacres and persecution expressed by the Moslems to Salam and other leaders; but that was not the only reason for Sheikh Bachir's ill-temper: he had also been given a talking-to such as he had not had for many a year. The days of quiet, well-mannered meetings with the Saudies seemed to be over: this time, King Fah'd had laid it on the line, with explicit orders and explicit threats. Once the Israelis withdrew, he said, Saudi Arabia accepted that Gemayel would be President, and that the Christians would once again be in control in Lebanon. That said, everyone living in the country – and there was no doubt that it was the Palestinians who were referred to – had to be afforded the full protection of the law; steps had to be taken to ensure that the Moslems of Lebanon could share in what was being done, rather than allowing a Christian hegemony to impose its own solutions on the country; and when it came to a withdrawal of PLO forces, as both the Saudis and Gemayel agreed that it would, there must be no attempts by the Phalangists to seek vengeance for past Palestinian misdeeds, and no interference with the guerrillas as they left.

This last point showed a long Saudi memory, for they had in mind a nasty ambush of a Palestinian funeral procession in 1970 by Christian villagers of Kahhaleh, which had left seventeen PLO men dead. The Saudis wanted nothing like that to happen to the thousands of PLO men who would have to take the road to Damascus, so Saudi demands were spelt out to Sheikh Bachir, and he was warned quite clearly that if things did go wrong, he would be held responsible, and Lebanon would find itself a lot worse off as a result.

The other important Saudi move of the time was to send the Foreign Minister, Prince Sa'ud, to Washington, in the unlikely company of Mr Abdel Halim Khaddam of Syria. The two ministers had some difficulty in arranging the trip, which had to be delayed several times, and when it did finally take place, they were clearly embarrassed by all the attention paid to it, and in particular, all the hopes which people in Lebanon were pinning on it. For though their talks in Washington were perfectly amicable, and may even have done some good in reinforcing President Reagan's slowly emerging idea of shifting American policy away from its total commitment to the Israelis, they could offer no concrete suggestions or instant solutions. More than most, their visit was a public relations exercise, a symbol to people so desperate now that any move offered some hope. In the words of Clovis Maksoud, the Arab League ambassador to the United Nations, uttered on another occasion in 1967: 'All activity is a victory in the context of defeat.'

For Syria, that aphorism certainly had an apposite ring. There was no doubt that the Syrian forces had been defeated, and even worse, that all that had happened and was happening was a complete reverse for Syrian policy. President Assad, who had assumed power in 1970 after a long period in which Syria had been racked by coups and counter-coups, upheavals and plots, had shown himself to be a practical man, capable of giving his country the stability it so badly needed. He was an Alawite, and naturally enough he had surrounded himself with people belonging to that small 12 per cent of the population which came from the same area and shared the same beliefs. The Damascus régime was certainly a minority government, but it was none the worse for that; its shortcomings were of the sort which could beset any régime: massive corruption, ham-handedness and excessive use of force in dealing with dissent, an obsession with the 'threat' posed by neighbouring Iraq and its rival wing of the Ba'ath Party, and a less than successful economic programme.

Assad's policy was to keep things quiet at home while doing what he could in the Arab world towards regaining his own lost territory, and perhaps in the process furthering the cause of the Palestinians. It was in that field that his personal attitudes played a part, for Hafez Assad cordially disliked Yasser Arafat. Assad was a professional soldier, a fighter pilot who had been commander of the Syrian Air Force, a man who felt at home in a regimented military environment. He did not like guerrillas, and he did not like short, tubby men with three days' growth of beard who insisted on embracing him in public. Assad, in his way, was a snob, and his dislike of the troubles caused by the PLO leaders was reinforced by his objections to their personalities.

Yet Assad needed the PLO. The course he pursued was a lonely one, requiring him to veto any action which ignored Syrian interests or appeared to him to bring closer the day when the Arabs would reach an accommodation with Israel without taking Syria into account. As a result he was a man with few friends. In desperation at his isolation he had formed 'The Steadfastness and Rejection Front', a group of those who, like him – though for very different reasons – would have nothing to do with what they called 'partial solutions': that is, anything which offered less than the total restoration of what had been the mandated territory of Palestine to the people who had lived there before 1948.

Those in this intransigent alliance besides Syria were Libya, Algeria, South Yemen and the PLO. Since these were not the most powerful or influential of Arab countries, President Assad was also trying other things: his was the only Arab state to back and supply Iran, on the grounds that anyone who caused trouble to his old enemies in Iraq was a friend of his. More importantly, he was also trying to put together an alliance which might prove more credible, and more of a threat to Israel, than that in which he found himself at present: he wanted a grouping of Lebanon, where his army, in the guise of the Arab Deterrent Force, was the most powerful factor, the PLO, and eventually, Jordan. For all King Hussein's sustained and enthusiastic backing of President Hussein in Baghdad, President Assad recognised that the King was deeply worried about the situation on the West Bank; that he still had hopes of realising his dream of a United Kingdom embracing both banks of the Jordan; and that he feared Israeli intentions towards the remaining part of his realm.

King Hussein was being wooed on all sides. He was formally bound by a resolution of the Arab Summit Conference in Rabat, which had given the PLO the sole right to negotiate on behalf of the Palestinian people, and he had adhered rigidly to that provision, giving his fellow Heads of State and the Palestinians themselves no cause for complaint. Yet it remained a prime American concern to involve the King in any talks going on, since they saw the so-called 'Jordan option' as the only remaining way forward. They believed that the only, faint possibility of getting the Israelis out of the West Bank would be to give Hussein control of the area once again, and the King, naturally enough, privately agreed with them. His public attitude had to be somewhat different; it was impossible for him to adopt the American line openly because more than half the people of Jordan were still Palestinians, and the King had no desire to see a repetition of the events of 1970. He had to be careful of Syria too, for after one more of those Arab attempts to unite, Jordan and Syria were once again at odds, with King Hussein being blamed by the Syrians for allowing Moslem Brotherhood training camps on his territory, and for permitting arms and ammunition to be sent into Syria from Jordan. In fact, the major support to the Brotherhood in Syria had been given by Saudi Arabia, which at the same time had been paying over huge amounts to President Assad's government – the Saudis believed in covering all the options, and were determined to be in an influential position if, as seemed likely, President Assad was overthrown and a new régime installed by force of arms.

King Hussein's answer to the Syrian threat was to side wholeheartedly with Iraq in the Gulf war; in a sense it was no more than siding with his enemy's enemy, though it did no harm to Jordan, which turned into the main supply route for Baghdad, and benefited accordingly. At the same time, King Hussein was quietly mending his fences with the Palestinians, in particular getting closer to Arafat and the moderates of Fateh, though he maintained a deep dislike of the extremists of the PLO such as Habash and Hawatmeh. Hussein feared that after the annexation of the Golan plateau, an Israeli success in Lebanon would lead on naturally to a formal proclamation of Israeli law in the West Bank and the establishment of yet more settlements there. He wanted an Israeli defeat; but at the same time it would obviously suit him to see the PLO humbled and made militarily impotent. Only under those conditions could Hussein hope to have a useful dialogue with the PLO – and useful in his terms meant leading to some form of power-sharing, for Hussein knew that although he could provide the international respectability and win the support of the Americans, only the PLO could persuade the people of the West Bank to accept Jordan once again as their ruler.

Egypt, the only Arab country to have concluded peace with Israel and to have direct links with that country, had perhaps the most difficult part of all to play during the invasion, yet carefully exploited the situation and gained a number of advantages. Under the direction of Osama el Baz, the brilliant theoretician of the Egyptian Foreign Ministry, President Mubarak rarely put a foot wrong. Egypt was swift and consistent in its condemnation of Israeli actions, yet at the same time made it plain to America and to the Arab world that it had no intention of going back on the agreements made at Camp David. Basically, what the Egyptians were doing was to stick to the letter of the promises they had made, while doing all they could to distance themselves from Israel and to move towards the Arab fold. Thus, together with France, Egypt sponsored a UN resolution aiming at a general settlement of the whole Middle Eastern crisis, which if it had come off, would obviously have cleared the way for a rapprochement between Egypt and its Arab critics.

Egypt also sought to link its acceptance of any Palestinians evacuated from Beirut with a global settlement of the affair, but here it was rather over-playing its hand. It failed too when it sought to push the Palestinians into setting up a moderate government in exile, which would have been welcome in Cairo; the PLO leaders realised very well that it would have been the kiss of death for them to put themselves under Egyptian control, or appear to be doing so.

Egyptian policy was clear: to do what it could to help resolve the crisis, and at the same time to show itself to be part of the Arab family of nations, and ready to move back into full relations with all the countries of the region. It did not work completely, yet at the end of it all, Egypt emerged with no additional critics in the Arab world, and had managed to maintain its close links with America and its basic formal relations with Israel. It was a difficult trick skilfully executed.

To sum up, every Arab country in its way had an ambivalent attitude to what was going on in Lebanon. As usual, only Colonel Gaddafy of Libya was out of step, with a firm policy, firmly stated. This he set out in a letter to Yasser Arafat:

I counsel you to commit suicide rather than be disgraced, because your suicide will glorify the Palestinian cause for generations to come, and your blood will form the fuel of the revolution spreading inevitably from the Atlantic Ocean to the Gulf.

It is shameful and inadmissible, no matter what the price, that the enemy should be given the privilege of negotiating our right to exist, not only in Beirut, but anywhere in Lebanon or the world, for the Zionists have arrogated to themselves the right to pursue you anywhere.

The Libyan leader went on to say that any negotiations should only be with the Lebanese authorities, and even then, no talks should be held while the Israelis were still in occupation of the country.

This was all too much even for Arafat, a man who made a main plank of his policies the avoidance of conflict with Arab leaders. In his reply, he wrote to Gaddafy:

We have not heard of a single demonstration of support, except perhaps in the West Bank, in any country 'from the Atlantic to the Gulf'. The encirclement of the Palestinians and the Lebanese by the Israelis, who are using the most modern American arms, has not provoked any reaction: on the contrary, the Arabs and the world seem to have given official approval to the siege imposed by the Israeli-American alliance. The fighters, Palestinian and Lebanese, who are taking part in the longest Arab-Israeli war ever, are waiting for the Arab countries at least to send them their planes, to protect their women and children and put an end to this blockade.

And Arafat added pointedly that 'if what we had discussed in our past meetings had been put into practice, there would have been no siege of Beirut' – a clear reference to earlier Libyan promises to provide troops, tanks and planes.

This ridiculous little exchange between Gaddafy and Arafat provided as clear an indication as any of the general state of relations between the PLO and its so-called backers. Arab unity, as usual, was a myth.

CHAPTER NINE

The Palestinians were at their strongest in Lebanon at the beginning of the Israeli invasion. They had been building up their strength steadily, and were getting all the arms and ammunition they could accommodate, some direct from Russia, some doled out by Syria, and some sent by Colonel Gaddafy to whichever group he happened to favour at any particular moment. Politically, too, the Palestinians were an important factor, both in Lebanon and throughout the whole Arab world. In the complicated Lebanese equation, it was the strength of their organisation which made them such a potent force, for they had a far better infrastructure than any of the other factions, apart from the Phalange. Again, like the Phalange, their position was mainly a result of the near-complete breakdown of the authority of the State of Lebanon. Just as in the Christian areas the Police, Gendarmerie or Army could operate only by the consent of the Phalangist leaders, so the same thing was true of the Palestinians in the Moslem areas of the country. This was the result of the Civil War of 1975–76, which had left the country shattered and physically divided.

The Palestinians began arriving in Lebanon in 1948 at the time of the first Arab-Israeli war. The first to leave their homeland were often the better-off, middle-class people: doctors, lawyers and businessmen, to whom the Lebanon was a natural haven, with its European outlook, its freedom of expression, and its commercial orientation. As a result, the first trickle of refugees had no trouble in integrating with local communities. It was only later that difficulties arose. After the 1956 and 1967 wars, the great mass-movement of the Palestinians began, and as the camps of Jordan filled up, the overflow travelled on to Lebanon, there to be reinforced three years later

by hard-core Palestinian activists when King Hussein subjugated the commandos in his country.

The first refugee camps in Lebanon were set up around
Beirut. This in itself was an indication of how little notice the
then authorities paid to this small influx, for in the 1970s it was
to become clear that the ring of camps around the city were
capable of strangling the capital, enabling the Palestinians to
cut the main road communications with the rest of the country.
In 1948 and the following years, as the refugees kept arriving,
the Lebanese policy was to give a qualified welcome to those
able and willing to integrate, though always regarding them as
second-class citizens. Meanwhile the very poor, the dispos-
sessed and those with no particular skills to offer were swept
into the camps, where they were out of sight of the majority of
the people, and certainly far from the homes of members of the
political and business establishments.

It was a case of out of sight, out of mind – for in the camps,
things were happening quite unbeknown to the government. In
Lebanon, just as in Jordan, the fledgling Palestinian commando organisations went to the camps to find their recruits
and supporters, as well as ready-made, secure bases from which
to operate. As early as the beginning of the 1960s, the camps
were becoming the centres of radical Palestinian thought, the
embryo arsenals of the armed movement which was soon to be
launched, and the breeding-grounds of the dissatisfaction and
determination to return to the homeland which was carefully
fostered by the emerging leaders.

The commando movement was actually born in the Gaza
Strip, a jam-packed tongue of Egyptian territory extending into
Israel, which contains nothing but orange trees and refugees –
400,000 of them. Yasser Arafat was born there in 1929, one of a
number of young men who later met to discuss what could and
should be done. Unlike many similar groups, this one actually
did something, for when the plotters split up and went off to
Egypt, the Gulf and the other Arab states, Arafat and his
colleagues kept in touch, and by means of persuasion, cajolery
and argument, managed to gain access to men who had money,
or weapons, or knew others who could supply them. Thus was
born Al Fateh, the main guerrilla group – its name is a

reverse-acronym of its Arabic title, Harakat al-Tahrir al-Watani al-Filistini, the Palestine National Liberation Movement.

Prior to this, a more formal organisation had been officially voted into being by the first Palestine National Congress, which had met in Jerusalem in 1964; this was the Palestine Liberation Organisation, headed by the lawyer and demagogue Ahmed Shukairy, and run by a fourteen-member Executive Council. At the same congress, a Palestine National Fund had been founded, which was to finance the PLO and its agencies, and a few months later an Arab summit conference in Alexandria had established the Palestine Liberation Army, which became known as the 'regular forces' of the Palestine Resistance Movement, though in practice the army was always under the control of the country in which its units were stationed.

Right from the beginning it was Al Fateh which made all the running. It launched its first offensive action on January 1st, 1965, with an attack into Israeli-occupied territory from Jordan. This had not been the original plan; at first it had been intended to send this mission into Israel proper, with Lebanon naturally being chosen as the jumping-off ground. But as early as this, even when Fateh was only a few months old, the Lebanese authorities were already eyeing it with suspicion, and one of the commandos who was to have made the raid was arrested by the army. A month later, there was a bland announcement that the man concerned had committed suicide while in prison – an unlikely story which was immediately denied by Al Fateh, which claimed the commando had been tortured to death. There were protests and demonstrations in the camps, but there was nothing the Palestinians could do, for at this stage they were still few in number, with only a handful of the more simple weapons, meagre ammunition, rudimentary organisation and little but the goodwill of their compatriots and the hostility of their enemies to sustain them. Still they kept up the attacks, and in 1966, Yasser Arafat himself was among a group of fedayeen – literally, 'men of sacrifice' – arrested as they were about to cross into Israel from Lebanon. Eventually, through Syrian pressure, Arafat was released after spending some time in the Sands Prison in Beirut;

nevertheless it was remarkable that the commander-in-chief of the Palestinian forces should have thought it necessary to take part personally in such a hazardous mission. There may well have been an element of bravado about it; the Palestinians, like most Arabs, are highly impressed by the 'macho' image, and proof of personal bravery has to be given by any leader. Arafat had already taken part in missions into occupied territory from Jordan, and was constantly having to demonstrate his personal disregard for danger; he moved not in a classic revolutionary style of a fish in the stream, but rather as a grain of sand in the Arab machine, an irritant which no-one liked and many tried to expel.

The Six-Day War of 1967 marked the beginning of public Arab acceptance of the commando movement, for after the massive, swift and humiliating defeat of their regular armies, the Arabs needed something on which to pin their hopes. Suddenly the commando movement became fashionable; what the massed regular forces could not accomplish, the guerrillas would. The image of the 'fedai', the young man with a keffiyah around his head and face, a rifle in his hand, and a burning determination to liberate his homeland in his soul, was a romantic concept which appealed to the youth of every Middle Eastern country. So the numbers of fighters gradually increased, with the vast majority of them stationed in Jordan, a country still officially at war with Israel. Jordan appeared determined to regain its own lost territory; Lebanon, on the other hand, had given up no land in the war and was plainly not going to do any fighting at any time if it could possibly avoid it.

In spite of the commandos' new-found popular appeal the build-up of the Palestine Resistance Movement was a slow process, and the commandos proved better at swaggering around Amman than infiltrating enemy lines or causing losses to the Israelis. Then came an unlooked-for opportunity which did far more for the movement than any raid it could have staged, transforming the fedayeen overnight into everyone's heros. The reason, in the usual paradoxical Arab way, was that the guerrilla forces had taken part in a set-piece battle with the Israelis in which they had, quite naturally, been beaten. This legend-making affair was the Battle of Karameh, a small,

pleasant town of white stone and small gardens on the bank of
the River Jordan near the Allenby Bridge. A group of guerrillas
had established their base there and the Israelis had decided to
move in and clean out this nest of 'terrorists'. A strong raiding
force was assembled and on March 21st, 1968, one group
crossed the river by the pontoon bridge which had replaced the
original Allenby Bridge, another crossed by the Damia Bridge
to the north, while a third unit was landed by helicopter behind
the town. Confident of success, for they rarely met any real
opposition from the still divided and ill-prepared Arabs, the
Israelis had made little effort to conceal their preparations, and
for days past their newspapers had warned that vengeance
would be exacted for the latest commando attack in which a
school bus had been blown up in the Negev and two children
killed. So confident were the Israelis that they had even laid on
coaches to take selected journalists into the town while they
conducted their search-and-destroy operation there.

This time, however, things went wrong. The Jordanian
Army had made its own dispositions, with artillery zeroed in on
all the approaches to Karameh, while tanks had been moved
into position in the surrounding hills. So when the Israeli
armour rolled forward with its tail of soft-skinned troop-
carrying vehicles, the Jordanian gunners were able to inflict
heavy casualties on the attackers. In the town itself, the Israelis
did not have it all their own way either. The Israeli troops who
landed from the helicopters were caught in a hail of crossfire
from the machine gun positions set up by the Palestinians, and
though the better trained, more disciplined and efficient Israeli
soldiers eventually prevailed, they suffered heavy losses.

As soon as the fifteen-hour Battle of Karameh was over, the
Palestinian propagandists swung into action, announcing a
great Arab victory at a time when the Arabs badly needed some
encouragement. Naturally enough, there was little mention of
the crucial part played by the Jordanian Army; rather, it was
the desperate image of Palestinian commandos firing their
red-hot machine guns until the ammunition ran out, and then
throwing their grenades before dying at their posts that was
carefully put out by the Palestinians. Total Israeli casualties
were admitted to be 28 dead and 70 wounded, though many

thought they must have been higher than this, while the Palestinians claimed to have lost more than 170 men – probably an exaggeration. Yet morally the battle was certainly won by the Palestinians, and their potent myth-making machine quickly capitalised on it to the full. Soon recruits were pouring in to join Fateh, and in Jordan and in Lebanon the still basically hostile governments had to tread more carefully in their dealings with their awkward guests.

In Lebanon, the Palestinian population had now reached 250,000, with some 90,000 people in the 15 camps scattered around the country, each with its commando affiliations and commando presence; and with the growth in population, the number of operations launched from Lebanese territory was mounting steadily. In the Arkoub, the barren, rocky wasteland around the foot of Mount Hermon on the borders of Syria, Israel and Lebanon, the Palestinians were setting up permanent bases, using the hundreds of caves there to store ammunition, and the few villages as their supply centres – much to the annoyance and fear of the local people.

Now not a week went by without some guerrilla activity; raids to blow up water culverts used by the hard-pressed Israeli farmers in the nahals, the armed settlements in Upper Galilee; ambushes of border patrols; grenade attacks on buses and lorries; roads mined and rockets fired across the border. At the same time, the leaders of the movement were establishing offices in Beirut and Amman, setting up training camps and supply bases, and sending envoys around the world to drum up support wherever it could be found. They were trying, too, to sort out their own differences, and to forge a new image of their movement which would be acceptable to the world beyond the Middle East, as well as to the Arab states.

The first step in establishing that new image of the PLO was to get rid of Ahmed Shukairy, a ranting figure who had done little to unify the movement or to make it effective, and had done a great deal of international harm by his wild oratory: he is best remembered for his promise to 'throw the Jews into the sea' – this at a time when the Palestinians hardly had the strength to catch the few scraps of support thrown to them. At a meeting of the Palestine National Council in Cairo some three months after the Karameh turning point, Shukairy was quietly and efficiently voted out of office, and Arafat elected.

As Arafat had already become leader of the military wing of Al Fateh, Al Assifa – 'the storm' – he was now in a virtually unassailable position: he had control of the money and the regular forces of the movement through his chairmanship of the PLO, and of the guerrilla forces through his command of Fateh. It was a position he quickly consolidated, for Arafat was always much more a politician and diplomat – only his admirers would say statesman – than a revolutionary leader in the style of a Castro; still less was he a Guevara. His early participation in raids into enemy territory, though occasionally necessary, must be seen as dictated by the need to establish a reputation. Once that was done, he was free to concentrate on building up his own position and that of the forces he represented, the moderate, middle-of-the-road section of the Palestinian movement.

Arafat reinforced his authority by putting his brother, Dr Fathi Arafat, in charge of the Palestine Red Crescent, the 'Army Medical Corps' of the movement, which was also responsible for assessing injuries and paying indemnities to those wounded or to the dependents of men killed. He also saw to it that a special fund set up by Kuwait to pay compensation and pensions was brought under his direct control; and in a third significant move, he took over the command of the Palestine Armed Struggle Command, PASC, the military police of the movement. This turned into his own private army – a force better paid, better trained and better equipped than the usual run of guerrillas, with recruits carefully chosen and owing allegiance directly to Arafat. This unit was to prove useful in quelling mutinies and arresting dissidents when necessary, and was always the most disciplined and reliable of the Palestinian forces.

For all the new surge of support for the Palestinians, they still faced difficulties in their two main theatres of operation, Jordan and Lebanon. In Jordan, King Hussein was gradually moving towards direct opposition to the commandos, and towards a bloody confrontation which was forced on him by Palestinian intransigence on one hand and the need to preserve his realm on the other. In Lebanon, the much weaker and more hesitant government was more concerned about the danger of Israeli reprisals than with the arrogance and lawlessness of the commandos themselves. Finally, however, it too was forced to act, and in March, 1968, it passed a law forbidding 'infiltration by Lebanese or Arab nationals living in Lebanon into territory occupied by Israel.'

This step by the Lebanese government was clearly designed more to mollify the Israelis than to have any practical effect. The Lebanese wanted to be able to say: 'Look, it's not our fault. We've told these people they are not allowed to attack you. Now please leave us alone.' For of course the tiny Lebanese Army, only 14,000 strong at that time, was quite incapable of securing the border with Israel, and was well aware that in the new conditions created by the battle of Karameh, any forceful action against the guerrillas would lead to possibly violent demonstrations of support for the Palestinians by some half of the Lebanese population. Nevertheless, the army did intervene when it came across some blatant instance of the law being flouted, and there were a number of clashes between army units and Palestinian commandos on their way to or from Israel. Just as regularly, Israel sent patrols into Southern Lebanon to blow up houses suspected of being used by 'terrorists', or shelled guerrilla camps, often doing more damage to farms than to the widely dispersed fedayeen.

Then in December, 1968, came the first of the massive Israeli 'reprisal raids' against Lebanon. These were clearly intended as much to force the Lebanese to act on Israel's behalf against the commandos as to 'punish' the country for the shelter it was reluctantly giving the Palestinian fighters. The excuse for this first show of Israeli strength was an attack carried out by two men of the extremist Popular Front for the Liberation of Palestine on an El Al airliner at Athens, in which an Israeli engineer had been killed. Picking an appropriate target, the politicians in Tel Aviv sent Rafael Eytan's helicopter-borne task force to Beirut Airport, where thirteen aircraft and a petrol storage tank were blown up, and damage estimated at £500 million was caused. The raiders met with no opposition at all; at one point Eytan even pulled a cowering airport gendarme from under a desk and demanded Lebanese 25-piastre pieces so

that he and his men could get some soft drinks out of a machine
– a remarkable display of propriety amidst so much devastation.

The Israeli attack on the airport was universally condemned,
and if its sole purpose had been to cause damage, it was not
much of a success: the Lebanese collected a huge insurance
pay-out and Middle East Airways were quickly able to re-
equip, going on to become one of the most modern and
profitable airlines in the area. But on another level the raid
achieved all that was planned, for there was an immediate
outcry in the country against the lack of action by the army and
its utter failure to protect the airport or to move against the
raiders during the time they were there. The Moslem and
left-wing parties, and of course the Palestinians, charged the
army with negligence at best, collusion at worst, and kept up a
barrage of criticism; the Right and the Christians argued that
the army did not have time to take effective counter-measures,
and anyway could not keep a sufficient force in every part of the
country that was under possible threat from Israel. As the
heated debate went on, the lines were drawn for the long-
running conflict which was to lead eventually to civil war and
Israeli invasion. The radical parties argued that the role of the
army was to defend the country and everyone in it, while the
Right said that given Lebanon's limited capabilities, the only
defence was to remove the cause of the Israeli attacks, a task that
should be given to the army. The Left answered this by pointing
to the long-standing fear in Lebanon that Israel wanted to
annex the south of the country up to the Litani river in order
to secure adequate water supplies for Upper Galilee – a
policy which Israel actually began to implement in 1982.

As the debate went on and the smouldering antagonisms
came increasingly into the open, Mr Rashid Karami, the Prime
Minister of the day and a realistic man who could see the logic of
both sides' arguments, was forced to resign. He acknowledged
that there were two points of view in Lebanon, the first time any
politician had accepted the polarisation of the country, and he
counselled a 'neutral' stand by the government to avoid causing
a split among the people. Yet he must have seen the impossibil-
ity of this; to be 'neutral', a government would have to abdicate

all responsibility and do nothing to curb lawlessness or to check the conflicts which were bound to develop between the two sides. The dispute steadily became more bitter and began to take on what were called 'confessional overtones' – that is, the supporters of one side were almost all Moslems, and began adding the basic demands of their community to their arguments in favour of freedom for the commandos; while on the other side, the Christians not only wanted the commandos to be controlled, they also wanted more to be done about the radical Lebanese parties, whom they saw as a threat to the established order and in particular to the dominant position of the Maronites.

As early as the Autumn of 1969, the Phalangist militia went into action against the Palestinians for the first time, the two sides trading fire across the Place des Martyrs, the main square of the commercial area of Beirut, where housewives crowded the souks and shops.

While the Palestinians and the Phalangists plunged Lebanon into the chaos which was to last for so long, Syria closed its border with Lebanon in pursuance of its traditional policy of causing as much trouble to its neighbour as possible. Every Damascus régime still harboured the dream of a 'Greater Syria' which would take in the Lebanon, a dream which played its part in the formulation of Syrian policy both at the time of the Lebanese civil war of 1975–76 and the Israeli invasion. Behind the move also was Syrian jealousy of Lebanon, which by greater efficiency and more forceful commercial practices was siphoning off trade which had traditionally gone to the Syrian ports of Latakia or Tartous. The usual reaction to all this came from Iraq, which offered any support needed to the Palestinians in Lebanon – a Pavlovian response prompted more by Syria's moves than by the plight of the commandos, and one which in fact had no practical effect whatsoever.

As the fighting spread to the whole country, it was clear that the army could not suppress the commandos and at the same time maintain order in the towns and cities; equally, it was obvious that the Palestinians did not have the strength to win in an all-out confrontation, even if they wished to embark on such a wild adventure. Some compromise had to be found, and after the intervention of President Nasser's chief troubleshooter, Mr Hassan Sabry al Kholi, both Yasser Arafat and General Emil Boustany, Commander of the Lebanese Army, agreed to meet in Cairo to hammer out some sort of accommodation. The fruits of their conference came on November 3rd, 1969, after two days of talks. In a joint communiqué they announced that agreement had been reached, and a way found to end the fighting. There was an immediate ceasefire, and both sides retired to lick their wounds – and to prepare for the further clashes which both knew were bound to come.

In fact, the agreement was a remarkable victory for the Palestinians, and a complete climb-down by President Charles Helou and his army backers, who in effect had to accept Karami's idea of 'co-ordination' and to promise the commandos much greater facilities. It was formally laid down that the Palestinians were granted control over the fifteen refugee camps in Lebanon, could use them as bases, and could install weapons there. The movement of commandos to and from the border was to be facilitated, and the supply route to the Arkoub, a track leading from Syria through Deir-al-Achayer and Rachaya known as the Arafat Trail, was to be kept open.

On the army side, the advantages were few. The Palestinian leaders promised to exert their authority over the lawless elements in their ranks, though both they and the army knew they were powerless to do so without provoking a war within a war; they undertook to see that commandos did not go armed or in uniform into Lebanese towns; and they agreed to give up a small and not very useful base at Dniyyah in North Lebanon. Perhaps the only helpful clause from the Lebanese point of view was a paragraph laying down that 'the Lebanese civil and military authorities will continue to exercise their full rights and responsibilities in all Lebanese regions in all circumstances.' It did not mirror the facts of the situation at the time or at any stage in the future, but it did at least provide a legal cover for when the army felt strong enough to take on the commandos once more.

Then came the Black September of 1970 in Jordan, when King Hussein was forced to move against the commandos, and in a series of bloody battles defeated them and threw them out of his country. Some went to Syria, but many more went on to Lebanon, and it was there that the main headquarters and offices of the organisation were set up. In Syria, control was too tight and the security forces too effective for the Palestinians; they needed a country that was weak enough to allow them to go about their own affairs without hindrance, and they also needed a country with a common border with Israel. Lebanon was the natural choice.

The growth of the power of the PLO in Lebanon was mirrored by the growth of the Phalangist Party and other right-wing Christian groups, notably Camille Chamoun's National Liberal Party, and his fighting force, the Tiger Cubs, led by his son Dany. The Phalangists, always the dominant force, were nominally Lebanese Nationalists, and had as a main plank of their programme the demand that all 'foreigners' – *i.e.* the Palestinians – should leave Lebanon. They blamed the PLO for all the Israeli attacks, and unlike the Moslems who wanted the army to defend all the people and all the territory of the country, they wanted the fledgling Lebanese Army to strike at the commandos, a task for which it was unsuited and ill-prepared. The real Phalangist aim, however, was undeclared: it was to maintain the Christian hegemony in Lebanon which had been established when the country had gained its independence from France in 1943.

At that time, a National Covenant had been drawn up which apportioned the various high offices of state among the different religious and ethnic groups, and laid down that there should be a six-to-five ratio in favour of the Christians in all governmental branches, army, policy and civil service. The President and the Commander in Chief of the army had to be Maronite Christians, the Prime Minister a Sunni Moslem, the Speaker of the Parliament a Shia Moslem, the Chief of Staff a Druze, and so on; even the Armenians were given their own parliamentary representatives. This was the system which the Phalangists were determined to maintain, for in spite of its apparent fairness, it effectively ensured that the Christians remained the dominant power in the land.

Then, in the mid-1970s, that concept was challenged. No census had been taken since 1932, but the Moslems were

convinced that the demographic character of the country had
altered, and that they were now the largest group – a view
shared privately by the Christians, who recognised that there
was usually a higher Moslem birthrate and that the Christians
were more prone to emigrate. The presence of the Palestinians,
most of them Sunni Moslems, was therefore a particular irritant to the Phalangists, who even at this time saw themselves as
the natural allies of the Israelis and did not hesitate to turn to
Israel for their arms supplies. The first arms deals done between Israel and the Phalangists were brokered by CIA men
who commuted between Tel Aviv and Jounieh, the Christian
'capital', by way of Cyprus.

The Palestinians, for their part, were forced into alliances
with the Moslem left. Arafat and the other leaders had no desire
to become embroiled in Lebanese domestic affairs, but they did
need to protect their offices, their camps and those living in
them. To do this, they had to have the support of the people
around them, and the only way to secure that was to help their
reluctant hosts. Thus, at the beginning of the Lebanese civil
war, the Palestinians, as an organised movement, tried hard to
remain on the side lines; it was only when the Christian militias
looked as though they might overwhelm the leftist forces that
Arafat committed his men to the battle.

The Palestinians and Lebanese leftists had only indifferent
success at first, so the Syrians were forced to intervene to
stabilise the situation and protect their left-wing allies. President Assad therefore sent Palestine Liberation Army units into
Lebanon to help the hard-pressed Moslem forces and try to
restore the balance. It was a bold move, for the PLA was in fact
part of the regular Syrian Army, officered by Syrians and under
the orders of the army command. Dispatch of the force was
bound to bring a reaction from Israel – which, sure enough,
quickly announced it would not tolerate Syrian 'occupation' of
any part of Lebanon.

For a while the Syrian move seemed to have eased the
situation, but then the fighting resumed, and this time the
Christians appeared to be in imminent danger of defeat. This
again was something the Damascus régime could not permit –
not because there was any particular liking by the Syrians for

the Phalangists and their allies, but because Syria could not allow the emergence in Lebanon of a Palestinian-dominated, socialist state. Such an entity on Israel's northern border could dictate the timing of any new conflict; and anything that happened in the area would be bound to embroil Syria, which was no more ready for a war then than it was eight years later. So the Syrians moved once more, in October of 1976, and this time in force: regular Syrian units were sent in with hundreds of tanks, in a full-scale invasion. This time, careful preparations had been made, and diplomatic messages sent via America assuring Israel that Syria had no expansionist aims and no desire to become involved in a war. The object, President Assad said, was merely to end the war in Lebanon and to impose an effective ceasefire which would allow for mediation between the rival factions.

To legitimise what had been done, a conference was called in Riyadh by King Khaled, attended by the leaders of Egypt, Syria, Lebanon and Kuwait, and Yasser Arafat of the PLO. This Riyadh 'restricted summit', as it came to be called, not only approved Syria's move into Lebanon, it also effected a rapprochement between Egypt and Syria, who had been at each other's throats over the previous year: Egypt had objected to what it saw as President Assad's efforts to exert Syrian hegemony over the whole of Lebanon, while also moving closer to Jordan and trying to control the PLO; Syria, for its part, had accused Egypt of 'throwing away the gains of the 1973 war' and breaking up the alliance with Damascus. The Riyadh mini-summit, perhaps influenced by the fact that a new administration was about to take over in Washington, managed to resolve this Syrian-Egyptian dispute, and also gave the green light for major Syrian involvement in Lebanon. The tanks rolled in, a full summit in Cairo rubber-stamped what had been agreed in Riyadh, the fighting stopped, and for once Arab leaders seemed to have moved swiftly, decisively and effectively. It was an illusion which did not last for long, for nothing had been done to settle the underlying conflicts in Lebanon, which were to resurface all too soon.

When the Syrians first moved into Lebanon in strength, all seemed well for a while, with Syrian troops taking over checkpoints, dismantling road-blocks and manning the crossing points between East and West Beirut. Soon, too, they were joined by token contingents from Saudi Arabia, the Sudan and from the Gulf states, though the Syrian troops continued to provide the bulk of what was called the Arab Deterrent Force.

There was, however, one potential region of conflict which could not be policed by the Syrians: this was Southern Lebanon, the area along the Israeli border. The Israelis had let it be known they would not tolerate Syrian forces there, and had laid down a 'red line' on the map, warning that any move south of this line by Syrian troops would draw an immediate Israeli response. As Syria had been intent on building up its position in the Arab world and anxious to avoid war with Israel, the Damascus government had quietly accepted the Israeli conditions.

This left a vacuum in the south, which had been practically untouched during the Civil War. The Lebanese Army there had now broken up, with Moslem units declaring themselves part of the Lebanese Arab Army formed by Lieutenant Ahmed Khatib, some of the Christian troops remaining in their barracks, drawing their pay, and taking no part in events, and others joining the militia established by Major Sa'ad Haddad. The Palestinians who had been in the border zone had left to fight in Beirut and other places, and refugees from war-torn villages further north had come south to take their place. As a result, the whole demographic pattern in the south had changed: before the war, the Christians had been concentrated in only three villages along the border, and in the towns of Marjayoun and Bint Jbail. At the end of the war, the Palestinians began to return, and sought once again to set up their bases and to take over houses or whole villages to use as jumping-off points for raids into Israel.

These moves were opposed by Major Haddad's men, who were increasingly supported by Israel, which had initiated a so-called 'good fence' policy. This was in practice a way of extending Israeli influence and direct control northwards into Lebanon for a few miles, thus creating a buffer zone along the frontier. Lebanese were encouraged to move into Upper Galilee to work each day, the sick and wounded were cared for at

specially set up clinics or moved to hospitals inside Israel, and
Israeli Army officers, usually with badges of rank and unit signs
removed, acted as liaison officers with the Christian militias,
procuring for them everything they wanted, from shoe laces to
heavy artillery.

Now that the fighting was over in the rest of the country and
the Syrian forces were firmly in control, more and more Palestinians moved south, and after a brief Syrian presence, virtually
took over the town of Nabatiyeh as a regional headquarters.
Beaufort Castle was occupied and began to be used as a firing
platform for attacks both on the Christian militias and the
Israeli settlements close to the border. The problems that Israel
now faced were of Israel's own making, for by refusing to
tolerate a Syrian presence on the border, it had created a
vacuum into which the Palestinians were inexorably drawn. If
the Syrians had been allowed to establish a presence in Southern Lebanon right down to the frontier, they would certainly
not have permitted the Palestinians to infiltrate unless they had
wanted them to do so – and at that time, and for years to come,
President Assad certainly had no desire to give the Israelis a
casus belli.

In a move later shown to be monumentally wrong, the
Israelis decided to rely on a force they had created and continued to control – Haddad's Christian-Shia militia. Even with
Israeli arms and know-how and a stiffening of experienced
Phalangist fighters shipped from Jounieh to Haifa and then
sent north into the enclave, this force was just not good enough
– and nothing like as efficient or ruthless as the Syrians would
have been. So the stage was set for Israel to launch the Litani
Operation, a cross-border incursion designed not only to kill or
capture as many Palestinian guerrillas as possible, but also to
clear the border of any Palestinian presence.

In the event, the Litani Operation failed in both those
objectives; the guerrillas faded away before the ponderous
Israeli advance, and when it was all over, the United Nations
force moved in, and Major Haddad declared his 'Free Lebanon' zone along the border. That narrow strip, nowhere more
than six miles wide, was never an effective security zone for
Israel, and Haddad and his men soon became in effect an

adjunct of the Israeli Defence Force, with their guns linked to the Israeli computers in the command post inside Upper Galilee. Nor did Haddad's writ run all along the border: there were still infiltration routes open to the Palestinians.

UNIFIL, meanwhile, had neither the strength nor the will to carry out its mandate in full: this was to maintain peace and to help to re-establish the authority of the Lebanese central government. In fact, it was years before a Lebanese battalion seconded to the UN was allowed to join the force. As it was, UNIFIL could not deploy its men right down to the Israeli frontier, as it was supposed to do, because Major Haddad refused permission for such a move. Also, for some reason, right from the beginning the UN men had been barred from one area, known as the Marjayoun gap. It was widely thought that Israel had insisted on this when it had agreed to the deployment of the international force, so as to give itself a possible invasion route if it should prove necessary again; in the event, however, when the attack was launched in 1982, the Israelis ignored this approach and rolled straight through UN positions. Yet another weakness of the UN presence along the border was that numbers were short and the force could not police a wide enough zone; consequently the Palestinians could and did fire over the heads of the UN men into Israel, or into Major Haddad's enclave.

While events in Lebanon were slowly but surely moving towards the much more widespread conflict which was to follow, developments far away were shaping Palestinian attitudes and positions. In 1978, President Sadat, Mr Begin and President Carter signed the Camp David accords, a piecemeal solution which effectively ignored the PLO, now endorsed by Arab states as 'the sole legitimate representative of the Palestinian people.' As Dr Fayez Sayegh said, the accords gave 'a fraction of the Palestinian people a fraction of its rights in a fraction of its homeland.' The Palestinians totally rejected the agreements brokered by President Carter, and were largely instrumental in crystallising the general Arab feeling that the Camp David proposals were thoroughly bad and had to be rejected. Yet they were implemented by Israel and Egypt – though only the provisions directly relating to those countries; talks were held, as required, on the granting of autonomy to the Palestinians of the occupied territories, but nothing at all was decided, and time after time one side or the other broke off the negotiations as new sticking points were reached. More and more, the Camp David agreement began to look like what the Arabs had suspected it to be all along: a treaty of peace between Israel and Egypt, restoring Egyptian territory in the Sinai in return for guarantees of peace for Israel. The net result was to diminish Arab bargaining power, for all the Arab countries combined could not hope to wage war against Israel without the support of Egypt, still the country with the largest and best of the Arab military forces.

As the Israeli withdrawal from Sinai continued in the stages laid down in the agreement, the Israelis gave clear signals of their intentions in the other occupied territories. More and more settlements were established in the West Bank, and those planted illegally by the fanatics of the Gush Emunim movement were quickly legalised by the Begin government. Harsh, repressive measures were sanctioned by the army in 'Judaea and Samaria', as Mr Begin insisted on calling them, and troops frequently fired live rounds at children and young people holding demonstrations. Bir Zeit University was closed almost as often as it was open; tear gas was used against protesting schoolgirls; there was a return to the old punitive methods of blowing up houses of suspected guerrillas or their accomplices without waiting for any proof or seeking legal permission. Yet when it was the mayors of Nablus and Ramallah who were the victims of bombings, not a single person was held for questioning, not a house was blown up, and not an arrest was made – a poor record for a régime which prided itself on its efficiency and good intelligence.

Soon the West Bank was put under 'civilian' administration, which meant in practice that Professor Menachem Milson sat in a chair formerly occupied by a senior army officer, while the army and the police continued to run the show. There was one notably dangerous development: General Sharon, the Defence Minister, sanctioned a change which allowed settlers from the West Bank to do their military service in specially formed units serving in 'the territories'. This meant that the zealots of Gush

Emunim were given a licence to carry guns, and to use them whenever there was some minor demonstration; this they often did. Professor Milson's main contribution was to try to arrange the spread of the 'Village Leagues', organisations of mayors and notables in the region which were supposed to supplant the PLO in the affections of the Palestinian people of the West Bank. The leagues were in fact a total failure, with no-one of any stature taking part, and those minor figures who did join having to be protected night and day from the vengeance of their own people.

It was when the final withdrawal from Sinai took place that Mr Begin gave his clearest indications of what the future held. Under the leadership of Marion Weizman, sister of the former Israeli Defence Minister, Jewish settlers around the town of Yamit organised a massive protest against the pull-out from Sinai. Petitions were circulated and a million signatures obtained; signs were put up, interviews given, and very soon the whole world knew of the strong resistance to the final Israeli evacuation from Sinai. There seemed little doubt that this well-organised campaign, which must have taken a considerable amount of money to stage, privately received official backing and support – General Sharon no doubt had a few secret funds at his disposal from which to dispense cash enough to finance the operation.

Finally, of course, General Sharon had to order Israeli soldiers to remove by force the small group of religious fanatics and extremists who tried to stage a sit-in when Yamit itself came to be cleared. With television cameras turning, dozens of reporters and photographers on hand, and crowds of interested local onlookers, the Israeli troops evicted the settlers. It was publicity which everyone welcomed: for what was being said, publicly and definitively, was that Sinai was the last Israeli pull-back; the idea that Israel would ever give up a single inch of the West Bank or Golan could be abandoned. And to underline that, only a short time later, in flagrant disregard of world protests and American pressure, Israel virtually annexed the Golan Heights: Israeli law was imposed on the area, which had previously been subject to the Syrian penal code, and amongst other things the inhabitants now became liable to

Israeli military service. The people, some 14,000 of them, all
Druze, staged a long strike, but to no avail. Israel had effectively taken over another huge slice of Arab land, just as it had
formally annexed Jerusalem and surrounding areas as early as
1967.

Back in Lebanon, another bitter little battle was taking place
which was to have a profound effect on the Palestinians. In
July, 1980, Bachir Gemayel launched a series of swift, vicious
and unexpected attacks on the positions of his allies, Mr
Camille Chamoun's National Liberal Party. From Jounieh
down to Beirut itself, the Phalangist militiamen struck without
warning, and after three days, the NLP was totally beaten. Mr
Chamoun conceded defeat, and his two sons, Dany, commander of the 'Tiger Cubs', and Dory, 'Foreign Minister' of the
party, went into exile.

The Phalangists, nominally headed by Sheikh Pierre
Gemayel but more and more under the control of the ruthless
and extreme Bachir, were now in total control of the Christian
areas from Beirut up to Jounieh, and only north of that, around
Tripoli and Zghorta, was there still an independent Christian
enclave. There, another former president, Suleiman Franjieh,
had his own private fiefdom and his own army. He rightly
blamed Bachir Gemayel for the particularly vicious murder of
his son Tony, who had been gunned down after being forced to
watch his own wife and child killed. Franjieh kept the
embalmed bodies of all three in his palace at Zghorta, and
swore not to bury them until the blood price had been paid.

Franjieh was an ally of the Syrians, who used him to maintain what pressure they could on the Phalangists of East Beirut.
Everyone was aware that Franjieh was quite capable of
launching a wholescale war as soon as he felt strong enough; as
the main architect of the immediate troubles which led to the
Civil War, he was not a man who baulked at spilling blood,
and was prevented from doing so only by the strength of the
Phalangist militias under Bachir Gemayel. Sheikh Bachir, as
his followers called him, took the Phalangists closer than ever
before to the Israelis, and the result was that his men were soon
equipped with everything they wanted from the Israeli arsenal.
Neither Franjieh, nor the Palestinians, nor even the newly-

reformed Lebanese Army would at that time have been a match for them.

The Palestinians themselves were as well-equipped now as they had ever been. There had been no set-piece battles with the Israelis or anyone else for years, so their stocks of weapons and ammunition had not been depleted. They had been given some forty tanks by the Russians, though many of them had been knocked out in Israeli air attacks before the invasion began, while the remainder never fired more than a couple of rounds before being destroyed or abandoned. The Palestine Liberation Army had three brigades in Lebanon; the Ain Jalloud, which had originally come from Egypt, the Bad'r Brigade from Jordan and the Hittin Brigade from Syria. All of them had Syrian officers, as usual with the PLA, and were mostly equipped with armour and heavy weapons. In Lebanon, they were concentrated around Beirut, where there were also some two thousand regular Syrian troops, as well as small detachments of special forces.

All the Palestinian leaders remained in Beirut throughout the siege. Arafat himself was away at the time of the attempted assassination of Argov and the first Israeli air attacks, but hurried back to Lebanon. Abou Iyyad and Abou Jihad, his two deputies, were in the city, as well as the leaders of the other factions, George Habash of the Popular Front, Ahmed Jabril of the Popular Front-General Command, and Nayef Hawatmeh of the Popular Democratic Front. Hani Hassan, Arafat's political adviser and the main liaison man with the Lebanese, was also there, so that no Palestinian of any real stature was outside the country when the war started. Another leader who hurried home when it all began was Walid Jumblatt, the Druze chieftain and head of the Progressive Socialist Party founded by his father, Kamal Jumblatt, who had been assassinated in 1977. Walid Jumblatt, with Marwan Hamadeh, Minister of Tourism and spokesman of the Lebanese Sunni radicals, was the leading representative of the left in all the concentrated negotiations which went on during the siege.

So on the day of the invasion, a full cast was assembled in Beirut. The Palestinians were fully mobilised; students had been called home from Europe and from the Arab countries, and there had been a general call-up of all the young men in the country; arms and ammunition were plentiful, and above all, morale was good. The Palestinians, that most political of people, understood very well that Israel had to eliminate the PLO if it was to have any success at all with its policies in the occupied territories. The PLO for their part were determined to remain the leaders and the spokesmen of all Palestinians, inside and outside the West Bank and Gaza.

The Lebanese, battered by eight years of almost continuous conflict, wanted no part of the fighting. There was no doubt that they would have preferred to see the Palestinians go without a struggle. They had been given a foretaste of what Israel was capable of the previous year in July, 1981, when Israel for the first time had bombed roads and bridges in Southern Lebanon and along the coastal highway to Beirut, and then, on the 17th of the month, had bombed Beirut itself. The targets had been buildings in the Fakhani district thought to house PLO offices, though, in the event, only apartments used by the Democratic Front and the Arab Liberation Front had been hit. The death toll had been high: 200 corpses had been taken out of the shattered buildings and others had certainly been left for dead. Of the 200, 175 were civilians, and of the 800 injured, 700 were also civilians, including nearly 200 children. But the Palestinians had also learned from the experience: many more buildings with safe, deep basements were found, and the various Palestinian offices and command centres were dispersed all over Beirut, while the leaders continued their policy of rarely sleeping in the same place on two successive nights. This demonstration of Israeli ruthlessness was a timely warning to the Palestinians.

The events of July of that year were in effect a rehearsal for the full-scale affair the following year. It had been a two-week war, though without the involvement of ground forces; in the end, five Israelis had been killed and 100 wounded; 386 Lebanese and Palestinians had been killed and more than 1,100 injured. It had also involved Mr Philip Habib, who had been touring the area in 1980 to try to defuse the crisis caused when the Syrians had installed their Sam missiles in the Bekaa Valley. This time, Mr Habib came very close to recognising the

Palestinians on behalf of the American government – something he resolutely refused to do a year later – for he managed to negotiate a ceasefire in Southern Lebanon. At the time, the only ones who were firing from the Lebanese side were the Palestinians; it was therefore difficult for Israel to maintain the fiction that the Palestinians did not exist and therefore could not be negotiated with.

The Palestinians themselves were not the monolithic group so often portrayed by Israel. It was accepted, in Israel and throughout the world, that the constituent organs of the PLO, all eight of them, had very different philosophies and beliefs; yet Israel constantly spoke of 'the PLO' as if they were a single group with a unified command and a political line followed by all their members. Of course, it was not like that at all, and even within Fateh, the largest and most important of the organisations making up the PLO, there were different and sometimes conflicting trends. Arafat himself, for all his devotion to consensus politics, was the leading representative of the moderate wing inside Fateh and the PLO; he was convinced that diplomacy was at least as important as continued 'armed struggle', and that wooing America was better than killing Israelis.

The most influential of Arafat's allies in pushing the 'moderate' line were the two brothers, Khaled Hassan and Hani Hassan. Hani Hassan stayed in Beirut with Arafat and acted as his adviser on relations with the Arab states and also negotiated with the Lebanese or Syrian governments; Khaled Hassan was based in Kuwait, the Gulf country with the biggest Palestinian population. Both these men carried considerable weight with large sections of the most influential sections of Palestinian society, the professional men both inside Lebanon and in the Palestinian diaspora throughout the Gulf. They were often, but not always, backed up by Salah Khalaf – Abou Iyyad – who, after being closely involved with the terrorist Black September movement in the wake of the Palestinian defeat in Jordan in 1970, had moved steadily to the right of the Palestinian political spectrum. Khalaf was one of the three founders of Fateh, the others being Arafat and Khalil al Wazir – Abou Jihad – the military commander. Wazir was, broadly speaking, the main spokesman for the militant wing of the organisation, and advocated continued attacks on targets inside Israel to ensure publicity and to lend weight to Arafat's efforts on the diplomatic front.

Other important constituents of the PLO – George Habash's Popular Front for the Liberation of Palestine, the Democratic Front led by Nayef Hawatmeh, and the Popular Front-General Command of Ahmed Jabril – all took positions well to the left of Fateh's official line. In Habash's phrase, 'The road to Jerusalem runs through Riyadh, Damascus and Beirut as well as Tel Aviv'; in other words, Habash and those like him were as much concerned with revolution throughout the Arab world and with sweeping away the old reactionary régimes, as they were with the liberation of Palestine. That was certainly the position of Hawatmeh, while Ahmed Jabril appeared to have no political philosophy at all; a former officer in the Syrian Army, he was much more 'the simple soldier', concerned only to take every chance of hitting the Israelis wherever they could be found. In fact, he was often very much under Syrian influence, just as the other groups, Saika and the Arab Liberation Front, were completely dominated by Syria and Iraq respectively – so much so that Saika men on occasion fought against the Palestinians of other groups.

Before the Israeli invasion of Lebanon, there had been some evidence of growing disenchantment among young Palestinians with the leadership of the movement, which had not changed since the creation of Fateh in the early 1960s. There was a feeling that the time had come for the old men to move on, and to allow younger leaders more in tune with the times to take over. But this was balanced by the perception that Arafat had achieved such an international image that any benefits gained by his departure would be far outweighed by the consequent drop in attention. It was also clear that if Arafat were to remain in power, then he would keep his old allies around him, for he depended on carefully balancing the personalities and powers of his associates in order to hold on to office.

In Lebanon, the PLO retained its old civil war alliance with the National Movement, though more in theory than in practice, until the Israeli invasion had the effect of uniting all the

Moslem left. Right up to that time, one of the main organisations of the Moslem left, Amal, the Shia Moslem party and its
militia, had actually been in direct and bloody conflict with the
Palestinians. Amal had originally been founded by the Imam
Moussa Sad'r, the Shi'ite leader who was murdered in Libya,
and had been set up to channel the frustrations of the mainly
Shia inhabitants of Southern Lebanon into productive action
and to diminish the power and influence of Kamal Assad, the
speaker of the Lebanese parliament and the old feudal leader of
the Shia. Because the Palestinians needed to use Southern
Lebanon as a base from which to keep up military pressure on
Israel, they were obviously at odds with the people of the
region, whose interests lay in a peace with their neighbours.
Even in Beirut itself, Amal was in conflict with the PLO, as
both tried to recruit from the same pool of young men, and
sought to exert physical control of certain districts.

The other main group in Beirut, the Independent Nasserites,
with their militia, the Mourabitoun, the 'Sentinels', were less
frequently opposed to the Palestinians, largely because their
presence was confined to Beirut, and because they had no
designs on each other's spheres of influence. In the event, the
Mourabitoun and Amal proved the best allies the Palestinians
had when the Israelis were at the gates of Beirut.

CHAPTER TEN

The only thing worrying Begin when the invasion was launched
was its timing, for the element of surprise, so often the hallmark
and key to success of Israeli military strikes, had already been
lost. This was thanks to Alexander Haig, who had authorised
his Press Liaison team in the State Department to make it
generally known that satellite surveillance of Israel's border
with Lebanon indicated that at least 25,000 troops were poised
to go in. Just why Haig, rightly regarded in Jerusalem as a
friend of Israel, chose to disclose this was never explained. The
Israelis had told the Americans in February of their plans and it
may have been that Haig was preparing an alibi if things went
wrong.

Whatever the reason, the Pentagon, and particularly Caspar
Weinberger, was aghast at the news, realising that Begin could
never carry out his promise of 'a clean surgical operation which
would last a week'. The Defence Department hierarchy, while
realising the value of combat-testing newly supplied equipment, was busy trying to persuade Reagan and Congress to arm
Jordan in the wake of the AWACs sales to Saudi Arabia.
Officials were only too well aware that Israel had learned hard
lessons from the blunders of the Yom Kippur War and the 1978
Litani campaign, and wanted to erase those traumas from the
national memory by re-asserting the country's 1976 super-
power image in the Middle East.

In the event, the ever-pragmatic Begin used the leak about
the build-up of troops to deceive others into thinking he was
crying wolf. He sent the theatrical and tricky Sharon, armed
with maps and carefully prepared 'background' material, to
tour the TV studios and newspaper boardrooms of New York
and Washington during the last week of May and emphasise
that Israel's frontier show of force was no empty threat. Begin
rightly calculated that the more it was talked about, the less

effective would be the message; in addition, he knew there was no way of concealing large troop movements from either the White House or the Kremlin, and was quite happy to use the presence of his army on the Lebanese border as a way of putting pressure on Reagan for concessions over arms deals with the Arabs. The prime aim of Sharon's Washington trip was to convince Reagan that it would be wrong for Israel's protector and ally to provide Jordan with mobile Hawk anti-aircraft missiles and F-16 jets. Despite intense lobbying on Capitol Hill, Israel had just failed to kill a Senate motion allowing the AWACs sale to the Saudis; now, in Israeli eyes, the Reagan administration was being panicked into supplying Amman with new weapons by the pro-Soviet noises from King Hussein.

The fast-talking Sharon opened his campaign with a fiery speech to the United Jewish Appeal dinner in the American capital on May 22nd, in which he virtually instructed the Jewish leaders to launch a massive lobbying campaign against the sales to Jordan. He also quietly hinted that something else was in the air: he told his audience that Jews in the British and Argentine armies had no business fighting each other in the Falklands; those Jewish soldiers, he said, should be in Israel where they were really needed. In his talks with administration officials, Sharon argued that Jordan was only a few miles from Israeli population centres, and that by refusing to join the Camp David peace process, Jordan had signalled its continued enmity. The Americans stressed Israel's 'qualitative' superiority in the regional arms balance and pointed out that it might be useful to offer King Hussein an inducement to join Camp David. The Americans had the final say; Sharon went home empty-handed, although in public he claimed that 'the United States and Israel have friendly and good relations.'

As events were later to show, Sharon was not the kind to take a defeat lying down. In the following week, he pressed the case for an immediate invasion of Lebanon. And to underline their belief that Israel was not a state to be ignored, Begin and Sharon timed the operation so as to create maximum embarrassment to Reagan, launching it slap-bang in the middle of his first major overseas trip, a journey carefully designed to symbolise the resurgence of American world leadership. Officials in the Israeli foreign ministry, who throughout the Lebanese campaign fought a steady rearguard action against Sharon, warned of the danger of personally upsetting Reagan, as well as of alarming Leonid Brezhnev; but Begin's mind was already made up. The invasion would go ahead. All he wanted was a pretext – and that was supplied by the shooting of Ambassador Argov. The attack on the London diplomat was duly used to justify the attack on Lebanon, despite the fact that Argov survived, unlike Yaacov Barsimantov, whose assassination in Paris two months before had provoked Israeli government rhetoric but little else. Begin was convinced that he had America's tacit approval, if not sympathy, for the invasion. This view was based on Washington's traumatic experience in Iran. The Israeli Prime Minister believed that the loss of such a strategic ally as the Shah had made it doubly important for Reagan, who was elected on a tide of resentment among Americans at their humiliation under Jimmy Carter, to keep faith with his only remaining dependable anti-Soviet ally in the Middle East.

In the twelve months prior to the invasion, Israeli warplanes had destroyed a French-built nuclear reactor in Iraq; the Air Force had bombed the headquarters of the PLO in Beirut, causing heavy casualties among innocent civilians living around the target; and Begin had annexed the Golan Heights, a move contrary to a generally understood agreement that any retention of Arab land would only be formalised in the context of a final peace settlement. Reagan had expressed official indignation at each of these Israeli actions, which contravened the US government's Middle East policies, yet his response had been limited. For instance, after the reactor attack, he temporarily suspended the shipment of four F-16s, although US-supplied weapons were used in the mission. As the *Wall Street Journal* wryly observed: 'From the time the raid occurred, the US behaved as if it were possible to walk right down the middle of this issue and get out with skin on both sides of the body unburned.'

Begin correctly surmised that there was little Reagan could do in the event of an invasion, for curtailing military shipments would have only a limited effect. Israel had never forgotten, or forgiven Britain for its 1973 ban on shipments of spare parts. As a result of that experience, Israel had become virtually self-sufficient in its arms industry. In any case, enough weapons were already in the pipeline from the United States, and above all, Reagan was unlikely to upset the Jewish lobby with mid-term congressional elections on the horizon.

To understand why Begin and his *alter ego* Sharon were so personally bent on such a radical solution as an attempt to wipe out the PLO, one has to go back to their upbringing as Zionists. Begin seemed to be suffering from a guilt complex brought about by having survived the Nazi slaughter of the Jews in Europe: the Germans killed his father, mother, brother and baby nephew. At the outbreak of the Second World War, he was the leader of the Zionist Revisionist Youth Movement, Betar, which became his Herut party after 1948. With his colleagues he took refuge in Lithuania, where, soon after the Soviet Union had extended its direct rule over the population, he was arrested at Vilna and exiled to Siberian prison camps. Paradoxically, the hardships of the camps, which did so much to form his rigid and abrasive manner, saved him from Hitler's Final Solution. Whatever the reason for his complex – if he has one – Begin is obsessed with the Holocaust. He refuses to be interviewed by German journalists, and in February, 1982, provoked an open rift with the West German Chancellor, Helmut Schmidt, by falsely accusing him of being among the viewers of a film showing the hanging by piano-wire of anti-Hitler German officers.

Begin's constant fear was that the Arab world was bent on annihilating his nation in a second Holocaust. Thus, despite his years as a fighter with the Irgun Zvei Leumi, or perhaps because of them, he consistently scorned the PLO as 'terrorists' and the 'scourge of the earth', and refused to accept that they had any redeeming features. In a letter to President Reagan, he went so far as to liken Yasser Arafat in Beirut to Hitler in his Berlin bunker. 'My generation, dear Ron,' he wrote, 'swore on the altar of God that whoever proclaims his intent to destroy the Jewish state or the Jewish people, or both, seals his fate, so that whatever happened from Berlin will never happen again.' Begin himself was one of the planners of the savagery at Deir

Yassin, a village near Jerusalem, where in April, 1948, some two hundred Arabs were massacred.

Sharon, a Sabra born on a moshav or agricultural settlement and a devoted family man like Begin, is as reckless in his attitude towards Arabs as Begin is obsessive. His '101' commando unit was once ordered to attack the West Bank village of Kibya and cause 'ten to twelve' casualties in retaliation for the murder of an Israeli woman and two children; Sharon reportedly blew up 46 Arab houses, killing 69 civilians, many of them women and children trapped in cellars. The then Prime Minister and 'father' of Israel, David Ben-Gurion, refused to authorise an investigation into the incident, despite a UN Security Council condemnation, the first ever directed against Israel. Perhaps Sharon was adhering to Ben-Gurion's edict: 'If you put into one hand all the ideas of the world and in the other the survival of Israel, I will choose the second. For the dead do not praise God'; or perhaps, like Begin, he believed the oft-quoted words of a Jew to a Gentile: 'What was done in the Holocaust haunts each one of us who is alive, and what was not done to prevent the Holocaust does not haunt you, and this separates you from us.'

The underlying reason for the invasion of Lebanon was the Begin-Sharon belief that the PLO had to be crushed and removed from the Middle East political process, so that Israel could proceed with its plans for subduing the West Bank. Mr Begin made no secret of the fact that he regarded the area occupied in the 1967 war as Eretz, the Biblical land of Israel, God-given territory that could never be relinquished. With Sharon, he had established sixty-two settlements on the West Bank; dismissing half the mayors who had swept to power in the 1976 elections as PLO sympathisers, and creating so-called 'Village Leagues' from the dregs of West Bank society as an alternative form of leadership for the territory. Local resentment to these moves was such that in the six weeks prior to the invasion of Lebanon, Palestinian youths stood up to troops time and time again, even though they knew that in all probability they would be killed. According to their superiors, the Israeli soldiers always acted in self-defence. Even the army spokesman in Jerusalem eventually made little pretence of explaining what was going on there, repeating, as if bored by the whole business, the usual explanation for casualties: that troops had been forced to shoot at the feet of teenage demonstrators – this in spite of the fact that the dead had head wounds. Arab newspapers, censored by the authorities, carried blank columns and the words 'we apologise' instead of editorials. And liberal Israel banned a thousand books in the West Bank, including Christopher Marlow's *The Jew of Malta*, because its cover read: 'We the Jews are prepared to be humiliated as dogs, but when we bare our teeth we bite.' Also prohibited were the diaries of Che Guevara and a volume entitled *The Archaeological Remains of Palestine and Jordan*.

On his return from the United States in May, Mr Sharon reported that according to Alexander Haig, there was still life left in the Camp David process, and that Haig was pressing for one more round of autonomy negotiations designed to give some hope to the Palestinians. With time running out for Israel to influence the coming Lebanese elections and install a Maronite-dominated government to protect its interests, Begin gave the green light for the invasion.

Several months before, Labour Alignment leaders Shimon Peres, Yitzhak Rabin and Haim Bar-Lev had been informed of the government's intention to embark on a comprehensive operation against the PLO. At a meeting in Jerusalem, Begin and Sharon had told them that it was unclear at that stage just what the campaign would entail – a simple operation to secure Tyre and Sidon, or even a full-scale assault on Beirut; Begin had insisted that they were simply 'tossing around ideas'. The opposition leaders had voiced alarm at the whole idea during this meeting and at two more conferences in the ensuing months. Word had also been passed to Philip Habib, who reported to his government that he thought an invasion to be 'a crazy idea'.

When it did eventually begin, the invasion was at first a political plus for Begin, for Reagan remained remarkably restrained, apparently following the advice of William Safire, the conservative American columnist, by 'keeping his cool on the Israeli rollback of the PLO.' The Reagan administration carefully linked Israeli withdrawal from Lebanon with the need to end PLO shelling of Israeli settlements. A State Department communiqué said: 'Israel will have to withdraw its forces from Lebanon and the Palestinians will have to stop using Lebanon as a launching pad for attacks on Israel.' Two nights after the invasion began, the US was even using its veto to block the passage of a UN Security Council resolution condemning Israel.

One reason for the muted response was that 'actuality' television pictures of what was happening in the south had yet to reach the outside world. The Israelis gave top priority to censorship: virtually every telephone call out of Israel was monitored by a huge staff of soldiers in offices in Jerusalem and Tel Aviv, and foreign correspondents on the first day of the war were kept under extremely close tabs. One British reporter was even interrupted while chatting to his news desk in London from a hotel in Metullah; he was just saying that four hundred tanks had rolled over the border when a voice butted in and said, 'This is the Israeli censor. You are not allowed to give this information. Please stop talking.' Another French radio reporter was gabbling away ninety to the dozen, when his call to Paris was cut off; the censor had simply pulled out the plug. Other reporters who submitted their copy to the censor often had it ripped to pieces. It was accepted by journalists that a good deal of military information had to be kept from the newspapers, but correspondents were even having arguments with the censors over the use of phrases like 'a massive force of Israelis': the censor would only allow the use of the word 'big'. While the actual cutting of copy gradually eased, for three months all calls made by British and American newsmen, even to their wives, were recorded or listened to by the official eavesdroppers. Television crews complained bitterly about the restrictions on satelliting material from Tel Aviv. On one occasion, ABC News was even banned from using the facility after evading a prohibition on an interview with Arafat in Beirut. Again, at one stage all women reporters were barred from Lebanon, even though several had survived wars in Vietnam, Algeria and Ireland.

What really hurt the Israelis was the tendency of US networks to screen film with a sub-title saying that Israeli censors had snipped the footage. According to cameramen, Israeli censors were particularly anxious to prevent pictures of wounded women and children being seen by the outside world, and photographers were forced to smuggle film out of the country under the pretence that it was unexposed.

Yet within Israel, a political consensus prevailed for the first two days of the invasion. When the operation began, Begin told Peres that a crucial reason for the attack was the intensive shelling of Northern Israel by the PLO forces. In fact, that shelling had begun only after Israeli air attacks on Palestinian bases near Beirut. In any case, Mr Begin's argument was specious: the best method of protecting the kibbutzim was the one found by Mr Habib the previous July: a ceasefire between Israel and the PLO. This had succeeded, in that for nine months not a rocket had been fired, even when Israeli planes had bombed Lebanon on April 21st. After another bombing in May, about a hundred rockets had been fired, which Israel admitted caused no casualties. The Palestinian fighters did not respond with full-scale barrages until after Israel's massive attack on Beirut.

In spite of all this, Labour leader Peres, usually a bitter critic of Begin's policies, seemed convinced. He declared: 'We believe it is the duty of Israel to do whatever is necessary to stop these attacks upon the population and life in the northern part of Israel. It is surely a matter of self-defence. I do not believe that Israel has any territorial ambitions as far as Lebanon is concerned, nor is Israel interested, or should be interested, in any war with Syria.'

Two days later, however, Peres, accompanied by Rabin, bearded Begin in his office in Jerusalem, having undergone a change of heart. They interrupted a cabinet session to voice 'grave reservations' about Sharon's handling of the war and fears that Syria would become involved. President Reagan, for his part, remained sanguine; all he was saying, during a visit to Rome, was that he was considering whether or not the Israeli action was 'a legitimate act of self-defence.'

Meanwhile, as the Chief Rabbinate was declaring the strike into Lebanon to be a 'milhemet mitzva', a divinely sanctioned war, trouble began brewing in Jerusalem. Sixty members of the left-wing student faction 'Campus' based at the Hebrew University, demonstrated against the war outside the Prime Minister's office. Police called on the protestors to disperse, and two, one a professor of physics, Dani Amit, were arrested. Pro-Begin students attacked another demonstration on Mount Scopus, police made more arrests, and it was clear that feelings were beginning to surface similar to those voiced a month before, when troops had been used to quell West Bank Palestinians.

At the time there was a smouldering anger about these incidents among numerous Jewish mothers. Gillian Hirsh of Kibbutz Nahshon wrote to the *Jerusalem Post*: 'I came here in 1972 and was proud to be an Israeli. Today I am ashamed. How can I explain to my son that he has to serve in an army whose purpose is to prevent his cousin from proclaiming his desire for independence, and to attempt to stem the tides of history? How can I give my children pride in a nation which is following the repressive and cruel path of all conquerors? Once I thought Israel would be different.'

The West Bank shootings also provoked resentment in the army. Two reservists, Segen Heled of Tel Aviv, and Frank Gampel from Jerusalem, pleaded 'reasons of conscience' when court-martialled for refusing to serve in the occupied territories. A senior officer in their unit said that both were apprehensive about the possibility of being involved in a confrontation with Palestinian protestors, while the reservists told the court it was contrary to their beliefs to act against civilians. Both were jailed for twenty-eight days.

Thus the emerging divisions at the beginning of the war. And it was clear these were reflected in the government – for while Sharon consulted each day with his cabinet colleagues, the suspicion quickly grew that he had deliberately understated the objectives of the assault. At the same time, right up to the fourth day of the invasion Alignment members of the Knesset's Foreign Affairs and Defence Committee were demanding to be properly briefed by Begin, and noting that no prime minister in the history of the state had left it so late to talk to them during the course of a military operation.

It then emerged that the cabinet meeting on the night of June 5th – the eve of the invasion – had not fully discussed the actual aims of the war, and that this omission had prompted Deputy Premier Simcha Erlich and Energy Minister Yitzhak Berman to abstain in the vote. They explained that they could hardly support an operation with such far-reaching implications when its objectives had not been defined. Interior Minister Josef Burg, Israel's chief negotiator with Egypt, was the one man who voted against the invasion; he was later to be accused by Sharon during another cabinet meeting of getting his information from his son, an army officer who led a move calling for Sharon's dismissal.

It was not until that Wednesday, June 9th, that the entire cabinet felt that they had a grip on events and were fully in control. As one minister said: 'It took a time to realise that Arik [Sharon] was trying to manoeuvre us along his own preconceived path while keeping the real truth from us.' This internal wrangling was to last many weeks: Berman and Communications Minister Mordechai Zipori, a former deputy defence minister, had begun insisting on talking of war goals on the Tuesday, but it was not until Education Minister Zevulun Hammer added his voice to the chorus of dissent that something was done. Sharon protested: 'You are peering over my shoulder with a ruler, measuring every metre.' He was later to complain that it was sometimes harder work fighting his cabinet colleagues than confronting the Palestinians.

On the international front, Weinberger, as expected by the Israelis, was accusing Israel of acting like Argentina in the Falklands. There was talk of Haig coming to mediate. Then, when Reagan realised that Begin had lied to him about the limited objective of the operation and was moving troops to surround Beirut, he sent an urgent note to Jerusalem on June 9th. This arrived at 2 a.m., and the Americans insisted that Mr Begin be woken up to receive it. In the message, Reagan called for a ceasefire to begin at 6 a.m. A cabinet meeting was convened in Jerusalem at 4 a.m. and the idea was rejected, because the Israelis wanted to push the Syrians and the PLO further north. In the end the truce did not come into effect until the following day.

Particularly surprising to Israel was the Soviet reaction. The Kremlin observed this setback to the PLO with almost complete indifference, and the Soviet media gave it very low priority: on the third day, news from Lebanon was relegated to second place on the English language broadcasts of Radio Moscow, and events were reported without dramatisation and with no campaign of protest being launched by the Soviet propaganda machine. This was a striking departure from previous policy; before, even minor actions against the PLO would rouse the Soviet Union to make apocalyptic pronouncements about Israel and force citizens to stage mass demonstrations.

This radical change in emphasis was attributed to two factors: first, the death of Mikhail Suslov, who had always regarded the PLO as a valuable instrument of Russian expansionist policy; and second, the fact that the Palestinians were allowing huge amounts of Soviet weaponry and equipment to fall into Israeli hands, including tunnel-building tractors which had never left the Soviet Union before. Of particular interest at this time was a report passed to the Mossad intelligence service that former KGB chief Yuri Andropov, now firmly ensconced in the Kremlin hierarchy, favoured improving relations with Israel – a suggestion which Yitzak Shamir, Foreign Minister, pursued soon afterwards during a trip to New York, via Switzerland.

When Israeli forces threatened to break through in the east of Lebanon and open up an invasion route along the road to Damascus, however, Brezhnev himself stepped in to register his concern for his Syrian allies. This was relayed to Washington, and it was then that Reagan called for a ceasefire. Begin managed to defer the truce for a day by assuring the Americans that his forces would do nothing drastic or of a strategic nature, but merely mop up and improve the Israeli lines. Begin later explained that he had received two letters from Moscow via the Finnish Embassy in Tel Aviv, and stressed that his reply had been conciliatory: 'We have no interest in provoking the Soviet Union,' he said. 'We have fundamental differences between us regarding our way of life, but it (Russia) is a great power.'

The first rumblings of what was soon to become a nationwide questioning of the war's morality came on Tuesday, June 16th, when Moshe Shahal, leader of the Labour Alignment faction in the Knesset, called for legislation regularising the conduct of war by Israel. More importantly, Peace Now decided to end its silence: a statement declared that now that the scale of the death and destruction had become clear, the movement had decided to speak out.

Apart from the news stories beginning to surface about censorship, with film smuggled out of Israel being played back on TV news broadcasts from Jordan, reservists began coming home. Soldiers with jobs linked to the Israeli economy, married men and those with 'serious personal problems' were allowed early leave, and many emerged from Lebanon distressed, especially those who had fought in the battle at Ain Hilweh, the Palestinian camp outside Sidon. They spoke of 'terrible things' happening during the fighting, in particular the involvement of civilians – this at a time when Sharon was said to be discussing with senior officers, at a meeting that lasted all night, how to avoid civilian casualties. He claimed that dozens of experienced commanders took part in the talks and all agreed 'we would not bomb Tyre and Sidon and turn them into ruins.'

Many of the reservists identified themselves with Peace Now, the movement begun by young veterans of the Six-Day and Yom Kippur wars, who openly criticised Begin in March, 1978, over his settlement policy and his handling of peace negotiations with Egypt. After Camp David, the movement had remained dormant until the West Bank disturbances had begun to gather momentum. Then Peace Now staged a rally in Tel Aviv's Square of the Kings at which tens of thousands surged through the streets to join in the first major public show of opposition to Begin. The Prime Minister told his cabinet he would not be intimidated, but to counter critics, his supporters took the trouble to organise a protest on the same site. Then, paratroopers from the unit which had carried out the raid on Entebbe to free Israeli hostages in 1976, wrote to Mr Sharon demanding his resignation; again, Begin said he was disregarding the criticism because it was against the national interest.

Later, the Prime Minister was bitterly annoyed when he learnt that Uri Avneri, the left-wing Israeli politician who edited the popular magazine *Ha'elam Hazeh*, 'this world' – a blend of politics, sex and scandal – had slipped through the

Israeli lines outside Beirut to interview Yasser Arafat in his bunker. To the consternation of the foreign ministry, Avneri described Israel's implacable enemy as 'calm' and 'fatalistic', and accompanied his article with a picture of Arafat with a child on his knee, apparently enjoying the novelty of talking to an Israeli.

Foreign ministry officials had been trying desperately to improve Israel's failing image in the world and so briefing officers, who always made sure that foreign correspondents were well supplied with propaganda, seized gratefully on the most recent syndicated column by the Americans, Rowland Evans and Robert Novak. The column began: 'Israel's accusation that the PLO is a rogue elephant whose arms and swagger created resentment and fear in Lebanon's largest cities was no fabrication.' It ended: 'In the aftermath of the Israeli invasion one conclusion seems to have been drawn: the PLO is justly accused of a grave disservice to the people whose country they used and to the people they represent. To themselves the disservice is greatest of all.' That column was a tonic to the tired officers who had the unenviable task of trying to convince sceptical reporters, a majority from the United States and Britain, that the world Press were lying about the situation in Lebanon. However, one article they failed to distribute in the huge amounts of documents thrust at correspondents day in and day out, was a *Washington Post* piece published at the same time, in which another noted American columnist, Richard Cohen, wrote: 'Doesn't anyone believe Israel any more? The answer, I regret, is no . . . Maybe it was just me – naive me – but Israel was supposed to be the place where the truth was told, where idealism thrived, where things were different from other countries. Israel was founded not on some lust for gold or territory but for moral reasons.'

The Labour opposition was also beginning to stir. Yitzhak Rabin, Israel's first native-born prime minister, who had been forced to resign in 1977, began to make the political running again, outmanoeuvring his old party rival, Peres, and pointing out that the operation in Lebanon had not achieved any of its three goals – goals for which, he claimed, he would never have gone to war in the first place. He opposed, he said, any full-scale

military action aimed at bringing about a new Lebanese political order, expelling the Syrians, or wiping out the PLO. The
articulate Cambridge-educated Abba Eban, foreign minister
when Rabin was ambassador to Washington, talked of the 'art
of war being to know when to stop.' Recalling Israel's history,
he noted that Begin and his followers had opposed all attempts
to stop fighting since the War of Independence: the Herut party
had tried to keep the Sinai campaign going, and in 1970, Begin
had taken Gahal (acronym for Gush Herut Veha-Liberalim,
bloc of Herut and Liberals) out of the National Unity government after Golda Meir had agreed to end the War of Attrition.
Furthermore, in 1973, Begin had led the Likud faction in
opposing Dr Henry Kissinger's proposals for ending the Yom
Kippur fighting. 'So you see,' Eban told a journalist, 'they don't
have much experience in stopping wars.' He recalled Chur-
chill's acid comment at the end of World War Two: 'If I
listened to my generals I would have to garrison the moon to
prevent an attack from Mars.'

A problem for both Peace Now and the Labour Alignment
was that their following was drawn mainly from the Ashkenazim from Europe, Israel's intelligentsia, whereas Begin
supporters were the Sephardim of the more backward countries
of North Africa and the Middle East. These oriental Jews, a
majority of the population, originate from poor areas and are
regarded as second-class citizens in the same way as black
people in the United States. Their unflinching loyalty to Begin
was reflected in polls during the war, which showed little
support for an alternative government. A 'Pori' institute poll
commissioned by *Ha'aretz*, the leading Hebrew daily newspaper, showed that two months after the war began, the
government was riding higher than ever: 56 per cent of Israelis
canvassed favoured Begin's government, as opposed to 45 per
cent immediately before the war. The number of people feeling
that the Likud represented the Israeli public rose from 51 per
cent to 63 per cent, and 74 per cent (60 per cent in June) wanted
Begin to stay in office for the full term; 76 per cent were certain
the Likud would win the next election, 17 per cent more than
prior to the invasion. Only 8 per cent predicted a win for the
Labour Alignment.

Not once did Begin seem to waver, although there were reports that he was hopping mad at opponents referring to him as 'Arik's first prisoner of war' or as 'the prisoner of Jerusalem.' These remarks were an allusion to a phrase used by Richard Crossman to describe Dr Chaim Weizmann's relationship with David Ben-Gurion. Begin was reminded that when he had first refused Sharon the post of defence minister, taking the portfolio himself after Ezer Weizman had quit the cabinet, he had said jokingly that he did not want to wake up one morning to find his office 'surrounded by tanks'. In public, however, Begin always backed Sharon, maintaining that his colleague was 'an excellent craftsman' who had been dubbed 'melech Yisrael,' king of Israel after he had led the crossing of the Suez Canal in 1973.

Following reports in July that the pair had crossed swords in the cabinet, Begin issued a categorical denial declaring that they had 'no basis whatsoever.' Rumours of a rift had begun to circulate after Shimon Shiffer, an Israeli radio correspondent, had announced details of the American plan to send Marines to Beirut. Israel had deliberately leaked the news, to the considerable annoyance of Reagan, who was in bed at his Santa Barbara ranch and had yet to sound out key members of Congress over the plan, for America was nervous about being sucked into another Vietnam. The blame for the leak fell on Sharon, who was said to have given the go-ahead for the broadcast, hoping to scotch the Washington initiative. Begin, according to a cabinet source, wanted a 'pax Americana' in Lebanon, and scolded Sharon, who was fiercely against involving the United States, for trying to torpedo the negotiations.

Begin was surprisingly restrained, considering the furore created in Washington, where the State Department must have begun to wonder if it was possible to keep anything secret in Israel. Yet the Prime Minister was clearly worried, as his recent trip to Washington had soon shown him that Americans were already wildly hostile towards Israel over the campaign in Lebanon. While Reagan refused to rebuke Begin, the Senate Foreign Relations Committee had had no such qualms. The Prime Minister's ninety-minute meeting on Capitol Hill was a catastrophe: Paul Tsongas, the Massachusetts Democrat said that in eight years he had never experienced such an angry session with a visiting head of state. Begin had got off on the wrong foot by adopting the 'lecturing' posture which had always so infuriated President Carter. Senators had considered him arrogant, and things went from bad to worse when an old friend of Israel, Joseph Biden, another Democrat, had forcefully complained about Begin's settlement policy, and had disputed Begin's insistence that support for Israel was never higher. This had touched a sensitive nerve in the Prime Minister, who had been hoping that pro-Israeli Congressional leaders would help him through the storm. Many of the thirty-six senators present had remarked on his condescending tone.

On his return to Jerusalem, Begin was reassured by a series of newspaper advertisements headed 'the voice of the silent majority.' Hundreds of housewives, technicians, secretaries, lawyers and clerks signed statements of support, urging the Prime Minister to be 'strong and of good courage.' They declared: 'Zahal [*the military*] will uproot the terrorist organisations from Lebanon that we may enjoy a secure future and for the sake of peace with our northern neighbour.' Buoyed by this support, an impassioned Begin delivered one of his characteristically rousing orations to the Knesset. He was at his demagogic best: he told a packed house that the world had been flooded with the 'abominations of falsehood.' He went on: 'Germans – destroyers, and the children of destroyers – are saying that the renewed Jewish army is perpetrating Nazi acts. Other nations talk of genocide and slaughter.' Quoting Thomas Carlisle, he said: 'A lie cannot last for long.' And the PLO he described as: 'An organisation that profanes the word liberation. There has not been one more contemptible than it from the time of the Nazis to this very day.' Cataloguing the nationalities of enemy guerrillas now in Israeli hands, Begin claimed they included 380 Bangladeshis and 23 Sri Lankans. 'What do the Bangladesh people have against us? What do the Sri Lankans want from us? We drink their tea. Why did they come to kill Jews?'

Even when Eli Geva, an admired combat colonel, who at thirty-two was the youngest tank brigade commander in Israel's history, refused to take part in any assault on West Beirut, Begin remained unperturbed. He summoned the colonel to his office in Jerusalem, and during a heated forty-five minute session, Geva spoke of his anguish as he had watched Beirut from a hilltop through binoculars and seen children on the streets. The Prime Minister asked him: 'Did you receive an order to kill children?' Colonel Geva shook his head. Mr Begin retorted angrily, according to the government version: 'Then what are you complaining about?'

Geva's protest created a sensation in the country, especially when it became clear that his words had fallen on deaf ears. He was a son of a founder of the Israeli army; his men talked of his heroism during the capture of Tyre and the Rashadiyeh refugee camp; he had even asked to be allowed to stay on to help with evacuating casualties. The normally taciturn Israeli army chief, General Rafael Eytan, went so far as to call him 'one of my most distinguished officers in the war'; but under pressure from Begin, he sacked the man.

Begin and Sharon seemed impervious to criticism. It emerged that another group, Soldiers against Silence, included the son of Dr Josef Burg, head of the National Religious Party and Begin's longest-serving cabinet colleague. Avraham Burg, a twenty-seven-year-old student of industrial design at the Bezalel Academy of Art, was a reserve lieutenant in a paratroop unit fighting the Syrians on the eastern front. 'My father and I share the same points of departure and the same aims,' he said. 'We differ over the ways of achieving them. And I cannot get out of my mind's eye the image of children with their hands held high in surrender because they were scared of me.' At a cabinet session, Sharon came under fire from Dr Burg for failing to consult colleagues on crucial military moves in Lebanon. Sharon was irked that Burg's son had gone as far as visiting Begin in order to present him with a petition signed by almost two thousand men from élite army units demanding that the Defence Minister be sacked. Avraham Burg was a graduate of a high school Yeshiva, an ultra-orthodox religious college, and groups of religious soldiers like himself took heavy casualties during the war: of the 369 Israeli dead, about 40 were from the Yeshivot Hesder, where religious soldiers study the Torah.

CHAPTER ELEVEN

Although the people of Beirut could hardly believe it, the savage pounding they received on August 12th, 1982, really was the last of the war. Gingerly at first, then with growing confidence, everyone began to pick up the pieces, getting things repaired, calling on old acquaintances in places further afield than they would have dared to go before. People still cautiously felt their way, still fearful, still expecting the worst. This time, however, things improved.

Up and down Hamra the pavements were jammed with suitcases as enterprising merchants brought out their stocks for the Palestinian fighters who crowded around. So they really were going, and the multi-national force was coming in. Suddenly, the Lebanese were certain the long ordeal was finished and turned their attention to the next crisis; everywhere, the one topic of conversation was the presidential elections.

The only candidate was Bachir Gemayel, who had pre-empted everyone else by formally nominating himself at a carefully stage-managed Saturday-evening rally in Achrafiyeh, which had been broadcast live on 'The Voice of Lebanon'. With Bachir in the field, no-one else dared to put his name forward, though at one time Camille Chamoun seemed to be ready to stand. Chamoun was a man who would be acceptable to the Moslems in a way Bachir never could be, for Bachir was disliked and feared in equal amounts, and the Moslems of the country held meeting after meeting to try to find a way of stopping him. At one stage Mr Michel Khoury, the governor of the Central Bank, was suggested as a compromise choice, but he firmly refused to run, so the Moslem politicians concentrated instead on preventing a quorum being assembled. Under the Lebanese system, the president was elected by the Chamber of Deputies, which had originally had 99 members. Now, with elections postponed so often, the number of deputies had been reduced by death to 92. In order to be elected, a presidential candidate had to secure two-thirds of the votes on the first ballot, or a simple majority on the second, and for the poll to take place at all, there had to be a quorum of two-thirds of the surviving members of the chamber. The only thing the Moslems could do was to try to persuade enough people to stay away, so that less than the requisite 62 would be there, and the vote could be postponed, giving more time for some compromise to be worked out. Bachir Gemayel, however, was having none of it: very firmly, he let it be known that he expected the election to go ahead as planned, and on time.

While the Lebanese were concerned with their own affairs, the Palestinians were busily preparing to pull out and engaging in last-minute bargaining over the deployment of the multinational force and the eventual destination of the guerrillas. Hamra, meanwhile, was crowded with shoppers as each day more and more goods came in – it was a big occasion when truck-loads of eggs, surely the most difficult commodity of all to smuggle in during a siege, suddenly appeared on the streets again. Vegetables were plentiful for the first time in weeks; the price of petrol dropped overnight, and after one hold-up, the Israelis allowed a tanker of fuel oil for the American University Hospital to cross into West Beirut. Philip Habib returned to Baabda from Israel; David Kimche, the director of the ministry of foreign affairs in Jerusalem was in Beirut, ready to settle last-minute points of detail; the stage was set.

The only hiccup seemed to be the negotiations for the release of the Israeli pilot, Aharaon Ahigaz. The Palestinians were quite ready to let him go, but naturally they sought to get what they could in return. The Israelis, in public, adamantly refused to offer any deal at all; in private, they said they would release some hundreds of detainees from Ansar, so long as the two events were not openly linked. The PLO had no choice but to agree to this and to abandon all hope of getting out Okamoto, the Red Army man whom George Habash of the Popular Front had been pressing the Israelis to release. Okamoto had been hired by the Popular Front, and Habash felt he might need to employ such people again: naturally they would be more ready to work for him in future if they saw that his organisation did all it could for people who had fallen into Israeli hands.

Israel in turn added to its demands; the bodies of nine Israeli soldiers also had to be found and returned by the Palestinians – four who had been killed in the Litani Operation four years earlier, and five during the 1982 invasion. General Sharon himself put in this request, an admission on his part of the severity of the fighting when his men had tried to move into West Beirut: the five bodies had lain for a full day at the Museum crossing point, and all efforts by the Israelis to recover them had failed because of the intensity of the Palestinian fire – even grappling hooks had been thrown, but they had failed to catch onto the uniforms of the dead soldiers. At night, the Palestinians had braved the Israeli fire to bring the bodies to their side of the line, knowing that Israel would want them back, and hoping to be able to use the dead, as well as the living, to secure the release of some of their men.

One week after the last Israeli air raids on Beirut, everything was tied up: the Lebanese government formally issued a request for the multi-national force to be deployed, the Israeli cabinet approved the schedule for the evacuation of the PLO and the Syrians from Beirut, and the International Red Cross successfully arranged for the captured pilot and the bodies of the nine Israelis to be returned.

At this point, the way seemed clear for the Lebanese to put their own house in order. But bitter divisions remained. At a meeting of Moslem leaders in Mr Salam's palace at Mousseit-beh, a formal decision was taken to boycott the presidential election. In the event this proved unnecessary, for others took more direct action to ensure that the election was postponed: a couple of shells were lobbed into the area around the Villa Mansour, the house near the Green Line which had been chosen as a makeshift parliament, the original parliament building in the Place d'Etoile being too badly damaged and in too sensitive an area to be used. Kamal Assad, the Shia Moslem house speaker who was popularly believed to have received some LL3 million as a reward for calling the assembly into session, announced that the election would be postponed: it would be held the following week at the Military Academy at Fayadiyeh, just off the Beirut-Damascus road in firmly

Christian territory. Café gossip this time was that the postpone-
ment and Mr Assad's announcement had earned the Speaker
another LL2 million.

Speculation about the election had now taken over from the
Israeli invasion as the main topic of interest for the Lebanese,
and many a joke was told and previous occasions recalled: how
Elias Sarkis had been brought to power by Syrian guns; how
Gemayel was going to be given the job under Israeli guns, while
Franjieh, people said, had secured the post with his own guns:
during Franjieh's election in 1970, he and his supporters in
parliament had reached for their pistols when the house
speaker of the time, Sabri Hamadeh – who was also a leading
hashish dealer – had decided that 50 votes did not constitute a
simple majority of the 99 members present.

For all the jokes and ribaldry, the Lebanese realised very well
that a serious issue was at stake here. Under the National
Covenant, the founding fathers had arranged matters so that
everything was divided between the Christians and Moslems,
with the Christians having an absolute right to the presidency.
However, they had to have the support of some Moslem
deputies for their candidate if he was to be duly elected. This
time, the Moslems, with very few exceptions, were united in
their opposition to Gemayel, the Christian candidate: yet
because of the deaths of so many deputies and the defection
from the Moslem camp of Emir Majid Arslan and his supporters, the Christians might just be able to secure the necessary
votes, and in effect force their man on the country.

Sunni and Shia politicians alike, as well as the religious
leaders of the communities, all objected to what was being
done; but they were even more concerned about the physical
consequences which might follow. In particular, they feared
that as soon as Bachir Gemayel was elected, he would seek to
demonstrate his strength by sending the Lebanese Army into
West Beirut, backed up by the Phalange militia. Any such
move, they knew, would lead to a bloodbath. The Moslems
were given some encouragement when the Saudi Arabian
ambassador, General Ali al Shaer, was sent back to Beirut after
being away from his post for months. This was taken as a sign of
support by the Sunni Moslems in particular. But in the event,

General Shaer was able to do little, and events overtook all his efforts.

While the politicking continued, there were still those who resorted to violence to decide matters. A car loaded with explosives was found outside the Palestine Research Centre on Rue Sadat, and when the PLO bomb-disposal expert could not be found, militiamen exploded it by firing an RPG into it. As they did so, another car bomb went off a few yards away. Soon came evidence that revealed who was behind these attempts: the next day, a blue Volvo turned into the car park of the ministry of information building in Hamra, driven by a pretty young girl who showed a government identification card, and said she was going to call on the secretary of the minister, whom she named. The Syrian guard allowed her in, then became suspicious when he saw the girl emerge again a moment later. The soldier ran up to ask the minister's secretary if she had just had a brief visit from a friend. The answer was no, and neither was she expecting one. The guard hurried downstairs again, shouted quick orders to others there, and with a comrade, drove the girl's car the few yards to the big empty car park behind the Central Bank on the other side of Hamra. Meanwhile, others found the girl half a mile away, buying shoes in a store. A bomb-disposal man was sent for, and inside the girl's car he found some 250 kilos of explosive, all neatly wrapped in canvas packs bearing Hebrew markings. The girl herself was identified as Mona Zohbi, though the name on her government ID card, which was plainly a forgery, was Nayla Negib Sarraf. She was a member of the Phalangist Party and a drug addict, acccording to those who questioned her. She has not been heard of since.

With French, Italian and American troops all on their way to Lebanon, there occurred a final snag which might have caused the whole delicate structure constructed by Philip Habib to collapse. A young Israeli soldier took the wrong turning when he left a forward Israeli observation post in Bourj Brajneh, and walked unconcernedly into the nearest Palestinian position. He was immediately 'arrested' and taken off to the same building in Sabra in which the captured Israeli pilot had been kept. Next day, only twelve hours before the evacuation of the PLO was due to begin, both were handed over to the International Red Cross.

Reporters crowded around outside the PLO information office in Fakhani as Avigaz and the soldier, Roni Haoush, were brought out by Abu Zaim, the Palestinian chief of intelligence. After almost three months with the Palestinians, Avigaz looked relaxed and fit as he joked in Hebrew with the Palestinian gaoler who had guarded him all through his captivity; Haoush, however, was plainly apprehensive after only two days in Palestinian hands. Abu Zaim made a speech which obviously bored the Israeli pilot as much as it did most of those standing about, then the two men were whisked away, to be brought back a little later and put in the care of John de Salis, the ICRC man, who then took them across to East Beirut and handed them back to their Israeli friends. They were flown by helicopter to Israel, where Avigaz said exactly as much and as little as he had said in Beirut; merely that he had been well treated and was glad to be free. The bodies of the nine dead Israelis were also loaded onto trucks for transport home, and with little ceremony, the way was cleared for the final evacuation of the PLO. Chafic Wazzan announced that he had received written guarantees that America would campaign for the release of Lebanese and Palestinian prisoners held by the Israelis, and also a promise that the Americans would see that the evacuation was fully implemented. Neither assurance amounted to much, but they helped the Palestinians to clothe their nakedness and showed that they were salvaging all they could from their military defeat.

And so at last, in the early hours of the morning of Saturday, August 21st, peace-keeping forces reached Beirut to supervise the departure of the Palestinians. First to arrive were the French; 350 men of the Second Foreign Parachute Regiment of the Legion, crop-headed, sunburned, rather short, tough men of half a dozen different nationalities, successors of the troops who had been dropped into Dien Bien Phu. The remarkably detailed plan worked out by Habib called for the French to arrive at 04.00 and to be deployed immediately in the inner port area of Beirut harbour, which should by then have been evacuated by the Israelis and occupied by the Lebanese Army.

When the French arrived, nothing of the sort had been done:
the Israelis were still there, the PLO men were at their positions
only a hundred yards away, and there was no sign of the
Lebanese Army. At first, the French commanders refused to get
off the ship and military attachés from the French embassy
tried to sort it all out; eventually, the Israelis, smiling sardoni-
cally, politely showed the French the positions they were to
occupy before taking themselves off to the eastern side of the
port, which was still in Israeli hands – from early in the
morning, General Sharon had taken up his position in a tall
building there, watching all that was going on through binoculars.

After an hour or two, some sort of order began to emerge, and
the French moved forward to take over posts held by the
Palestinians. The men at the front in this sector were all from
the PLA, so as each defensive position was abandoned by the
Palestinians and occupied by the French, there was a brief
ceremony in which French and Palestinians formed up in two
lines opposite each other, the French non-com in charge rattled
off to his officer the strength and name of his unit, and the officer
saluted, turned, and saluted his Palestinian opposite number.
The Palestinians had an even more elaborate drill: the men
stood at ease, came to attention, and presented arms a few
times; then they chanted slogans about returning to Palestine,
before finally doubling off, to be seen moments later casually
removing helmets and guns and searching for tea.

By mid-morning, the French had secured the whole western
side of the port area, and a small sector previously occupied by
Israel on the east; meanwhile, in West Beirut the first contingent of Palestinians had gathered in the dawn half-light in the
stadium close to the Arab University, among the devastated
wreckage of one of the worst-hit areas of the whole city. No-one
was left in the apartment blocks to watch them prepare to leave,
but from all over the Palestinian districts, families gathered to
see their men off. The fighters themselves were from the Bad'r
Brigade of the PLA, which had come to Lebanon from Jordan
and was returning there; they were joined by units of the
Iraqi-controlled Arab Liberation Front and some Fateh men
with Jordanian passports.

As everyone milled about, women sang patriotic songs, leaders bellowed speeches through loudhailers to boost the morale of the men who were going, and the men themselves kissed and hugged their children – children they were leaving behind and thought they might not see again for months. Many who lived in Sabra and Chatila were never to be seen again. Wives and mothers keened and ululated as the confused and emotional leave-taking went on, then eventually everything was ready, and the fighters climbed aboard the PLA and Lebanese Army trucks which were to ferry them down to the docks. As they moved out of the stadium there began a deafening cacophony of gun fire which was to go on for days: Palestinians and Lebanese alike emptied clip after clip into the air as the convoy moved slowly through the devastated streets of Beirut, the traditional farewell of departing heroes, a sign of both rejoicing and of mourning.

It was certainly both on this occasion: the people of Beirut, the Lebanese who had endured so much so long, were very glad to see the Palestinians leaving at last; the Palestinians, those going and those staying, knew they had put up a valiant fight and had created the legend their leaders had wanted. They knew too, just as the politicians did, that it was the end of an era. After 76 days of combat, the time of organised armed struggle was over. Seventeen years after Fateh had launched its first operation into occupied Palestine, and 12 years after the PLO had moved its headquarters to Lebanon, the Palestinians were being dispersed around the Arab world, unwelcome guests accepted only on sufferance and as a result of emollient applications of Saudi money and American diplomacy.

None of this was allowed to show as the first contingent of troops left. All of them had been carefully chosen, not only according to their destinations, but for their appearance too: these were young, smart, fit and tough-looking, not a defeated army but a detachment of troops in good heart. As the first convoy made its snail-like way to the docks, the small arms fire was punctuated with the sound of grenades being flung into the sea, RPGs fired into the air, and heavy mortars being let off. This demonstration was intended not only to be a celebration, but also to show that there was no shortage of ammunition

among the Palestinian fighters, and that they could have kept
up the fight if they had been required to do so. At the head of the
procession walked some of those who were to stay behind,
leading the slogan-shouting, orchestrating the celebration; in
the lead was the sector commander of the Hamra area, wearing
a sports shirt with the words 'Palestine is my country' em-
blazoned on it. Pictures of Arafat and Palestine flags were
hoisted aloft every time a camera appeared: this was a propaganda exercise as much as anything else, and nothing had
been left to chance.

Eventually, the troops arrived at the port and boarded the
Cypriot ferry *Sol Georghios* for the short trip to Larnaca. At 2.15
in the afternoon the vessel pulled out, and the days of the
Palestine Resistance Movement as an organised fighting force
were at an end. In the streets of West Beirut now it was the men
of the Mourabitoun and Amal who were in charge, as the
Palestinians concentrated on preparations for departure. For a
while the Joint Forces Police, composed of some of the best men
from both the Palestinian and Lebanese militia movements,
continued to maintain security and to carry out general police
duties, but gradually they too were withdrawn from the streets.
This force, identified only by a yellow brassard on the arm, had
been responsible for 'conventional' policing in West Beirut
throughout the siege, and were polite and efficient. At the
forward Palestinian positions at the crossing points, they were
scrupulous in searching cars, but always explained why, and
apologised for the need to check all vehicles. When they
stopped the few cars moving late at night, again they recognised
all the different passes issued by the various groups, but were no
less thorough, tapping doors and wings of vehicles to make sure
that no explosives had been packed inside. They invariably
went out of their way to be polite to foreigners, and often
paradoxically, Arabs with whom one was travelling had to be
persuaded to keep quiet and to allow their Western friends to
negotiate the road blocks: it was always quicker that way.

The first group of Palestinians to leave Beirut disembarked in
Larnaca that day, again with flags flying and heads held high
for the benefit of the television cameras. There, they boarded
planes to take them on to Jordan and Iraq, the majority of

them, some 265, arriving at a Jordanian air base near Mafraq. There, King Hussein himself welcomed them, surrounded by most of the top figures of the Jordan government, a discreetly hidden force of Bedouin troops and a specially invited posse of cameramen and reporters; the ordinary people of Jordan were notably absent. The King greeted each Palestinian personally, and on Jordan television one PLO officer was clearly heard to remark as his men lined up: 'Please brothers, just one kiss and keep moving.'

Jordan's welcome to the Palestinians made a remarkable public spectacle which was intended to expunge the memory of 1970, demonstrate the King's confidence and strength, and underline his quiet, undeclared claim to be the only one willing and able to act for the Palestinians and to be their champion in international negotiations. It was a risk for Hussein: he had agreed to take a total of 2,000 fighters, a considerable number in a country where at least 65 per cent of the 2.3 million inhabitants are Palestinians, and where the 750,000 people of the West Bank still in theory form part of Hussein's kingdom.

Hussein, however, was now a more mature and experienced man than the vacillating figure who in 1970 had eventually been forced into allowing his army commanders to do what they had wanted to do for so long. He was now confident that his Bedouin Army could see that his orders were obeyed, and regarded the arrival of the fighters as strengthening his hand, rather than posing any threat. Nevertheless, the Palestinians were put in carefully controlled camps well away from population centres and in close proximity to all-Bedouin Jordanian forces. There were also forceful words for General Abdul Razzak al Yahya, the PLA commander in Jordan, when he announced that the Palestinians would launch new raids into Israel from Jordan, and described Jordan as no more than 'the bridge to the West Bank.' General Yahya was summoned by the army commander, General Zeid bin Shaker, and told discreetly but firmly that he was under the orders of the Jordanian Army command, that nothing would be done without the sanction of that command and that serving soldiers should not make political statements. General Shaker, a close

relation of the King, made it plain that he expected his orders to
be followed, and from then on General Yahya stayed remarkably silent.

As the evacuation of the Palestinians from Beirut went ahead
over the next ten days, problems did emerge. The Israelis
carefully noted every group leaving and were quick to seize on
any suspected violations of the agreement. The entire operation
had to be stopped for a while when Israel complained about a
number of jeeps which had been loaded on one ship: the jeeps,
they claimed were carrying armaments and capable of being
adapted as fighting vehicles. In Cyprus, UN men examined
them and found that the boxes the Israelis said held weapons in
fact contained nothing more lethal than old typewriters and
papers: the jeeps were intended for use by the PLO bureaucracy which was to be established in Tunis. Nevertheless,
Cypriot Customs impounded them as a way out of the dilem-
ma, and the men on board ship were allowed to go on to
Tunisia.

The Israelis also complained that a number of women and
children dressed as fighters were leaving Beirut with the guerrillas. This was certainly true – Mahmoud Labadi's American
wife was one who went to Tunis by sea – but the Palestinians
could see nothing wrong in this, and privately, nor could the
Americans or any others involved. For some reason, instead of
being glad to see the Palestinians go, the Israelis seemed bent
on causing troubles and difficulties right up to the end. There
had even been argument over the military designation of the
days leading up to the departure of the Palestinians: the Americans and officers of the multi-national force described the first
Saturday as D-day, for departure day. The Israelis objected on
the grounds that D-day had heroic Second World War overtones; they wanted 'E' for expulsion, or at least evacuation.
When Sharon met Mr Habib during the Palestinians' departure, he asked the American: 'How is the expulsion going?'
Habib replied: 'The evacuation is proceeding according to
plan.'

Israeli intelligence officers who watched each contingent of
Palestinians boarding the ships in Beirut harbour were several
times joined by attachés from the Western embassies which

were now established in East Beirut. Using high-powered glasses, they tried to scrutinise each man as he walked up the gangway, and frequently referred to photographs they had with them. It was no use: too many of the Palestinians kept their keffiyahs over their faces and disappeared into cabins as soon as they were aboard. The anonymous 'attachés' watching were sure that the international terrorist 'Carlos', Ilyich Ramirez, had been trapped in Beirut during the siege and had got out in this way; others, too, were thought to have left disguised as Palestinians.

The most serious threat to the evacuation came when fighting broke out near the Beirut-Damascus highway, the route which had to be taken by the majority of the Palestinians and Syrians leaving the city. The Israelis said they were not involved, and blamed Phalangist militiamen and Syrians; others said it was Druze and Christians who were responsible. Whoever it was, the incident held up the departure of the men travelling overland by a full day. Then, when the departure by road did finally begin, over-keen Israelis almost wrecked it: they objected to the rather perfunctory way in which the Italian troops of the peace-keeping force were counting the men and the truck-loads of Palestinians, and delayed the convoy for half an hour before allowing it to go on.

As the Palestinians arrived at the Syrian border, there were scenes as wild as any that had taken place in Beirut. As before weapons were fired into the air, this time with the Palestinians in the trucks loosing off their clips, perhaps in a subconscious demonstration to their Syrian brothers that they had no intention of doing anything to annoy them, and so had no further need of any ammunition. As it turned out, the Palestinians were to be given very little opportunity to cause trouble: after their tumultuous welcome on the border, and similar scenes for those who had arrived by ship in Tartous, they were packed onto buses and taken off to Dumayr, a bleak camp some forty-five miles north of Damascus. Next to it was a Syrian Air Force base, and when the Palestinians arrived at their new home, they noted that it was rather more heavily populated than usual – and also that the watchtowers around the perimeter, which overlooked their accommodation, were all fully manned. It

seemed there was not all that much difference between Dumayr
and Ansar.

Yasser Arafat himself stayed on in Beirut for a week after the
evacuation began, formally taking leave of the Lebanese politicians who had negotiated on his behalf for so long, and less
formally of the dozens of supporters in the background who
were often the ones with the biggest influence on PLO policy –
the Palestinians who had integrated into Lebanese society, the
rich, well-travelled and well-connected, whose worldly experience, expertise, and influence were a considerable factor in all
PLO calculations. In the end Arafat went by sea to Greece,
after an emotional send-off at the dock-side: 'I am leaving this
city, but my heart will always be in Beirut,' the chairman of the
PLO said as he stepped aboard the Cypriot ship. On arrival in
Athens, he was welcomed personally by the Greek Prime
Minister, Mr Andreas Papandreou, whose left-wing government had been one of the main supporters of the PLO in
European councils.

In the end, more than 9,000 Palestinians left Beirut, as well
as 3,500 Syrian soldiers, who returned home with heavy guns,
some tanks on transporters and various other equipment, thus
showing that they too had no shortage of armaments. The
Palestinians were supposed to hand their heavy weapons over
to the Lebanese Army; in fact, as they had always intended,
they allowed Amal and the Mourabitoun to take what they
wanted. The PLO would have had difficulty in surrendering
weapons to the Lebanese Army in any case, since Lebanese
forces were still not in West Beirut. As it was, the Moslem
militias had the pick of the Palestinian arsenal, and were only
inhibited in their selection by the shortage of men able to
handle the weapons.

The few Palestinian fighters who did stay behind had more
use for silenced pistols and grenades than for long-range guns.
They meant to carry on a secret war while their comrades were
dispersed throughout the Arab world, for the manner of the
Palestinian withdrawal made it unlikely, if not impossible, for
them ever to regroup and form a new conventional fighting
force. The Palestinians went to Syria, Tunisia, Jordan, Iraq,
South Yemen, and North Yemen, with the wounded being

taken to Cyprus, Greece, Syria and Egypt. The Egyptians stuck to their decision not to accept any Palestinians except in the context of an overall settlement of the whole Middle East crisis, and so took only a few of the most seriously injured for treatment. They also paid the tolls for the five ships which took the guerrillas through the Suez Canal to Jordan and the two Yemens.

Arafat was the only Palestinian leader not to go to Damascus – a careful decision on his part, but one which infuriated President Assad. George Habash, Nayef Hawatmeh, Ahmed Jabril, Abou Iyyad and Abou Jihad all went by sea to Tartous or Latakia, and then on to Damascus; Arafat adamantly refused to do so. With Hani Hassan, his personal bodyguards, and about a thousand picked men of Fateh, he sailed for Greece, and after a day there went on to Tunis, to be greeted by President Habib Bourguiba and formally to proclaim Tunis the new headquarters of the PLO.

In fact, the Tunisians, like the Syrians, took no chances: they set up a special camp for the Palestinian guerrillas at Beja, sixty miles from Tunis, and requisitioned the Salwa Hotel at Bourj Cedria, sixteen miles from the capital, for Arafat and his entourage. This luxury hotel with its swimming pool, bars and all the rest was a considerable change for Arafat and his men, who had always been used to the rough conditions dictated by security needs in Beirut, and who during the siege had sometimes slept on floors and often in cellars and basements. The Tunisians had also reached a quiet understanding with the French: in the event of any serious trouble with their Palestinian guests, the Tunisians would appeal to France, which guaranteed the dispatch of combat units at twenty-four hours' notice.

As the evacuation went on, the blockade of Beirut came to an end, and the same Israeli Army engineers who had plunged the city into darkness now returned to the electricity station and switched the power back on again. The water had been restored a fortnight earlier, to come gushing out of shattered mains all over the city. Now new traffic jams formed at the crossing points into West Beirut, as thousands returned to see if their homes were still intact, or to try to repair apartments already known to be damaged. Food was allowed in again, and fuel for the generators, for although the electricity was now restored, there were hundreds of cables to be repaired, and even then, electricity had to be rationed because of the chronic shortage in the country.

For most people left in Beirut, there was a feeling of new beginnings in the air. Everyone in the western sector of the city was determined to pick themselves up and try to get back to normal, while in the east, the mood was one of delight that at long last the hated and feared 'foreigners', the Palestinians, had been forced to quit. The Palestinian civilians and dependants, the old men, the women and children, drifted back into the camps they had been forced to leave, trying to find places to live among all the rubble, and to work out how to exist now that the protection and support of the PLO had been removed. The various relief organisations did what they could, but it was an uphill task, and for weeks people were still hungry and sleeping in deplorable conditions. Now, the Palestinian families who stayed behind were forced to see the reality behind all the bluster and show: this was no victory, but a bitter defeat, it was the end of a long period in which the PLO had been a state to match the Phalangist state, a time when the only authority they recognised was Palestinian authority. Now they had to depend for protection on Lebanese militias, and they had to take their orders from Lebanese. It was an unhappy experience.

Others at the opposite end of the social scale noticed the departure of the Palestinians too: the Central Bank, and the 83 commercial banks which had made Beirut their headquarters, all felt the effects. The main bank used by the PLO was the Arab Bank, and in the two weeks before the departure of the Palestinians, it had moved some 800 million dollars to various countries, though most to Tunis to act as the central reserve of the PLO in its new headquarters. The PLO was one of the richest of 'liberation' organisations, funded not only by special donations from the rich Arab oil states, but also by set taxes in Kuwait and various other countries, so as to provide a regular, assured income.

During its twelve years in Beirut, the PLO had bought hotels and apartment blocks, set up factories, and taken interests in various other enterprises. Some were designed to be used as front organisations to conceal the supply of special commodities the organisation needed – printing equipment, advanced electronic gear, explosives, radio and all the rest, while the Red Crescent had departments to import drugs and medical supplies. These businesses, which had often been started solely to service the needs of the PLO, had often expanded into profit-making companies in their own right, adding to the considerable revenues amassed. Factories and home industries had been established to provide work for the dependants of those killed in action, or for the old or the sick who could not find a place in the overcrowded Lebanese economy. These, too, often turned into profit-making operations.

The removal of the PLO reserves from Beirut was noticed, but hardly caused a tremor in the remarkably buoyant Lebanese economy. Throughout the siege and the blockade, the lira never lost its value: it was traded every day not only in Beirut, but also in the world's leading money markets, notably in Switzerland. The Lebanese Central Bank, under Michel Khoury, continued to act as usual in spite of the conditions, intervened in the markets when necessary, and saw to it that the lira never fell too far or rose too much. Even with only 40 of their regular 500 staff working at the Bank on Hamra in West Beirut, still the Governor and his administrators managed to keep everything under control; the Bank's computer, served by special generators, was able to operate even when shells hit the building and killed and wounded employees.

The only real fear was that someone might wish to take over the Bank: then, for all its impressive appearance, not much could have been done about it. A senior security man there said that by his reckoning, the collection of lethargic Lebanese security men on duty, the Bank's own guards, and the electronic alarm system and steel doors, might delay an attacking force for thirty minutes. What he did not say was that the gold and foreign currency reserves which were the main causes of the stability of the lira, were of course far away. Apart from the risk of people trying to break in, the only other worry the Bank had was an Israeli demand for identification of certain people in the south of the country who received regular payments from

particular political parties: Bank officials indignantly and categorically refused to give this information: the Lebanese banking
system was more secret than the Swiss, they said, and they had
no intention of allowing a temporary phenomenon like an
Israeli invasion to breach their confidentiality and thus damage
the system.

For a country importing 85 per cent of all its needs, including
oil, Lebanon had a remarkably healthy economy, regularly
showing a balance of payments surplus because of the huge
remittances sent home by the three million Lebanese abroad,
and through invisible earnings. To the canny Lebanese
businessmen, the real long-term Israeli threat was not the
physical danger posed by their soldiers, but what they saw as an
Israeli attempt to annexe the Lebanese market, and to link their
currency, with its vast inflation rates, to the relatively stable
Lebanese lira.

It was considerations like these which exercised the
Lebanese as they picked up the pieces after the last Palestinians
left and the French, Italians and Americans prepared to follow.
Only a few of the more wary Moslem politicians were still
fearful of what might happen; for most people, it was the
beginning of a new era, not still part of the end of the old.

CHAPTER TWELVE

The election of Bachir Gemayel was a foregone conclusion, provided enough Deputies could be found to attend the adjourned session of parliament at the Fayadiyeh Military Academy. The question was, how to persuade them to go there – or, in the case of the Moslems, how to get them to stay away. At a meeting of all the Moslem leaders at Saeb Salam's house, tactics were worked out, and each of the politicians present was asked to visit all the friends he had among the members of the assembly, and to explain to them why they should not vote. It was not a question of boycotting parliament, argued Salam and the others; merely of forcing a delay in which a compromise in keeping with the National Covenant could be worked out. If anyone was guilty of embargoes and the like, it was Sheikh Bachir and his supporters, they said, since he had effectively prevented anyone else from standing by his early declaration of his own candidature. All other possible presidential candidates were too frightened to run against Gemayel, who would have 'physically eliminated' anyone who dared to do so.

On the Christian side, the arguments were quite different. In their view, Bachir Gemayel filled all the qualifications needed for the presidency of the republic, and in addition, he was young, strong and dynamic – just the man the country needed at such a critical time. The Moslems were the ones who were flouting the National Covenant by their decision to stay away from the electoral meeting of parliament.

Then, in the Lebanese way, the affair began to move from arguments to action, and the first thing to happen was that the telephone cable linking the eastern and western sectors of the city was cut. The Phalangists blamed the PLO for doing it, and the Moslems blamed the Phalangists. Certainly it seemed to benefit the Phalangists more, by preventing consultations between the Moslem Deputies in the west and the Christians in

the east, and it was difficult to see any advantage the Palestinians might have derived.

Soon, events took a more serious turn. Mr Hussein al
Husseini, a Shia, was said to have been threatened with murder
when he was stopped at a Phalangist checkpoint, though he
immediately denied this. Later, there was further drama, when
another Deputy, Mr Hassan Rifai, a Sunni Moslem representative from the Baalbek district, was shot in the chest and leg by
gunmen who called at his home. From his hospital bed in
Damascus, where he was taken by a Syrian military helicopter,
he roundly accused the Phalangists of being the authors of the
attempt on his life. Mr Rifai said that the men who had called
on him had asked if he intended to attend the parliamentary
session: he had said no, whereupon the men said that he should,
then drew their pistols and shot him – a very Lebanese form of
political canvassing.

Mr Raymond Edde, the Deputy for Jbail and absentee leader
of a moderate parliamentary bloc, said that Deputies living in
the east had told him they were subject to 'menaces and
constraints'. Speaking from the haven of his self-imposed exile
in Paris, Mr Edde urged the British and French parliamentary
delegations which had been invited to witness the elections to
meet the Deputies and find out what was going on; they never
did so. Another Deputy, Mr Najah Wakim, claimed that 'millions of dollars' had been accepted by certain members of
parliament to persuade them to attend the session; he men-
tioned in particular the speaker, Mr Assad, the Druze leader,
Majid Arslan, and certain Deputies from the south of the
country.

The Emir Majid himself was determined to attend parliament, and declared himself firmly for Sheikh Bachir, who he
said was 'brave, ambitious, and from a good family.' Arslan's
rival, Walid Jumblatt, took a very different view: 'If Bachir
were elected, he would turn Lebanon into one big prison for the
leftist progressives, and might try to liquidate them physically.
His election would mean the abolition of freedom of the Press
and political liberties, and there would be an attempt to impose
a one party system.' This was good electioneering rhetoric, but
what mattered was the numbers.

On Monday, August 23rd, the whole country was glued to the television as the proceedings of parliament were broadcast live, with the commentators constantly giving the numbers of Deputies present, like some high football score.

After the arrival of the committed Phalangist Deputies and their known allies, the rest were extremely slow to trickle in. At first, all was jollity and back-slapping as the Deputies met and began their usual interminable discussions and chats. Then things grew quieter as the numbers crept up towards the magic 65 mark – then stuck at figures well short of the quorum needed. There were hasty consultations in back rooms, and a number of telephone calls were made which even the Phalangist Deputies described as 'forceful'.

While all this was going on, the Green Line between the two halves of Beirut was all tension for the first time in days. Traffic was stopped, and even Lebanese wishing to cross on foot were prevented from doing so. It was not clear who had imposed this restriction, though Phalangist militiamen were reported to have turned back a car driven by a Lebanese, while allowing foreign nationals to cross – after some argument. This time, however, it would obviously have been to the advantage of the Moslems to prevent any Deputies crossing from West to East Beirut.

Up at Fayadiyeh, the assembly was still four short of a quorum two hours after the session should have begun. By now, telephone calls were no longer enough, so Sheikh Bachir's elder brother Amin set off with several bodyguards to call on a number of Deputies. This last-minute persuasion did the trick. Five more Deputies were brought in, the old and infirm solicitously supported on the arms of the tough young Phalangist guards, others who had found pressing engagements elsewhere tracked down and equally carefully escorted into the temporary parliament building – some almost frog-marched. Just before 2 p.m., Mr Assad announced that a quorum had assembled and that a vote could be taken. Immediately there was rejoicing all over East Beirut and in the Christian areas to the north, for everyone knew that given a quorum, their man was bound to be elected: it was unlikely that all 55 Deputies present would vote for Sheikh Bachir, but once there was a quorum, he would need only a simple majority on the second count, and of this he was assured.

So it proved. On the first poll, four brave Deputies wrote 'Abstain' on their ballot papers, and one wrote in the name of Raymond Edde, a perennial candidate, though he had not bothered to nominate himself this time. The second ballot was obviously a formality, but it was held nonetheless, and Bachir Gemayel was duly elected. Perhaps the real reason for the second ballot was the old Lebanese parliamentary custom whereby Deputies who had promised their votes to a certain candidate and been rewarded for their loyalty wrote the name of their choice in a particular manner to show that they had delivered as promised. Nothing in Lebanon was ever taken on trust.

As the last few votes were announced on the television screens, East Beirut erupted in a wild outburst of joy every bit as noisy and alarming as that which accompanied the exodus of the Palestinians from the west. Down at the Phalangist head-quarters in Achrafiyeh, clerks and messengers seized the guns stored there and dashed outside to fire off their ammunition into the air, watched admiringly by the smartly uniformed girls who served in the militia. Cars dashed hooting through the streets, quickly plastered with huge posters of Sheikh Bachir. Now, however, new posters had been rapidly distributed: gone was the unsmiling, dour-looking Bachir wearing khaki fatigues and cradling a sub-machine gun, the Bachir of the Civil War days, the militia commander. Now the picture was of a neatly-suited, smiling Bachir, thinner, more suave. Bachir the politician had taken over from Bachir the gunman. That at any rate was the image being projected – though in West Beirut, few were convinced by this sudden metamorphosis.

Saeb Salam and his allies met on the afternoon after the election, welcomed the conciliatory statement the new presi-dent-elect had issued while deploring the way the ballot had been conducted, and in effect said they would wait and see what happened. Mr Begin did not help matters by sending a particu-larly warm message of congratulation to his 'dear friend', though his move was slightly offset by the correct, but much more welcome message from Washington.

Bachir himself retired to his family home at Bikfaya to receive the good wishes of his supporters and to plan his first moves. He was conscious of the need both to extend his authority over the whole of the country and to secure the withdrawal of all the armies still occupying it, Syrian and Israeli, as well as some remaining Palestinian forces in the north. There was also the problem of his old rival, former president Suleiman Franjieh, who had responded to events by immediately declaring the area he controlled around Zghorta yet another 'Free Lebanon' and by sending his militiamen to cut the roads to the south. He was joined in this desperate enterprise by Mr Karami, a moderate and far-sighted man not known for such extreme gestures.

As the exuberant celebration of the election went on in East Beirut – the firing there cost five dead, compared to some twenty-seven killed in West Beirut during the send-off for the Palestinians – the normalisation of Beirut began to speed up, with new crossing points opened, the glass merchants doing a brisk trade as shops finally dared to take down the shutters and replace windows, and thousands who had fled the carnage of the siege returning to their homes. By September 2nd, the evacuation of the Palestinians had been completed, Sheikh Bachir was quietly preparing to take over the country, and the Americans, Italians and French were looking forward to their own departure from Beirut.

It was at this point that President Reagan launched his new proposals for the Middle East – proposals which seemed to signal a remarkable shift in American attitudes, and which were formulated as a direct result of all that had happened in Lebanon, and as a response to the decision by the Palestinian leaders not to sacrifice their men and the people of Beirut by standing fast and inviting an Israeli onslaught. President Reagan's address to the nation on the Middle East created an immediate flurry in Israel, the Arab world and Moscow. The Soviets in particular regarded it as a most dangerous move, for it effectively kept them out of the equation, while raising the possibility of a global settlement which could give the United States a dominant position in the region. It was a radical change in attitude for the American administration and is worth considering in some detail. This is what the President said:

> While events in Beirut dominated the front page, America was engaged in a quiet behind-the-scenes effort to lay the groundwork for a broader peace in the region. US diplomatic missions travelled to Mid-east capitals and I met at home here with a wide range of experts to map out an American peace initiative for the long-suffering peoples of the Middle East, Arab and Israeli alike.
>
> It seemed to me that with the agreement in Lebanon we had an opportunity for a more far-reaching peace effort in the region, and I was determined to seize that moment . . . The strategic importance of the region to the US is well known, but our policy is motivated by more than strategic interests. We also have an irreversible commitment to the survival and territorial integrity of friendly states. Nor can we ignore the fact that the well-being of much of the world's economy is tied to stability in the strife-torn Middle East.
>
> The Lebanon war, tragic as it was, has left us with a new opportunity for peace. We must seize it now and bring peace to this troubled area while there is still time.

The President went on to say that a month earlier, even before the PLO evacuation from Lebanon had been started, he had directed that a review of the whole American policy in the Middle East should be begun.

> Two consequences of the war in Lebanon are key to the peace process: first, the military losses of the PLO have not diminished the yearning of the Palestinian people for a just solution of their claims; and second, while Israel's military successes in Lebanon have demonstrated that its armed forces are second to none in the region, they alone cannot bring just and lasting peace to Israel and her neighbours.
>
> The question now is how to reconcile Israel's legitimate security concerns with the legitimate rights of the Palestinians, and that answer can only come at the negotiating table. Each party must recognise that the outcome must be acceptable to all and that true peace will require compromises by all.

It looked as though President Reagan's rhetoric was going to wind its way to a platitudinous conclusion once again, but this time, the President meant what he said: there were new American positions and proposals.

> I call on the Arab states to accept the reality of Israel, and the reality that peace and justice are only to be gained through hard, fair, direct negotiations.
>
> The war in Lebanon has demonstrated another reality in the region. The departure of the Palestinians from Beirut dramatises more than ever the homelessness of the Palestinian people. Palestinians feel strongly that their cause is more than a question of refugees. I agree.
>
> There must be a period of time during which the Palestinian inhabitants of the West Bank and Gaza will have full autonomy over their own affairs.
>
> The United States will not support the use of any additional land for the purpose of settlements during the five-year transition period. Indeed, the immediate adoption of a settlement freeze by Israel, more than any other action, could create the confidence needed for wider participation in these talks. Further settlement activity is in no way necessary for the security of Israel and only diminishes the confidence of the Arabs that a final outcome can be freely and fairly negotiated.
>
> It is clear to me that peace cannot be achieved through the formation of an independent Palestinian state in the West Bank and Gaza. Nor is it achievable on the basis of Israeli sovereignty or permanent control over those territories. So the US will not support the establishment of an independent Palestinian state in the West Bank and Gaza, and we will not support annexation or permanent control by Israel. But it is the firm view of the United States that self-government by the Palestinians of the West Bank and Gaza in association with Jordan offers the best chance for a durable, just and lasting peace.

This was the Palestinians' reward: a real shift in American policy, a moving away from total support of Israel, however much that had been wrapped up in the past. The American move was also carefully timed, for the resumed Fez summit conference was due to convene only three days later, and there was no doubt that the President's statement would be bound to be at the centre of all the informal discussions there, even if it could not be part of the formal agenda.

As it turned out, even before that, President Reagan's proposals drew a considerable response, not least from Israel, with Mr Begin immediately and predictably rejecting the whole American package. The Israelis were particularly upset because the Americans had managed to keep their ideas secret from them, though they had discussed them in advance with Saudi Arabia and Jordan. At an emergency meeting, the Israeli cabinet swiftly and categorically turned them all down: 'The government of Israel has resolved that on the basis of the American positions, it will not enter into any negotiations with any party.' Begin himself said that settlement of the West Bank was 'a Jewish inalienable right and an integral part of our national security. Therefore, there shall be no settlement freeze.' And to back up his tough talk, the establishment of eight new settlements in the West Bank was quickly approved.

The Arab states gave a cautious welcome to the proposals, which were clearly designed mainly to involve King Hussein in the peace process. Hussein himself expressed interest, but pointed out once again that he could not negotiate for the Palestinians or the West Bank unless given a mandate to do so. At Fez, the King did not get it: on the contrary, the summit reiterated its support of the PLO as the sole legitimate representatives of the Palestinian people, called for Israeli withdrawal from all Arab territories, the dismantling of settlements established after 1967, and the establishment of a Palestinian state with Jerusalem as its capital. The one ray of hope was a clause calling on the Security Council to guarantee 'peace among all states of the region, including the independent Palestinian state.' Arab diplomats explained that this meant that Israel would be recognised once a Palestinian state was set up, which did not square at all with President Reagan's proposals.

Yet for all the rejections, the tough talking, the defiant words from Jerusalem, there was no doubt that America had moved significantly to take a more active and a more even-handed role in Middle East negotiations. There was a feeling everywhere that the time of armed struggle, of punitive raids and swift retaliation, was over, and that the politicians now had to take over from the soldiers.

It was a mood which did not last long. For even as the Lebanese Army was cautiously preparing to move into West Beirut, isolationist voices on Capitol Hill were agitating for the Marines to be pulled out, a move which swiftly paved the way for the horrors which were to follow. Both France and Italy wanted to keep their men in Beirut for the full thirty days which had been the original time promised, but American planners, jubilant that the Palestinian evacuation had gone off so smoothly, were determined to get their troops out. As a result, September 10th was the date set for the multi-national force to be withdrawn.

On that day, the American Marines, demonstrating the remarkable naivety of which soldiers and politicians are capable, signalled 'mission accomplished' as they boarded their landing craft to leave Lebanon. Of course, it had not been. Nothing had been done to ensure the safety of the Moslems of West Beirut; no attempt had been made to help the Lebanese Army establish its control over all the city; no moves had been made towards disarming the various militias of both right and left; and the Palestinian civilians left in the refugee camps were as vulnerable as ever. The American argument was that their job had been merely to oversee the evacuation of the PLO, and that this had been done; yet when the Marines had first landed, it had been well understood that this was a symbolic American presence designed to show that if things did go wrong, America was ready to act with real clout. Conversely, the premature American withdrawal was taken as meaning that the US was interested only in getting the Palestinians out of Lebanon, and once that was done, had no further interest in what happened there.

Even as the Marines left, people who resented the apparent turn for the better in Lebanon were preparing to upset things once more. Secret meetings were held, large amounts of money changed hands, and Habib as-Shartuni began moving quantities of explosives into the apartment he shared with his father. That apartment was in the Phalangist party headquarters at Achrafiyeh, where Shartuni's father was the caretaker. As a result, Shartuni was regularly in and out of the place, and the dozens of Phalangist guards and the Israelis who had taken up position in the street outside soon after they moved into East Beirut paid no attention to him.

By September 14th, some hundreds of kilos of explosives had been moved in, transported in all sorts of ways – in boxes of groceries, in cases of drinks, in consignments of office stationery. They were laid out as Shartuni had been shown, the sophisticated detonator set up, and the radio which was to trigger it all off moved into a room above a patisserie a street away. That day the party faithful began assembling, and there was a roar of applause when Bachir Gemayel strode in to take his place in the centre of the notables on the platform. Now that he was among his own, he was every inch the militia commander again: tough, down to earth, not the President of the country, but a feudal leader surrounded by his people. Across the street Shartuni watched and waited: and at just the right moment he sent the radio signal pulsing into his own apartment, to set off the massive explosion which blew the building to pieces and killed Gemayel and some thirty of his followers.

In the first chaos, it was thought that Sheikh Bachir had escaped, for someone looking just like him was seen staggering out of the building. Members of the Gemayel family and his party men toured the hospitals, trying to find where he had been taken, so convinced were they that their leader had got out alive. In fact, Gemayel lay buried under tons of masonry, right under the centre of the explosion. Those who had arranged it all had been experts, and experts with detailed local knowledge. They had made no mistake.

Shartuni himself hurried back to the building as soon as the explosion occurred and helped the rescue workers. Within hours, however, investigators had established that it was not a car bomb that had killed Sheikh Bachir, as first thought; it was soon obvious that it was an inside job – and Shartuni was picked up as a prime suspect.

The Phalange investigators who interrogated Shartuni said he had 'links with the Palestinian Intelligence Department headed by Abou Haoul, and had previously worked with Syrian Intelligence. While in Paris he joined and worked with one of the international terrorist networks.' This was all very vague coming from people who would be totally ruthless in finding out what they wanted to know, once they had the culprit in their hands. The inference to be drawn is that the information given to them by Shartuni was too damaging and dangerous to reveal, for those who benefited most from Sheikh Bachir's death were certainly not the Palestinians, nor international terrorists. Those who stood to gain were the Israelis, or factions within the Phalangist Party opposed to Bachir, or followers of Suleiman Franjieh bent on revenge, on the Syrians.

Certainly the Israelis were ready to act as soon as the death of Bachir Gemayel was confirmed. Within two hours of the announcement, their troops began to move into West Beirut. According to a spokesman for Mr Begin's office in Jerusalem, the move was 'to keep West Beirut quiet and prevent dangerous developments.' The army, even then, had a different version: the advance into West Beirut, according to the IDF, was needed because 'certain elements' in Lebanon wished to create anarchy once again; under such circumstances it would have been 'immoral' for the Israeli Army not to go in, said the spokesman.

As the Israelis once again pounded positions in West Beirut from land and sea – this time the air force only buzzed the city as a warning of what might happen, and did not actually bomb – a final Israeli consensus emerged: the reason they had gone into West Beirut was to preserve the peace and prevent violence in the wake of the assassination of the President-elect – though at the same time, officers in Tel Aviv were trying to justify it all by talking of '2,000 Palestinian terrorists' who had stayed behind after the bulk of the PLO pulled out.

If that had been true, the Israelis might have had a tougher time than they did when they finally entered the city they had besieged so long. As it was, they met only small arms fire and some RPG attacks as they advanced cautiously into the old Palestinian areas from the south, and into Ras Beirut from the port. Fortunately for them, the two main Mourabitoun strongpoints, the Murr Tower and the shattered, burnt-out Holiday Inn, previously held by the PLA, had been handed over to the Lebanese Army, which took no action as the Israelis moved in. Even so, two Israeli tanks were knocked out, two Israeli soldiers killed and five wounded as they cautiously made their way

forward, blasting buildings used as firing positions by the
defenders, then sending foot patrols in to make sure that
everyone had been cleared out.

The only organised groups in the city now were the Mourabitoun and Amal, some small groups of Communist Party militiamen, and some members of Jumblatt's Progressive Socialist
Party. They were no match at all for the Israelis. Groups of
frightened boys gathered at crossroads to get their orders from
only slightly older men, who knew as little as they did; individual fighters stayed at their posts and died; but most simply
faded away as the Israelis advanced just behind their artillery
barrage and shells from the gunboats – more accurate this time
than previously.

By nightfall on the first day, it was virtually all over. Israeli
officers made their way to Walid Jumblatt's house, where he
was meeting with leaders of other parties and militia groups,
and demanded that all fighting end immediately; if it did not,
they threatened to call in air strikes to clear the remaining
pockets of resistance, and they could not guarantee that that
would not cause civilian casualties. The men assembled at
Jumblatt's house refused to talk to the Israelis and walked out,
leaving Jumblatt alone with them; then an hour or so later, they
sent messages saying they had agreed to give up. The city
quietened down, though there was still a little fighting next
morning around the Corniche Mazraa. All in all, some thirty-
two Lebanese were killed during the Israeli take-over of West
Beirut.

On the Wednesday, the day the Israeli attack began, Mr
Wazzan had sent messages to President Reagan saying that
they were deliberately breaking the agreements worked out for
the evacuation of the PLO; these had explicitly stated that
Israel would refrain from entering West Beirut in return for the
departure of the PLO. Israel justified its attack on the city by
saying that it was the Palestinians who had broken the agreement by leaving units behind, and again spoke of the 2,000
fighters still in the city. President Reagan agreed with Mr
Wazzan: there had been a breach of the agreement, he said, and
he called on Israel to withdraw its forces. Israel replied with a
series of statements issued in Jerusalem: 'Israel took over West

Beirut', the first said, 'to prevent the danger of bloodshed, violence and anarchy. This danger was indeed averted. Israel will hand over to the Lebanese Army when it is ready to assume control.'Another statement accepted that there had been an agreement with the Lebanese government over West Beirut, but said that 'it was no longer operative' because PLO units had remained in Beirut. 'Our purpose is to prevent bloodshed and to give Lebanon a chance to resume its progress towards the formation of an independent Government after the murder of Bachir Gemayel.'

On Thursday, September 16th, Israeli Army radio reported that Israel controlled all main intersections and roads in the city, and only houses inside various neighbourhoods remained to be 'purged'. This same broadcast said that the refugee camps in West Beirut 'which were harbouring terrorists' had been encircled and closed by Israeli forces, and it had been decided to send Phalangist militiamen into the camps to clear them of Palestinian fighters.

It was on this day, Thursday, that the first units of the Phalange went into Sabra and Chatila. They formed up near the airport after driving into Beirut from Chouefat, and their advance squads set up a tactical headquarters near the Arab University. Many of the men concerned in what was to follow came from Damour; others were the Phalange special security squad under Elias Hobeika, a former close aide of Bachir Gemayel and the contact man between the Phalange and Mossad, the Israeli Intelligence Service. Other Christian commanders involved were Joseph Edde, leader of militia forces in the south, Dib Anastas, head of the Phalange Military Police, Michael Zouein, who had led the 1980 attack against the Chamoun forces, and Maroun Mischalani, an East Beirut militia officer. In all, between 300 and 400 Christian militiamen went into the camps, including some of Sa'ad Haddad's men from Southern Lebanon. They were virtually unopposed; a few Palestinians who had kept their Kalashnikovs tried to defend themselves and their homes, and were instantly shot down by the far superior force coming in, but in general, the Christians had little difficulty; as Israeli gunners fired flares over the camp, the Phalangists were able to go about their work fairly silently, carrying out the first few dozen killings with knives, bayonets and rifle butts. Then as the work went on through the night and into the next day, the guns took over. Whole families were gunned down in their homes, or as they tried to flee; children were shot hiding behind their mother's skirts; men were lined up against walls and executed; in a stable, the horses were killed as well as the men tending them. Dozens of people tried to take refuge in the Gaza hospital, where the twenty or so foreign doctors and nurses were led away by militiamen and harangued about their wickedness in helping the Palestinians; one Palestinian auxiliary who tried to stay with the foreigners was spotted, pulled out, taken down a nearby alley and shot; the fate of those who tried to hide in the hospital was never established.

By the Thursday night and Friday morning, little attempt was being made to hide what was going on: flares were again fired and the crackle of rifle fire could be heard for hours as more men, women and children were shot. According to later testimony, the Israeli northern commander, General Amir Drori, had sent troops in to stop the massacre at midday on the Friday, but for once, the Israeli soldiers seemed to have been remarkably ineffectual. On that day bulldozers were taken into the camp to dig mass graves, and some of the first Phalangist units were rotated with fresh ones brought in from East Beirut.

It was on Friday, too, that outsiders began to realise what was happening. Reporters several times tried to get into the camp, and quite close to the edge saw mechanical shovels carrying scoop-loads of bodies. Diplomats and relief workers who went to the camps reported that 'a large number' of people appeared to have been killed. In Tel Aviv, Israeli reporters were beginning to hear about it, and one of them, Zev Schiff, military correspondent of *Ha'aretz*, telephoned 'a senior personality'. Schiff later wrote: 'I know that this person acted immediately. In other words, the massacre had started already on Thursday night and what was known to me on Friday morning was undoubtedly known to others before.' Schiff said that his information came to him from an Israeli in Beirut.

On Friday night the Phalangists pulled out, and on Saturday reporters were able to go into the camps for the first time that week. They described a scene of carnage: bodies lay everywhere and in the centre of the camp two mass graves had been only roughly covered over. In all, 400 people were known to have been killed and a further 900 were missing, presumed killed. One relief worker said the only way to find out the true figure would be to count the living, since it would have been impossible to find all the dead.

As the first dispatches went out on news agency wires, the storm broke. President Reagan was reported to be 'shocked and stunned', having just sought mildly to justify the Israeli action in going into West Beirut in speeches he had been making during a tour of New Jersey. George Shultz called in Moshe Arens, the Israeli ambassador, for a stormy meeting, though it was clear the ambassador knew nothing at all of what had been going on: like most Jews, he had spent the day quietly at home, celebrating the New Year.

Throughout the world, leaders expressed their shock and horror at what had happened, while in Jerusalem, conflicting statements came from Israeli politicians, soldiers and spokesmen. For once, Mr Begin seemed to misjudge the mood of his countrymen, and for days stoutly resisted the growing pressure for a full judicial inquiry to be set up. Eventually he had to give in, and the full story of what happened on Thursday and Friday, September 16th and 17th, was examined by a High Court Judge, Chief Justice Yitzbah Kahan.

The immediate result of it all was that President Reagan agreed to send the Marines back to Beirut, and the French and Italian units returned with them. The Israelis were forced to pull back from the immediate areas of West Beirut, the camps and the airport, and finally to agree to allow UN observers into the city. Camille Chamoun withdrew his bid for the Presidency, and on September 23rd, Amin Gemayel was sworn in unopposed to take his younger brother's place, with the support this time of Moslems as well as Christians in the national assembly. The dreadful bloodshed at Sabra and Chatila, a repetition of the massacre of Palestinians by Chamounist militiamen at Tal Zaatar six years earlier, seemed to mark the end of a time out of life for the Lebanese and Palestinians, a season in purgatory.

It was too, the end of the war between the Israelis and the Palestinians. Only minor skirmishes would be possible once the Palestinian forces were spread around the Arab world, isolated terrorist incidents and reprisals for them. By brute force and ruthlessness, the Israeli Army had effectively smashed the fighting capability of the Palestinians. By gross miscalculation, overweening arrogance and disregard for the opinions of the world, the army commanders and the Israeli politicians in control had made it all worthless. They lost the war the soldiers had won.

INDEX